THE UNITED KINGDOM

THE UNITED KINGDOM

RAY HUDSON

Senior Lecturer in Geography,
University of Durham

ALLAN WILLIAMS

Lecturer in Geography,
University of Exeter

WESTERN EUROPE:
ECONOMIC AND SOCIAL STUDIES

Harper & Row, Publishers
London

Cambridge San Francisco
Mexico City   São Paulo
New York   Singapore
Philadelphia   Sydney

Harper & Row Ltd
28 Tavistock Street
London WC2E 7PN

British Library Cataloguing in Publication Data

Hudson, Ray
  The United Kingdom. — (Western Europe : economic and social studies)
  1. Great Britain — Economic conditions — 1945–
  I. Title II. Williams, Allan III. Series 330.941'0858 HC256.6

ISBN 0-06-318350-1

Typeset by Burns & Smith, Derby
Printed and bound by Redwood Burn Ltd, Trowbridge

CONTENTS

PREFACE

Our concern in this book is to provide an account of changes in the postwar geography of the United Kingdom. From the vantage point of 1984–1985, when the book was written, sharp contrasts are evident between the UK in the immediate postwar years and in the early 1980s. Our main aim is to analyse the changes in economy, society and politics that link these two benchmark periods and to show how they have both been shaped by, and helped to shape, the internal geography of the UK. Furthermore we wish to emphasize that the problems and policies of the 1980s are best understood in the context of the postwar evolution of the UK.

Labour's electoral victory in 1945 and the national rejection of the wartime Prime Minister, Winston Churchill, were grounded in the economic and social conditions of the interwar years. Agricultural and industrial depressions, the misery of widespread poverty and long-term unemployment, appalling health and housing conditions and a series of confrontations between labour and capital, notably the crushing of the working class in the 1926 General Strike, left a residue of bitterness and a widespread determination to build a better future after the war. A strengthened spatial policy would have to be an integral part of any attempt to build a fairer society because the interwar years created a deep and persistent North–South divide. It was an apparent contradiction of that period that, while mass unemployment prevailed in the traditional industrial regions, a new generation of industries producing consumer goods (such as cars and electromechanical household appliances) expanded rapidly in the Southeast and Midlands. While rotting tenements and slums still dominated cities in the industrial North, there was unprecedented suburbanization in the South. While industrial land lay derelict in peripheral regions, there was growing concern in the Southeast over the disappearance of rural England under sprawling, uncontrolled, speculative, semi-detached housing developments. It was against this background, as well as the immediately preceding experiences of the war years which helped produce a sharper class division in voting patterns, that Labour was elected in 1945 with a landslide victory. It had broad urban, rural and regional support, and a manifesto, *Let Us Face The*

Future, committed to radical social and economic reorganization via a greatly increased role for the State. In 1945 there was an air of optimism that the experiences of the interwar years need not be repeated, that a fairer and more caring society could be constructed.

One of the most striking features of the early 1980s is the similarity, in terms of mass unemployment and the divisiveness, to the interwar years. While the regional divisions of the 1930s were a product of differential economic growth, the deep and growing divisions in the 1980s between urban and rural areas and between the South and the rest of the UK were linked to the spatially differentiated effects of national economic decline. This was sharply reflected in spatial polarization in support for the Conservative and Labour Parties in the 1983 General Election and 1985 local government elections – between rural and/or southern Tory areas and urban and/or northern Labour ones. To the economic evangelists of the 'New Right' (for whom competition between people is the motor of social progress) that dominates the economic policy-making of the Thatcher government, such divisions are not only inevitable but desirable. The 'old' solutions of the postwar social democratic consensus – Keynesianism, State intervention, the Welfare State – are seen by them as the 'cause' of the UK's decline in the global international economic order. Denationalization, deregulation and privatization are the order of the day – irrespective of the short-term negative impacts on national economic performance and the longer-term social and political consequences of a bitterly divided society. These policies are not unique to the Thatcher governments; indeed, their roots lie in earlier government strategies. Whether there is a viable alternative to such policies is a question of vital importance and one to which we return in Chapter 5, but it is nevertheless worth stating the obvious at this point: the question of what constitutes an 'adequate' set of policies cannot be divorced from our concept of the type of society we wish to see in the United Kingdom.

What is undeniable is that the spirit of social harmony and national unity of 1945 (even if more apparent than real) has been replaced by the re-emergence of deep cleavages in UK society, and this has been reinforced by the pursuit of the political economy of Thatcherism. The exception was a brief, but electorally significant period during and after the Falklands/Malvinas campaign when nationalistic fervour was the order of the day. While social conflicts have developed on cross-class lines over a wide variety of issues – ecological, environmental, anti-nuclear, etc. – the UK remains a deeply class-divided society. Events in the early 1980s, such as the 1984–1985 miners' strike and increasingly violent racial conflicts in the cities — and the way in which such conflicts were settled – are painful reminders of this. So too is the continuation of 'the troubles' in Northern Ireland, now extending over almost two decades with still no sign of a military, let alone viable political, solution.

So far we have emphasized the differences between the UK in the immediate postwar years and in the early 1980s, not least the political ones. Yet over much of the intervening period there was a considerable measure of consensus between governments of different parties over a broad range of economic and social affairs, while many features of UK society in the 1980s had their roots in developments in the 1970s, the 1960s or even earlier. To understand the changing geography of the UK over the postwar period, it is necessary to relate intranational to national level changes (and vice versa). But to understand both of these, one must look beyond the UK itself to the changing international political and economic order, the changing global pattern of capital accumulation and the UK's changing status in the world order – changes that were partly a product and partly a cause of government economic policies. For just as the 'old' regional divisions of the UK in the 19th century were intimately bound up with a growing imperial role, so the changing internal geography of the postwar period is closely related to the UK's relative decline in the international order and successive governments' responses to it. But these are not one-way relationships, for the pattern of spatial differentiation produced within the UK in the prewar years has both been modified by relative decline in national economic performance and, in the course of this, offered opportunities to private capital that have helped shape the way in which the changing international economic order has evolved.

The organization of this book reflects an emphasis on two main themes: the inter-relationship between economic, social and political processes, and the links between different spatial scales – the international, national, regional, urban and rural. We hope to identify major strands in the transformation of the United Kingdom and show how these have affected the UK as a whole, different regions and urban and rural areas. This does not mean that the same analyses of economic, social and political events are repeated mechanically at each spatial scale. Different processes have different relevance at each spatial scale. Therefore, as we progress from national, to regional, to urban and, finally, to the rural levels, so there will be some shift in emphasis from economic to social matters, and from production to consumption issues. We would emphasize that we see the national, regional, urban and rural not as mutually exclusive levels of analysis but as inter-related approaches to coming to terms with the postwar transformation of the UK.

The task that we have set ourselves is clearly an ambitious one and the available space precludes any attempt at a comprehensive analysis. Instead we have included what we consider to be the major features of the human geography of the postwar UK. Determining this, in itself, has been one of the main challenges of the book, as we have discovered over the past six months of constant, occasionally frenzied, exchanges of letters and telephone calls between Durham and Exeter!

Whatever progress we have made towards fulfilling our aims has, of course, been the outcome of the help and cooperation of a number of other people. Chief among these have been Terry Bacon of the Drawing Office at Exeter, who prepared the many illustrations quickly and efficiently, while Joan Fry, Heather Hughes and Debbie Clough have shared the burden of typing our manuscripts. Pat Richmond made useful comments on Chapter 4 and Eleonore Kofman offered sound general editorial advice on the final text but, as always, the ultimate responsibility for any errors or omissions rests with the authors.

Ray Hudson
Allan Williams

Durham and Exeter,
July 1985

ONE

The United Kingdom
in the Changing Postwar World

1.1 Introduction

The final years of the Second World War and the immediate postwar period seemingly promised a better future for most people in the United Kingdom. Having defeated Fascism and the enemy without, an attack could be mounted on the enemies within – want, disease, idleness, ignorance and squalor. Central to this were the proposals of Lord Beveridge, significantly a Liberal peer. The commitment to maintain 'full employment' – or, to be precise, a 'high and stable' level of employment – given in the 1944 employment policy White Paper (Cmnd 6527) was followed by the passage of seemingly radical reforming legislation by the postwar Labour government, which translated many of Beveridge's 'welfare state' proposals into practice. In addition, significant industries were nationalized and while these were not quite the 'commanding heights' of the economy, generally being technically backward and unprofitable, they provided goods and services that were vital to profitable production in other industries. While to a degree simply an outcome of extending wartime controls on production, nationalization apparently offered better conditions and security of employment to those working in these industries and more scope for government directly to influence national economic development.

The creation of physical and land-use planning mechanisms, following the reports of the wartime Scott and Uthwatt Committees and the influential Barlow Committee report, *The Distribution of the Industrial Population* (see Rhind and Hudson, 1980, pp. 216–219), presented the opportunity to create more attractive and healthy living environments. An expanded public sector housing programme would improve housing conditions for many, if not quite providing homes fit for heroes, once the immediate problems of postwar reconstruction were overcome, and it was expected that most new housing would be in the public sector. The commitments to create a welfare state held out the promise of a more egalitarian, caring society. This is best epitomized by the loosening of the link between ability to pay and access to health care via creation of a National Health Service, and a new system of unemployment benefit to replace the pernicious Poor Law. This would ease the severe distributional inequalities resulting from allocation via market forces, though it failed to break the link between wage incomes (or lack of them) and lifestyles and living conditions for the great majority of the population.

The legislative programme and social and economic goals and policies of the postwar Labour government in many ways delineated the parameters within which economy and society in the UK would develop over the next three decades. Succeeding governments, Conservative as well as Labour, reaffirmed commitments to 'full employment' and the Welfare State, and to a significant but precisely defined role for the State in relation to the economy and to civil society. Although important party political differences emerged over specific issues, such as the nationalization of road transport and steel, or the scope of public sector housing provision, in general the consensus prevailed. It was not until 1975 that Harold Wilson's Labour government began to break the mould of class compromise of the social-democratic consensus, albeit unwillingly. The election in 1979 of Margaret Thatcher's Conservative government heralded a vigorous and deliberate assault to shatter this mould irrevocably. What had seemed to be the solution to the social and economic problems of the 1940s was now seen as a central reason for the UK's relative economic decline.

In the remainder of this chapter, we sketch out the main lineaments of the political economy of the UK in the postwar period.

1.2   The United Kingdom's changing position in the world economy

The United Kingdom's declining share of world industrial output and trade is a long-established trend. As the world's first capitalist industrial nation, the UK's relative position inevitably had to decline although its location at the core of a global empire guaranteed that this would be first revealed in terms of output rather than trade. The USA overtook the UK in terms of production by the 1880s; Germany did the same in the 1890s (Rostow, 1978). It was not until the late 1930s that Germany briefly took a slightly larger share of world trade in manufactured goods but the Second World War did increase the USA's share of the world trade above that of the UK (Figure 1.1).

Even so, after the immediate problems of postwar reconstruction and the 1947 economic crisis had been overcome, it seemed that long-term secular decline in the UK's share of world trade in manufactures had been reversed. Although the longer-term effects of wartime indebtedness to the USA and the exhaustion of the economy remained to be tackled, the UK's major international competitors other than the USA were in an even worse condition. Thus the UK still had over 25 percent of world trade in

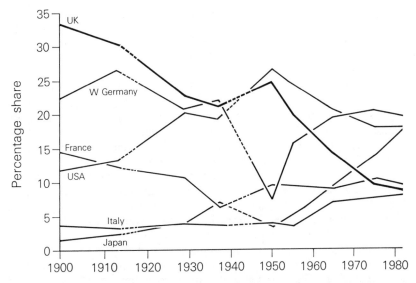

Figure 1.1   Shares of world trade in manufactured goods, 1900–1982 (Atkinson, 1983).

manufactured goods (Currie, 1983, p. 104), while manufactured exports as a proportion of Gross Domestic Product (GDP) rose sharply compared to the interwar years and imports continued to fall (Atkinson, 1983).

Governments of both major parties were also committed to maintaining the UK's old international political and economic role. This raised decisive choices on two fronts: the priority to be attached to the interests of domestically tied capital and the domestic economy as against those of internationally oriented finance and industrial capital, and the areas to which UK external allegiances and policies would primarily be directed. On the first point, the interests of international capital have been prioritized. Regarding the second, the UK apparently emerged from the war with its formal and informal (the 'sterling area') empires largely intact, its horizons global, its perspectives imperial.

This perception of the UK's international position had important effects in shaping governments' defence, foreign and trade policies. The military and defence costs of preserving an international strategic role diverted potential resources from restructuring the domestic economy. Preoccupation with the benefits of the 'old' international division of labour led to rejection of the European Economic Community (EEC) in the 1950s – the UK wished to retain the competitive advantages to manufacturing industry arising from Commonwealth preferences, cheap food imports and guaranteed or preferential access to markets for manufactures. When attempts to transform the embryonic EEC into a more limited industrial free trade area failed, the UK government turned towards formation of the European Free Trade Association (EFTA), shorn of anything resembling the EEC's Common Agricultural Policy.

By the late 1950s it was becoming clear that the UK's position in the international economic order had deteriorated sharply, undermined by changes both at home and abroad. Rowthorne (1983) suggests that '... on almost all fronts British capitalism was in difficulties by the end of the 1950s' (p. 67). Symptoms of these difficulties, both for capital and the State, were numerous: for example, the UK's share of world trade in manufactures had fallen to 16.5 percent by 1960, the balance of payments position was increasingly fragile (Figure 1.2) and sterling crises were becoming endemic. What had happened? By this time the UK's formal and informal empires were disintegrating. Over the preceding postwar years, UK companies had enjoyed captive markets in the countries of the Empire – some 75 percent of their imported manufactures were supplied from the UK in the early 1950s. Many potentially dangerous competitors in Western Europe and Japan were still recovering from the physically destructive impacts of war and its aftermath. By the end of the 1950s – as the 'winds of change' began to sweep over Africa, for example – competition intensified in the markets of the newly independent ex-colonies, not only from the USA but from West Germany, France, Italy, The Netherlands, Japan and non-contestants in the Second World War such as Sweden. As manufacturing capital rebuilt productive capacity in these areas, up-to-date technologies were installed which often gave them a competitive edge over UK rivals. Import penetration rose, with manufactures accounting for 31.8 percent of UK imports in 1960 compared to 19.4 percent in 1950. Japan and West Germany both sharply increased their share of world trade in manufactures, the latter exceeding the UK's falling share by around 1960 (see Figure 1.1). Moreover, presaging a much more general pattern of future changes, decline in certain branches of manufacturing – cotton textiles and shipbuilding, for example – was not just relative but absolute and this was associated with the re-emergence of the 'regional problem' (see Chapter 2.2).

Imperial decline also created difficulties for finance capital and the City of London. In the 1950s the prosperity of banking and commercial capital still rested on sterling's role as an international reserve currency, which presupposed the UK's continuing hegemony in its formal and informal empires. When this began to be eroded, the vulnerability of sterling increased with immediate implications for the balance of payments and seemingly longer-term ones for London's future as an international financial centre. The UK's share of 'world' trade in invisibles and private services began to fall:

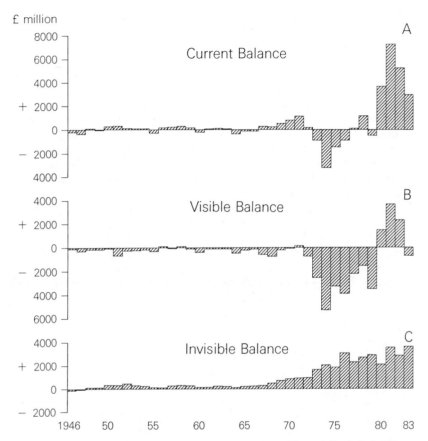

Figure 1.2 The UK balance of payments, 1946–1983 (Central Statistical Office, 1984, *Economic Trends*).

from 24.9 to 20.9 percent and from 26.3 to 20.3 percent, respectively, between 1955 and 1960 (Brown and Sheriff, 1979, p. 246).

The UK's changing role in the world economic order was not without its paradoxes. Major UK manufacturing firms began to invest heavily overseas, in sharp contrast to competitors in Western Europe and Japan: in 1950 23 UK-based multinationals had at least six foreign subsidiaries but, by 1960, 30 had so (Channon, 1973). This in itself was significant in terms of the UK's falling shares of manufacturing output and exports. Early transnationalization of production by UK firms in pursuit of enhanced profits exemplifies growing convergence between their interests and those of finance capital in an 'open' economy with only limited government controls on capital movement, and the growing conflict between their interests and those of the national economy. At the same time, 'full employment' conditions led to the UK being integrated into international migration patterns in a new way, with large migrant inflows from the New Commonwealth leading to net immigration for a time (Figure 1.3; see also Chapter 3.4.3 on the significance of immigrant concentrations in particular urban areas). In contrast, when continental Northwest European countries became increasingly linked with those of Southern Europe and North Africa via international labour migration in the 1960s (King, 1984), this took the form of temporary movement as 'guestworkers' rather than of permanent settlement as citizens. This difference would be important in relation to their economic dynamism and the UK's continuing relative decline.

By the end of the 1950s, then, there was growing recognition of the progressive deterioration of the competitiveness of manufacturing in the UK, manifest especially in recurrent balance of payments problems. This helped bring about a major reorientation in national economic policies from 1962 (discussed in the next section) but such policies failed to produce their intended effects. Symptoms of deindustrialization became more intense as the

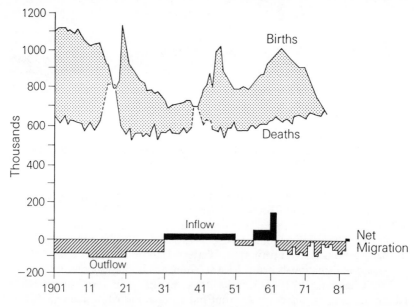

Figure 1.3   Emigration, immigration and population change, 1901–1981 (adapted from Lawton, 1982).

pace of investment abroad by UK manufacturing capital accelerated (Channon, 1973) and, particularly after the election of a Labour government in 1964, balance of payments and sterling crises became more frequent and severe. This called into question the viability of the postwar international financial and monetary order as well as posing acute political choices for central government. The overriding importance attached by government to preserving sterling's international exchange rate necessitated tackling balance of payments problems in the short term by abandoning modernization policies (and the 1965 National Plan), and adopting severely deflationary domestic economic policies, to try and boost exports. Abandoning the attempt at coherently 'planned' industrial modernization implied a continuing deterioration in the international competitiveness of manufacturing in the UK, however. Eventually, and not without irony, the sacrifices in terms of domestic economic policy proved to have been both insufficient and unnecessary as sterling was anyway devalued in November 1967. This decision had important consequences for the UK's international role: defence commitments outside Europe were substantially cut to ease balance of payments pressures and, in 1968, the Basle agreement signalled the end of sterling's role as a reserve currency (Shanks, 1977, p. 50).

Devaluation did offer opportunities for some sections of manufacturing capital in terms of import substitution and/or export growth. Retaining the competitive advantages it conferred necessitated new emphases in domestic economic and foreign policies, however. Increasing emphasis was placed on incomes policies as the route to increased competitiveness and profits on the domestic front. Attempts to join the European Economic Community were renewed, following French rebuffs earlier in the 1960s, as the EEC was much more significant to the UK in actual and potential international trade than was EFTA. The UK joined the EEC on 1 January 1973, along with Denmark and Eire, and has since had an uneasy relationship with the rest of the Community. There is continuing domestic debate as to whether to leave, persistent criticism of the size of the UK's net budget contribution and a refusal to join the European Monetary System after its formation in 1979 (Parboni, 1981, pp. 141–168). However, entry to the EEC, which later became the European Community (EC), has been associated with a reorientation and increasing concentration of the geographical pattern of the UK's international trade, further integrating the UK economy with that of the Community at the relative expense of links with the USA and Commonwealth, while increasing the disparity between UK imports of manufactures from the EC and exports to it (Table 1.1). The appearance by 1982 of Nigeria and Saudi Arabia among the top ten national export markets and of Japan as a major source of manufactured imports is, in different ways, a telling reminder of the changes that took place in the international economic

Table 1.1 The changing geographical patterns of the UK's trade in manufactured goods, 1970–1982

(a) Major trading blocs

	% Exports		% Imports	
	1970	1982	1970	1982
Centrally planned economies	4.0	2.0	4.9	1.5
Developing countries	23.3	29.3	11.6	9.0
European Community	28.9	37.2	32.8	50.8
Non-EC Western Europe	16.3	12.0	18.1	15.4
Other developed economies	27.5	19.5	32.6	24.1

(b) The top ten national trading partners

Export markets: % total exports

1970		1982	
USA	11.0	USA	10.2
West Germany	5.9	West Germany	9.1
Netherlands	4.7	France	7.6
Australia	4.7	Netherlands	5.1
South Africa	4.5	Belgium*	4.8
Sweden	4.3	Irish Republic	4.7
Irish Republic	4.2	Italy	3.9
France	4.2	Saudi Arabia	3.1
Belgium*	3.6	South Africa	2.9
Canada	3.6	Nigeria	2.8
Total	50.8	Total	54.2

Import sources: % total imports

1970		1982	
USA	18.9	West Germany	18.1
West Germany	10.9	USA	13.7
Canada	7.5	France	9.1
Netherlands	5.2	Japan	6.9
Sweden	5.2	Netherlands	6.3
France	5.0	Belgium*	6.2
Switzerland	4.1	Italy	6.2
Italy	3.7	Switzerland	4.2
Belgium*	3.4	Sweden	3.4
USSR	3.1	Irish Republic	3.2
Total	67.0	Total	77.3

* Includes Luxembourg.

Source: *Barclays Review* (1983).

order in the 1970s, partly linked to the major crude oil price rises of 1973–1974 and 1979–1980 (Mandel, 1978; Frank, 1980, pp. 20–101).

At the same time, the UK's share of world exports continued to fall to 5.3 percent in 1982 (8.8 percent in 1955). This largely reflected further manufacturing decline and, without North Sea oil, the fall would have been more pronounced. The UK's share of world manufacturing exports dipped below 10 percent around 1970 (see Figure 1.1); even though manufacturing exports grew absolutely to 1975, imports of manufactures, especially finished goods, grew more sharply (Figure 1.4). This divergence became even more marked after 1975 when exports fell absolutely (−8 percent, 1975–1980) while by 1980 almost two-thirds of imports were manufactured goods. The absolute decline in manufactured exports partly reflected the unprecedented post-1979 collapse in UK manufacturing output, but the longer-term divergence between export and import growth rates reflected the increasing uncompetitiveness of manufacturing in the UK. There was a growing gap in

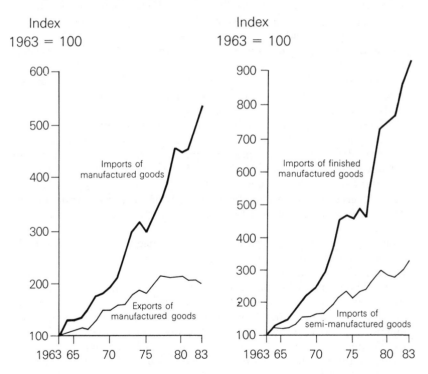

Figure 1.4   Volume growth of UK exports and imports of manufactured goods, 1963–1983 (Atkinson, 1983).

labour productivity between manufacturing activities in the UK and elsewhere, itself reflecting lower rates of fixed capital investment and research and development (R & D) expenditures; by 1978 value added per employee in manufacturing in the UK was less than in Italy, less than one-third of that in West Germany, and less than one-half of that in Japan and USA (*Barclays Review*, 1981).

By the first half of 1983, for the first time the UK recorded a deficit in the trade balance in manufactured goods (*Barclays Review*, 1983) and this was linked to accelerating and widening import penetration. While increased import penetration for products such as clothing has been associated with the selective industrialization of parts of the Third World – 'the new international division of labour' (Edwards, 1979; Fröbel et al., 1980) – by far the major sources of competition are other advanced capitalist countries (Table 1.1). One effect of these changes has been a growing dependence on imports of key 'high-technology' products. Despite the 40 percent appreciation of the dollar against sterling during the period 1982–1984, USA exports to the UK rose substantially (Beresford and Pearson, 1985); 33 percent of these (by value) were in computing and related fields by 1984.

What has been the broader significance for the UK's declining position in the international economic order? The 1970s were characterized by a chronic visible trade deficit, especially after 1973 as a result of the sharply increased price of oil imports and the steadily eroding positive balance in manufactured goods. Although there was a considerable surplus on 'invisibles', this was insufficient to compensate wholly for the visible trade deficit.

It is symptomatic of the UK's changing position in the international economy that international tourist receipts and revenues from civil aviation and travel became increasingly significant as a source of invisible earnings (*Barclays Review*, 1982), while more traditional sources of invisibles such as financial services and maritime transport declined in relative importance. By the early 1980s annual receipts from foreign tourists were well in excess of £5 billion (Sandles, 1985).

The persistent balance of payments problems had a marked impact on the domestic economy, especially after abandonment of a fixed sterling exchange rate in 1972 (see Chapter 1.3). A succession of major deflationary measures from 1975 onwards, while partly induced by direct external pressure from the International Monetary Fund (IMF), mainly reflected the priority given by government to international and financial interests in shaping economic policies, a priority partly necessitated by the very weakness of UK-based manufacturing. When the balance of payments position subsequently improved, this was almost entirely through exploiting North Sea oil reserves, considerably reducing oil imports and enabling expansion of oil exports. Energy imports fell from over one-half to less than 10 percent of consumption between the early 1970s and 1980s while, by 1982, oil and petroleum accounted for 19.2 percent of exports; to put this in perspective, in 1900 coal accounted for 12.5 percent of exports. Both these effects benefited the visible balance of payments, countering the reductions in the invisibles balance because of profit repatriation by USA oil companies and the UK's net transfers to the European Community.

North Sea oil had another effect, however. The conversion of sterling to a 'petro-currency' pushed up the exchange rate, further reducing the competitiveness of manufactures produced in the UK. This is but part of the explanation for the UK's accelerating deindustrialization, however.

In certain well-publicized cases, increased import penetration undoubtedly has reflected dumping practices (for example, see Beresford and Pearson, 1985). However, both government domestic economic policies (discussed in the next section) and trade policies have been more important reasons, with the UK government adopting a much less protectionist stance than, say, the French or Japanese. At the same time, continuing overseas investment by UK manufacturing capital has exceeded the volume of inward investment to the UK by foreign-based multinationals such as Ford, Nissan and Philips. This net inward investment has been made for a variety of reasons such as relatively cheap labour by EC standards and getting behind EC tariff barriers, though the UK's 'free-trade' policies have at the same time led such companies to supply UK markets from production sites elsewhere in Europe (for example, Ford and General Motors from Spain) or the Third World. While such inward investment has often been of great local or regional significance, the net deficit on direct investment in manufacturing tended to expand over the 1970s (*Barclays Review*, 1982). The suspension of exchange control regulations from 1979 by the Conservative government, totally removing restrictions on direct investment overseas and considerably relaxing those on portfolio investment, dramatically increased this deficit. The overall deficit exceeded £8 billion in 1981 alone, almost half of which was in the form of direct investment – 'an unprecedented deficit' (*Barclays Review*, 1982).

Many City of London financial institutions such as unit trusts and investment companies now hardly invest at all in manufacturing activities in the UK, having switched to investing abroad. The rationale underlying this behaviour was clearly spelled out in an advertisement in *The Sunday Times*, 10 March 1985:

There has never been a sterling crisis for investors in the Overseas Equity Pension Bond ... we've achieved tax-free growth of 40% per annum to date in this top performing fund ... somewhere in the world, there's always somebody making money. Whilst one stock market is out of favour another may be booming. By maintaining the flexibility to move your pension investment between world markets, the Overseas Equity Pension Bond aims to provide steady growth through the ups and downs of individual market sectors.

But what is good for the welfare of individual pensioners is not necessarily good for the UK's productive base in manufacturing activities. Over the period 1981–1983, there was net annual disinvestment of about £2 billion from manufacturing activities in the UK in contrast to the modest net investment of the 1973–1981 period (Henry, 1984). Manufacturing output and employment collapsed though labour productivity and profits rose a little; manufactured imports surpassed exports for the first time. It was against this background that the Conservative government embarked in 1982 on the Falklands/Malvinas campaign. Memories of imperial grandeur were revived and sentiments of jingoistic nationalism recreated, as militaristic ventures abroad breathed new life into Margaret Thatcher's authoritarian populism (Barnett, 1982).

1.3   Central government economic policies and the changing national economy

The UK's postwar economic history has been characterized by a recurrent gap between the aims of government national economic policy and the trajectory of national economic development. An important reason for this is the growing internationalization of economic life, relative to the limits of State economic intervention. The increasing dominance of the world economy by a few major multinationals has even led some (for example Radice, 1984) to question the validity of the notion of a 'national economy'. However, for much of the postwar period there has been a party political consensus that governments could and should intervene to influence national economic performance, although after 1979 the Conservative government altered the balance between State policies and the forces of international competition. A persistent theme in the consensus has been the implementation of 'stop-go' policies, the switch from go to stop generally coming in response to international pressures as the UK's position in the international economic order deteriorated.

1.3.1   Full employment policies, 1944–1962

Conscription dramatically abolished interwar unemployment problems and by late 1942 wartime production was threatened by labour shortages. The coalition government responded to this threat by enhancing its powers to direct and control production, creating a 'command economy'. Policies were devised to seek out labour reserves, particularly female ones: by the end of 1943 all women aged 18–50 were being registered and directed to war work, unless prevented by compelling domestic reasons. Of necessity, the government reorganized the social services and set up day nurseries. It was against this background that the debate on postwar society was conducted. What sort of guarantees could be given to working people who were winning the war that the poverty and misery of the interwar years would not be repeated? The response was the highly influential White Paper on employment policy (Cmnd 6577), and the challenge to postwar governments was how to devise macro-economic policies, along Keynesian demand-management lines, to sustain in peacetime the 'full employment' created by the wartime economy.

The significance of memories of interwar unemployment seemed to be confirmed when the 1945 General Election rejected Churchill's Conservative Party, returning a Labour government on a seemingly radically reforming programme. This government then used relatively unsophisticated, though effective, wartime economic planning machinery to reconvert the economy to peacetime production. It was apparently committed to 'planning' the economy but, by 1948, 'planning' had been transformed to accommodate the requirements of capitalist interests and Treasury hostility to increasing public expenditure (Rowthorne, 1983, p. 66). The decisive moment came in 1947. No sooner had the newly created National Coal Board begun operating than an energy crisis erupted. Almost all primary energy requirements were met by coal (Figure 1.5) but coal stocks at power stations had been reduced to 8.5 million tons in 1947. Abnormally severe weather at the start of 1947, combined with the inability of the rail system to move enough coal to power stations, meant that soon all but essential industries in London and the Southeast, the Midlands and Northwest were without electricity. About two million workers were temporarily laid off. The immediate crisis lasted well into 1947 and the drop in industrial output contributed to the 1947 balance of payments crisis (see Figure 1.2). Government response to this was selectively to restrict public expenditure and shift the emphasis in industrial production to import substitution and export growth. Given the priority attached to defence expenditure, which still accounted for 7 percent of Gross National Product (GNP) in 1948, the cuts fell disproportionately on other programmes such as education, health and housing. Sterling's devaluation against the dollar in 1949 reflected both the government's commitment to domestic industrial production and its unwillingness to seek to guarantee this by stronger interventionist planning. Instead, measures such as wage restrictions had to be introduced to try and preserve the competitive advantage conferred by devaluation. This implied a price for those working in industry and for the government in terms of political support.

The economic policy shifts initiated from 1948 ushered in the era of 'Butskellite' policies that dominated until 1962 (Keegan, 1984, pp. 20–24).

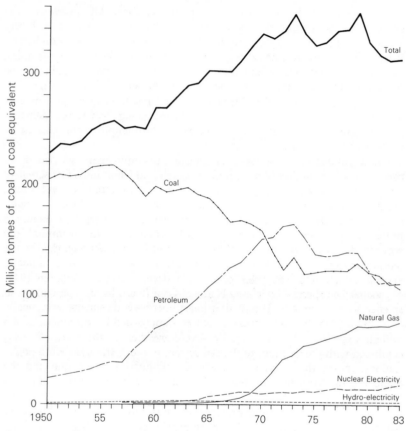

Figure 1.5   Primary energy consumption in the UK, 1950–1983 (Central Statistical Office, 1984, *Economic Trends Annual Supplement*).

Conservative governments between 1951 and 1962 accepted many of the changes introduced since 1945. Most of the nationalizations of basic industries were accepted. These were seen as vital to national economic recovery but offered little hope of profit for, and so investment by, private capital; the only instances of denationalization – road transport and steel – were in industries where prospects for profits seemed good (Brown, 1962). They also endorsed the creation of the Welfare State and the commitment to full employment although the means of attaining these goals altered. The emphasis on holding down public expenditure strengthened – it only rose from 21.5 to 22.3 percent of GDP between 1950 and 1960 (Brown and

Sheriff, 1979). But a dramatic cutback in military spending meant that this could be done without sacrificing the Welfare State, workers' wages or industry's profits – at least for a time. Maintaining full employment increasingly rested on 'fine tuning' the economy, regulating domestic demand via changing taxation levels.

Butskellite policies seemingly produced their desired results. The economy grew strongly while annual inflation rates fluctuated around 2 percent. Industrial output grew sharply, although manufacturing output as a proportion of GDP fell as a result of more rapid expansion in other sectors. Moreover, profitability was restored in manufacturing and investment recovered strongly in relation to the interwar period. At the same time, full employment conditions prevailed, with the number of employees in employment increasing and very low levels of registered unemployment (Figure 1.6). Indeed, growing labour demands could only be met by selective immigration (from the New Commonwealth) and an expansion in female activity rates, drawing many married women into waged labour, often for the first time (Table 1.2).

Some important changes were also occurring in the structure of the economy during this period. The organizational structure of manufacturing was changing, with growing centralization of control in increasingly vertically integrated major corporations: by 1963 the top 100 companies controlled 38 percent of national manufacturing output, compared to 21 percent in 1953 (Hannah, 1976). Centralization and concentration were also evident in parts of the private service sector, especially retailing. These had important implications for the geography of employment and economic activity as well as for governments' capacity to manage the economy.

Within broad sectors such as manufacturing and services there were important changes in output and employment (Table 1.3). In agriculture, the combination of output growth and employment decline reflected greater penetration of capitalist relations of production and new techniques such as factory farming, increased mechanization and new strains of crops and fertilizers (Newby, 1980, pp. 83–96). The changes in agriculture partly reflected the government's 'cheap food' policy and further integrated agriculture with key branches of manufacturing such as chemicals and engineering. This policy involved retaining access to cheap imports from the Commonwealth and other areas as well as holding down the prices of domestic food production via the 'deficiency payments' scheme of the 1947 Agriculture Act. Keeping food prices down was one mechanism whereby wage increases in industry could be contained, but, at the same time, this lessened the incentive to invest in new production techniques.

Employment cuts in mining and quarrying largely reflected a change in government energy supply policy from 1958. The *Plan for Coal* (National

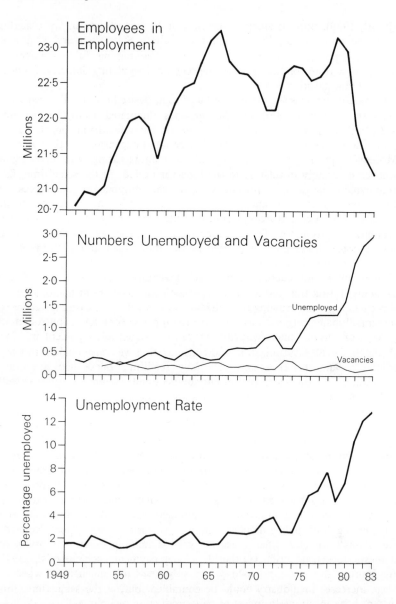

Figure 1.6 Employment, unemployment and vacancies, 1949–1983 (Central Statistical Office, 1984, *Economic Trends Annual Supplement*).

Table 1.2   Activity rates, 1931–1981

| | Male | Percentages | | |
		All	Female Married	Non-married
1931	90.5	34.2	10.0	60.2
1951	87.6	34.7	21.7	55.8
1961	86.0	37.4	29.7	50.6
1966	84.0	42.4	38.1	49.2
1971	81.4	42.7	42.2	43.7
1976	80.6	45.7	49.0	41.6
1977	79.8	47.4	50.4	42.1
1979	78.6	46.9	49.6	42.5

Sources: Central Statistical Office (1978, 1982).

Coal Board, 1950) was intended partly to resolve the medium-term problems of energy supply via reconstructing production around 250 of the NCB's 900 collieries. Investment would be concentrated on these, maintaining output while cutting the unit costs of winning coal – and so those of electricity. However, reconstruction posed more severe problems than were anticipated. Policies of maximizing coal output introduced in 1947 were continued and the NCB was not allowed to raise coal prices as it wished. Towards the end of the 1950s, though, when many newly reconstructed collieries were beginning to produce coal in substantial quantities, a cheaper source of primary fuel became available. Military intervention over the Suez Canal secured access to cheap oil supplies from the Middle East and energy policy switched from supplementing to replacing coal with oil in electricity generation (T. Hall, 1980, pp. 67–87). Consequently, from the late 1950s the NCB began to close collieries and run down manpower at an accelerating pace.

Within manufacturing there were considerable differences between branches (Table 1.3). Symptoms of deindustrialization were already apparent in falling employment in clothing, leather, textiles and shipbuilding in the 1950s, but there was expansion of chemicals, electrical engineering, motor vehicles, paper, printing and publishing and 'other manufacturing', encompassing both consumer goods and the means of production. Similar points can be made about the services sector. Against a background of overall expansion, employment in transport (mainly rail) and public administration fell in the 1950s. The former reflected government transport policies, particularly encouragement of road transport in general and private car ownership in particular, underpinned towards the end of the 1950s by motorway investment. The latter reflected more general policies towards

Table 1.3   Percentage changes in employment, Standard Industrial Classification Order Groups, 1952–1982

				Percentage change			Absolute nos. in 1982
		1952–1960	1960–1966	1966–1971	1971–1975	1975–1979	1979–1982	
1	Agriculture, forestry and fishing	−17.6	−22.4	−25.3	−5.6	+13.6	−3.5	354*
2	Mining and quarrying	−12.2	−25.5	−30.2	−12.2	−3.1	−6.6	326
3	Food, drink and tobacco	+10.6	+2.1	−4.0	−6.4	−5.6	−11.4	622
4	Chemicals and allied industries	+14.6	−1.6	−2.5	−2.2	−7.9	−13.5	416
5	Metal manufacture	+6.1	−0.8	−11.3	−10.3	−11.2	−33.2	295
6	Mechanical engineering	+11.7	+11.6	−2.6	−8.8	−18.0	−21.1	728
7	Instrument engineering	+21.5	+7.5	+0.6	−6.3	+3.2	−15.6	130
8	Electrical engineering	+31.0	+15.6	−3.8	−3.9	−11.4	−14.7	649
9	Shipbuilding and marine engineering	−6.2	−26.9	−8.2	−4.0	−9.8	−16.0	147
10	Vehicles	+27.0	−6.5	−4.4	−7.3	−2.2	−24.8	559
11	Other metal goods	+8.9	+7.5	−8.1	−4.6	+4.1	−19.7	432
12	Textiles	−9.2	−11.9	−18.1	−14.9	−15.9	−33.0	314
13	Leather goods	−8.5	−6.1	−19.7	−11.3	−21.2	−32.4	29
14	Clothing and footwear	−0.6	−8.0	−10.5	−11.4	−16.0	−26.8	273
15	Bricks, pottery, glass, cement, etc.	n.c.	+2.3	−8.6	−10.3	−10.8	−20.1	211
16	Timber and furniture	+1.6	n.c.	−6.6	−2.0	−12.3	−19.5	266
17	Paper, printing and publishing	+17.9	+6.1	−4.1	−5.4	−6.7	−9.5	498
18	Other manufacturing	+21.3	+12.0	+4.7	−2.8	−6.4	−24.0	244
19	Construction	+9.6	+11.9	−22.9	+4.0	−4.1	−18.6	1049
20	Gas, electricity and water	n.c.	+12.8	−12.5	−6.4	−1.4	−2.3	340
21	Transport and communications	−5.4	−3.2	−3.3	−3.5	−2.3	−7.7	1383
22	Distributive trades	+19.9	+5.1	−11.0	+5.7	+0.6	−5.7	2706
23	Insurance, banking and finance	+22.8	+17.5	+11.6	+10.8	+57.6	+4.8	1321
24	Professional and scientific services	+22.2	+26.6	+16.0	+18.8	+14.3	+0.1	3768
25	Miscellaneous services	+11.7	+17.4	−1.6	+11.2	+1.9	+0.2	2554
26	Public administration and defence	−2.5	+8.8	+6.8	+9.7	+1.8	−4.2	1549

* Includes seasonal and temporary workers.

n.c. = No change.

Sources: Fothergill and Gudgin (1978); Central Statistical Office (1985).

Note: The emphasis on employment and the selection of the particular dates in the Table reflect a wish to connect discussion of changes at national level with those at regional level (see Chapter 2) and the availability of regional level data. Regional output data are notoriously unreliable in the 1970s as output is allocated between plants of multiregional firms on the basis of employment.

controlling public expenditure and deregulating the economy, thereby reducing the numbers employed by central government. Conversely, increases in government employees in professional and scientific services, mostly in education and health, reflected commitments to the Welfare State. In both consumer and producer services controlled by private capital, expansion reflected overall economic growth and rising consumer expenditures. Producer services increasingly became organized as a separate economic sector associated with the growth of office employment and the social division of labour.

By the end of the 1950s several paradoxes were apparent in national economic performance and its relationship to government policies. Successive 'stop-go' cycles were having deleterious effects on manufacturing investment and economic modernization while such cyclical policies were made necessary by regional economic imbalances. Levels of national demand that produced full employment in the Development Areas stoked up inflationary pressures in the Southeast and Midlands, which were then transmitted more generally throughout the economy. In contrast, setting demand at levels that had less inflationary impacts left significant pockets of unemployment. Further, while national output growth rates were impressive compared to those attained in the interwar years, they paled in comparison with those of most of the UK's international competitors (Hudson el al., 1984, pp. 80–82). No fundamental modernization of the economy was taking place on a scale comparable to that in, say, West Germany or Japan. As a result, the UK's share of world manufacturing output and trade began to fall sharply. It seemed that a postwar golden age had been achieved in the UK in the 1950s, enabling the interests of capital, labour and the State to be satisfied simultaneously but this had been based on very specific circumstances. Those who believed they could continue indefinitely were living in a fool's paradise (Rowthorne, 1983, p. 66).

1.3.2 Modernization policies, 1962–1975

Around 1962 the Conservative government began markedly to change its practices and ideology as it sought to generate faster economic growth, sustain full employment and improve international competitiveness. A general election was required within 2 years and a 'depressed' economy with 'high' unemployment (maybe 5 percent) did not seem a recipe for electoral success. This, together with misperception of the successful French experience of indicative planning, influenced the development of new policies. These centred on securing tripartite agreement between government, big industrial companies and trade unions about national growth targets. The National Economic Development Office and Council were created in 1962 to provide the institutional setting in which to pursue this corporatist approach to national economic policy formation. The aim was to provide an environment in which major companies could confidently invest while trade unions moderated their wage demands. Government for its part agreed to selective increases in public expenditure – which then rose rapidly, both absolutely (Table 1.4) and as a percentage of GDP – as an integral component of its new planning approach.

Following vague references by Labour's leader, Harold Wilson, to the cathartic effects that the white heat of new technology would have on the UK economy, the new government greatly strengthened the economic planning and policy tendencies established between 1962 and 1964. Structural intervention in industry and State subsidies to private capital to invest in new plant and machinery were increased, notably via the 1966 Industrial Development Act. The government's planning aspirations were encapsulated in the new Department of Economic Affairs (DEA), headed by the Deputy Prime Minister, and most coherently presented in the National Plan (Department of Economic Affairs, 1965). In a sense, the Plan merely expressed pious hopes as government lacked the powers needed to implement its proposals but, in practice, this proved irrelevant as the Plan was *de facto* abandoned only months after publication. The deflationary package of July 1966 cut back planned public expenditure increases, which meant that the Plan's crucial national output growth targets were forfeited. As it happened deflation proved insufficient to counter pressures on the balance of payments and sterling, which was devalued in November 1967.

If creating the DEA signalled a commitment to coordinated modernization policies, its abolition in 1969 unambiguously confirmed their abandonment. Industrial restructuring policies were continued from 1966 but in an increasingly chaotic, uncoordinated way. The rundown of the coal industry accelerated after 1965 in response to pressures on public expenditure and because of continuing attempts to cut energy prices, as natural gas and nuclear power provided additional competition to domestically produced coal (see Figure 1.5). There was a further dimension to this, however. Reducing coal-mining employment had been seen in the National Plan as releasing labour required by an expanding manufacturing sector. Abandoning the intended manufacturing growth rate meant that labour released from the mines became translated into unemployment growth.

The government remained committed to manufacturing expansion and restructuring but strictly within limits dictated by the balance of payments position. The Labour Party no longer displayed the same enthusiasm for nationalization as in the immediate postwar years, which meant that this was largely rejected as a restructuring mechanism for manufacturing – with the significant exception of bulk iron and steel production, renationalized in

Table 1.4   Public expenditure by PESC categories, 1969–1983

	£million, current prices					
	1969–1970*	1974–1975†	1975–1976	1978–1979	1979–1980	1982–1983
Defence	3,775	5,151	5,403	7,495	9,226	14,103
Overseas aid	483	873	772	1,832	2,107	2,139
Agriculture, forestry and fisheries	502	1,555	1,481	1,027	1,277	1,833
Industry, energy, trade and employment	1,634	3,299	2,882	3,480	3,387	6,530
Government lending to nationalized industries	2,013‡	3,212‡	3,749‡	693	1,857	1,114
Roads and transport	1,314	2,570	2,656	3,038	3,650	5,049
Housing	2,181	5,057	4,203	4,650	5,865	4,692
Other environmental services	1,200	2,302	2,388	3,099	3,657	5,100
Law, order and protective services	798	1,528	1,620	3,077	3,792	5,560
Education and science, libraries and arts	3,674	7,060	6,968	9,781	11,246	15,408
Health and personal social services	3,125	5,794	6,199	9,225	11,057	19,000
Social security	5,755	8,620	9,517	16,918	19,986	36,550
Miscellaneous	1,436	1,770	3,069	1,801	2,129	3,760
Total	27,790	49,791	50,907	65,477	78,521	123,340

* 1974 prices.
† 1975–1976 prices.
‡ Refers to total capital expenditure by nationalized industries.

Source: Various public expenditure White Papers.

1967. However, establishment of the Industrial Reorganization Corporation and the provisions of the 1968 Industrial Expansion Act created new channels through which to pursue modernization goals, including encouragement of mergers. Such initiatives had some impact, though not always the intended one as some newly merged companies invested overseas rather than in the UK. However, modernization of manufacturing generally proceeded more slowly than in the UK's major competitors. The government also increasingly regarded incomes policy as the mechanism by which to restore national economic growth, investment and profits. This had the political effect of alienating significant sections of its supporters, as the 1970 General Election revealed (see Table 1.9).

The new Conservative government essentially remained committed to the 'old' social-democratic aims but initially switched more to market forces as an economic steering mechanism. However, once it became clear that this switch in policies was contributing to national economic recession, it began to move away from them. The first step was to recognize that not all 'lame ducks' could be allowed to die, with Rolls Royce being rescued from bankruptcy via nationalization in 1971. The intensity of the U-turn was revealed in the 1972 Industry Act, which contained a more powerful package of interventionist measures than that of the preceding Labour government. But, like its predecessor. Edward Heath's government came unstuck over its policies towards incomes control and the trade unions, losing the February 1974 General Election on the issue of the miners' strike (T. Hall, 1980, pp. 166–221).

Whereas a Labour government was returned in 1964 because it seemed better equipped to implement modernization policies, the one in 1974 was returned because it seemed better placed to cooperate with trade unions. The new government initially seemed committed to more powerful interventionist policies than those introduced in 1972, although the most radical demands of the Labour Party's pre-election national conferences were effectively neutered (Coates, 1980, pp.2–11). A new interventionist agency, the National Enterprise Board (NEB), was created in 1975, but its budget and powers were strictly limited. In practice the NEB mainly became another mechanism for rescuing lame ducks, notably British Leyland, though it and its successor, the British Technology Group, also came to have a minor role as a source of venture capital for small 'high-tech' companies until the latter was wound up in 1984. More generally, the impact of soaring domestic inflation and the international recession, intensified by the 1973–1974 oil price rises, produced a radical redefinition of the government's economic philosophy and policies, abandonment of its commitment to full employment and a preoccupation with tackling inflation.

Perhaps the most dramatic single indicator of these changes was a precipitate fall in the rate of profit in manufacturing while that in services remained high (33.2 percent in 1966 and 31.6 percent in 1976; Brown and Sheriff, 1979, p. 251). Gross Domestic Product continued to grow though rather more haltingly, unevenly and slowly than in other major capitalist countries (Hudson et al., 1984, pp. 82–85). Output in services generally grew consistently and strongly. Growth in industrial production and manufacturing output lagged behind this and compared poorly to manufacturing growth in other countries, especially after 1966 (Rowthorne, 1983, p. 69). The weaknesses of industrial production in the UK were clearly visible prior to the mid-1970s' general recession in the world economy, and the share of manufacturing output in GDP continued its secular decline. Manufacturing investment per capita in the UK also remained well below that in other major industrial countries, as did the growth rate of labour productivity (Brown and Sheriff, 1979, pp. 247–249). While an improvement on past performance in the UK, it was insufficient to halt the falling share of world exports. Consequently, modernization investment meant job shedding while failure to modernize often meant total closure and redundancies.

The combined effects of these tendencies was that manufacturing employment began to fall absolutely from 1966 (see Table 1.3) while employment in agriculture and mining also continued to fall. These losses exceeded net growth in service sector employment so that the total number of employees in employment fell by over 700,000 between 1966 and 1975 (see Figure 1.6). Associated with these changes, female activity rates further increased (see Table 1.2) while the proportion of women, especially married women, who worked part-time was also rising: by 1966 46 percent of all married women working for a wage did so on a part-time basis while 80 percent of all part-time female workers were married. The net result of these changes in the levels and patterns of labour demand was that unemployment rose considerably (see Figure 1.6). Inflation also accelerated sharply from the start of the 1970s; by 1975 'wage-settlements of 30 percent or more ... [were] ... becoming normal' (Shanks, 1977, p. 75). Simultaneous increases in inflation and unemployment confounded Keynesian economic orthodoxies, posing acute policy choices for government; we consider these in the next section.

Before doing so, however, we wish to examine in more detail some changes in economic structure between 1962 and 1975. Governments' policies helped accelerate centralization of control via encouragement of mergers and take-overs. By 1970 the top 100 manufacturing companies accounted for 46 percent of all UK manufacturing output; well over half of these were multiproduct companies, having grown and diversified by mergers and acquisitions (Hannah, 1976). Similar processes were occurring in private sector consumer and producer services. Foreign multinationals were becoming increasingly significant; by 1970, 300 USA-based companies controlled 15 percent of UK manufacturing output. This growing interpenetration of major capitalist economies and the concentration of production were reflected in trade patterns and, by 1973, 30 percent of UK exports were intra-company flows (Hood and Young, 1979). Increasingly national economic performance seemingly depended on decisions by a relatively small number of major multinationals, christened the 'meso-economic sector' by Holland (1975).

In addition to these changes in the forms of organization and ownership of capital, others were taking place both between and within manufacturing and services. The broad switch in capital, output and employment from manufacturing to services generally reflected profitability differentials. Considerable changes were also occurring within these broad sectors, which can be illustrated by employment (see Table 1.3). As employment loss became more common after 1960 and generalized after 1966, branches of manufacturing became differentiated via their pace of decline. Small absolute job increases were recorded only in instrument engineering and other manufacturing between 1966 and 1971, and these were reversed after 1971. Employment thus fell in all Standard Industrial Classification Order Groups between 1971 and 1975, most heavily in clothing and textiles. In contrast, the general trend in service employment was upwards and more and more women were drawn into the labour force, especially on a part-time basis. Employment in producer services, most notably insurance, banking and finance continued to grow while that in consumer services, both private and public sector, generally rose. The greatest absolute and relative increases were in professional and scientific services, reflecting levels of public expenditure on education and health (see Table 1.4) and growing socialization of the costs of reproducing labour power. This assumed great significance as planned public expenditure increases were cut as part of the crisis management deflationary package adopted in 1975.

1.3.3 Disinflation policies and abandonment of the commitment to full employment, 1975–1983

The April 1975 Budget confirmed that the government's economic strategy now centred on restraining the growth of public expenditure (see Table 1.4), cuts in real wages and rising unemployment as deliberate policy choices. Domestic deflation to improve the balance of payments position was seen as unavoidable, given the 1972 decision to adopt a floating sterling exchange rate. As Dennis Healey, Chancellor of the Exchequer, stated in his Budget speech, 'This is not a matter of choice or of political decision. It is a fact of the world we live in – a fact for which I must budget. Our overseas deficit must be removed – and the world must know if it will be removed' (*Hansard*, vol. 890, col. 283, 5 April 1975). Yet again the interests of internationally oriented capital took precedence over those of jobs and production in the UK. The Budget statement forecast correctly that unemployment would rise above one million as a result of the proposals it contained (see Figure 1.6). In this way the government explicitly signalled the rupture with the commitment to full employment given in 1944 and since shared by governments of both major political parties.

Some claim that the Labour government was 'blown off course' by pressures imposed by the IMF in 1976 but it had chosen to alter course sharply prior to that point (Bosanquet, 1980). However, it decisively shifted the terrain for the political debate about economic policy. It no longer centred on the most appropriate means of attaining full employment and output growth – these aims had already been jettisoned – but on reducing inflation – though, as before, preoccupation with the balance of payments was never far away.

From 1975 planned public expenditure increases were successively cut (see Table 1.4), while control of public expenditure was increasingly centralized, reducing the autonomy of local authorities. Had the 1975–1976 share of public expenditure been maintained until 1978–1979, current expenditure would have been £3100 million higher and capital expenditure £4700 million higher over the intervening period (Ormerod, 1980). These cuts were intended to allow private sector investment to grow. It did, but private sector investment in the UK rose by only £1700 million, partly because of investment abroad. Faith in market forces generating growth in investment, output and jobs within the UK was clearly misplaced.

The government's revised policy for 'the regeneration of British industry', based on a reheated corporatist approach to industrial policy, failed to produce its intended results. It did produce some unintended ones, however. For a time, the government successfully converted its social contract with the trade unions into a restrictive incomes policy, with the acquiescence of senior trade union leaders, passing the costs of industrial regeneration onto the working class. Average real wages fell by 8 percent between 1975 and 1977 (Ormerod, 1980, p. 59), helping profitability to recover somewhat. Subsequently, increasing frustration with real wage cuts and rising unemployment led to widespread rank-and-file militancy, especially in parts of the public sector. The collapse of the social contract in the 'winter of discontent' in 1978–1979 was an important factor in the government's defeat in the 1979 General Election, and in the arrival of Margaret Thatcher as Prime Minister.

The Thatcher government is distinguished from its predecessors in that its '... electoral ideology, far from being discarded having served its purpose, formed the basis of the economic programme the Government intended to implement' (Gamble, 1983, p. 22) despite the fact that the circumstances facing it when it took office had altered, as governments in the USA and West Germany recognized in pursuing more expansionary policies. To some extent the government simply intensified tendencies visible in the policies of its Labour predecessor: generally restricting public expenditure but selectively increasing funding (notably for defence and law and order) while reducing the Public Sector Borrowing Requirement (PSBR); increasing the scope of the private sector at the expense of the public sector as companies such as British Aerospace, British Telecom and Jaguar have been privatized; and reaffirming the primacy attached to reducing inflation. In some respects, notably intensified pressure on local authority expenditure and associated cuts in public sector housing provision (see Table 1.4), the quantitative changes were of such magnitude as to amount to qualitative changes in policy. Other policy elements were entirely new, especially the open assault on the organized power of trade unions, which became combined with the aim of cutting back the public sector via elimination of nationalized steel and coal production (Sadler, 1984; Hudson, 1985). Overall, though, what perhaps distinguishes Thatcherite economic policies from those of the Wilson/Callaghan era is not so much a radical change in the direction of policy as a radical change in style, in the accompanying rhetoric. The debate became abrasive and the style adversarial; for example, drawing on imagery derived from the Falklands/Malvinas campaign, striking miners in 1984–1985 became 'the enemy within' (Beynon, 1985).

While several elements of the government's overall economic and political programme have been implemented, many have not. The 'social market' strategy threatened significant sections of labour and capital – perhaps most vividly revealed by Sir Terence Beckett, Director General of the Confederation of British Industry (CBI), who threatened a 'bare knuckle fight' over interest rates in 1980. There was also growing disagreement within the Conservative Party itself, associated with Party luminaries such as Lord Stockton (the former Harold Macmillan), Edward Heath and Francis Pym. Rather than risk an all-out assault, the government settled for a 'war of position' on several fronts. It has often displayed considerable tactical acumen in choosing when to push forward – no more so than in avoiding confrontation with the National Union of Mineworkers in 1982, waiting until 1984 when circumstances were in its favour (Beynon, 1985). But a result of this approach has been growing difficulty in retaining overall strategic control and, by the 1981 Budget, the government's strategy was in disarray on most fronts, though inflation and interest rates had begun to fall (Gamble, 1983,

p. 129). By the 1982 Budget, the Medium Term Financial Strategy (MTFS) was disintegrating. Concern over the political costs of rising inflation led to relaxation of monetary targets. This increased pressures to adhere to the fiscal part of the MTFS and further reduce the PSBR. Even so, government borrowing rose, as did public expenditure from 39.5 percent of GDP in 1979–1980 to 42.5 percent in 1983–1984. Widespread cuts in regional and industrial aid, in nationalized industry and in Welfare State spending, failed to compensate for the growth in pensions with the 'aging' of the population, planned increases in expenditure on defence (including maintenance of an independent nuclear deterrent) and law and order, and unplanned ones on social security as a result of mass unemployment. At the same time, the emphasis on cutting capital rather than recurrent spending led to the emergence of a crisis in infrastructure provision, with the charge being levelled at the government that 'the infrastructure, ill cared for and vulnerable in 1980 is now sufficiently unkempt and at risk to give rise to public alarm' (Mauser, 1985). It says much about the mood of the electorate, the political alternatives on offer, the Falklands/Malvinas campaign and the UK electoral system, that Margaret Thatcher was returned with a massive majority of seats in Parliament in June 1983. This election result appears all the more remarkable when set against the background of the impacts of the policies pursued since 1979 on the economy – though as we show in later chapters, it is less surprising if one considers the people and areas that suffered most heavily as a result of them – but these must themselves be seen in the context of changes between 1975 and 1979.

Between 1975 and 1978–1979 there was weak, patchy recovery in manufacturing output but by 1979 this stood well below the level of 1973–1974 and the share of manufacturing output in GDP continued to fall. Labour productivity grew very slowly, especially compared to that in other countries, reflecting continuing low levels of new fixed capital investment. Increasing productivity differentials were a key reason for falling international competitiveness. Manufacturing employment fell as companies shed labour in restructuring production within the UK, switched production abroad, went bankrupt in the face of growing competition or switched capital out of manufacturing. Manufacturing employment fell sharply between 1975 and 1979 (see Table 1.3), especially in metal producing and using industries, clothing and textiles.

In aggregate, the economy recovered rather more steadily and strongly, and this becomes clear if different sectors are considered. One effect of the UK's entry to the European Community was a boost to agricultural production because of the increased levels of price support provided by the guarantee section of the Common Agricultural Policy (CAP). The increased profitability of agriculture led to important changes in its organizational structure. While small family farms continued to predominate, the trend to bigger units continued; these dominated in terms of output, more emphatically than elsewhere in the Community (Hudson et al., 1984, pp. 52–54). Formally independent, family farms were increasingly tied into the interests of agribusinesses and food processing companies via contracting arrangements (see Chapter 4.2). This, along with technological changes, has helped promote specialization of production. The net result has been to reinforce the productivity gap between the UK and the rest of the Community (Centre for Agricultural Strategy, 1980).

The 1973–1974 oil price rises led to an apparent re-evaluation of the role of coal in energy supply, with coal production stabilizing in the short term and plans for major new investments in the longer term. Of greater significance was the development of North Sea oil reserves and the subsequent rapid rise in oil production. In the services sector both output and employment continued to grow strongly – the latter amounting to over 50 percent of all employment by 1979. The startling growth of jobs in insurance, banking and finance, at a time when those in manufacturing fell, mirrored increasing government preoccupation with monetary control rather than production in the 'real' economy. The changing pattern of sectoral demand for labour was linked to falling male and growing female employment, especially part-time work for married women. Over one million women were added to the labour force in the 1970s, almost the entire net increase in it, while the labour supply was also increasing as a result of demographic factors and the 1955–1960 'baby boom'. As a result of these changes in labour demand and supply, unemployment rose sharply (see Figure 1.6), despite the effects of a variety of temporary job schemes introduced by government from 1976, such as the Job Creation Programme (Lonsdale, 1985, pp. 43–53).

Worse was to follow after 1979. The removal of capital export controls and an appreciating 'petro-pound' further eroding competitiveness were instrumental in precipitating a massive collapse of manufacturing activity in the UK. Output plummeted to below the levels of the late 1960s. Labour productivity grew but only as a result of wholesale labour shedding and the reorganization of work practices, often associated with corporate mergers to cut capacity (Churchill, 1985), rather than through investment in new capacity and technologies. Manufacturing investment slumped – indeed net disinvestment prevailed – as capital was switched overseas. The growing technological backwardness of manufacturing is encapsulated in the UK's 4.6 percent share of the world robot population in 1983, compared to 43.9 percent for Japan, 21.3 percent for the USA, 12.8 percent for West Germany, even 4.8 percent for Italy (Rodger, 1984). Such was the severity of the decline in manufacturing and construction output that despite the rising output of North Sea oil and in agriculture and services, GDP declined between 1979 and 1981.

The impact of the post-1979 recession on the labour market was equally severe. Severe employment decline became generalized. The greatest rate of job loss was in metal manufacturing (see Table 1.3) and this, along with the greatly accelerated pace of job decline in the recently nationalized British Shipbuilders and British Leyland – both major metal users – is highly symbolic. It mainly reflected the British Steel Corporation's major closure programme, brought about by the government's intention to cut public expenditure and the scope of the State sector, and attack trade union power. The continuing fall in manufacturing employment generated considerable public debate, not least because of the readily visible links between this, trade policies and import penetration in products such as cars, electrical consumer goods, clothing and textiles. This led to calls for protectionism in the late 1970s and early 1980s, which often united sections of capital and labour but met with limited success.

Partly because of downward multiplier effects from loss of manufacturing jobs and partly because of government public expenditure policies, total service sector employment also fell between 1979 and 1982. Largely because of this, female activity rates stabilized while more and more service employment was on a part-time or casualized basis (Wainwright, 1984, p. 204). As in manufacturing, job losses were often associated with mergers, especially in distribution, while in banking and finance employment growth was accompanied by growing centralization of control (Churchill, 1985). It is highly revealing of the character of the changes that had occurred that, by the early 1980s, an estimated 1.3 million people relied directly or indirectly on tourism for employment, making it the biggest single employer and growth industry (Sandles, 1985).

Employment decline in all sectors resulted in the number of employees in employment in 1982 falling below the 1960 level. Self-employment rose by 32 percent between 1979 and 1984, to almost 2.5 million, most of the increase being of women (Manpower Services Commission, 1985). Notified vacancies fell sharply, though, while registered unemployment more than doubled in four years (see Figure 1.6). Within the growing mass of unemployed, long-term unemployment was becoming increasingly prevalent and generalized across all age and both gender groups. By 1981 government temporary job schemes were absorbing about half of all school-leavers (Stafford, 1981). Currently well over half a million people annually are taking part in the Youth Training Programme, Community Programme and other special employment schemes (Manpower Services Commission, 1985) for a few months prior to an existence on supplementary benefit for many. Against this background, immigration to the UK virtually ceased while emigration rose as those with appropriate skills became international migrant workers in the new centres of accumulation in the Middle and Far East. The government's response to mass unemployment is to harangue the unemployed into pricing themselves back into work (cutting the real level of State welfare benefits to encourage this) or into setting up their own small businesses. Thus the ultimate answer to capitalism's failure to generate sufficient jobs at socially acceptable wage rates is to urge everyone to become a capitalist, but the fact that, objectively, most people will be unable to do so is then conveniently skipped over.

1.4   Changing living conditions and lifestyles

As an integral part of changing economic and employment structures, there have been important alterations in class structure with the growth of a new middle class and a recomposition of the working class. Linked to these changes there has been a series of profound changes in lifestyles and living conditions. As Harold Macmillan (now Lord Stockton) put it at a garden fête in Bedford in 1957: 'Let us be frank about it. Most of our people have never had it so good' (cited in Keegan, 1984, p. 21) – a phrase that came to be a *leit-motif* for much of the postwar period. Such changes both reflect and have helped to shape economic and employment changes. There has been a more or less steady increase in average per capita disposable real income and consumer expenditure (Figure 1.7), accompanied by changes in work practices, shift patterns and increasing leisure time and paid holidays. This and the growing numbers of two-income households have helped change consumption norms, the division of domestic and waged labour, and household lifestyles (Pahl, 1984). Recently the relative decline in the UK's position in the international economic order has been reflected in newspaper headlines such as 'UK living standards trail in world league' (Wilkinson, 1985). Within the UK the gap in living standards between those in work and the unemployed has taken on an increased significance – unemployment has risen sharply and welfare benefits have been cut in real terms – while changes in taxation policies have widened differences among those in work.

In this section we examine changes in housing provision, private consumption and collective consumption and Welfare State provision. The boundaries between private and public sector provision have been the focus of a major political debate as to what sort of society the UK ought to become, the most recent manifestation of which is the dispute about redefining the boundary between the private sector and Welfare State in service provision. These consumption cleavages also have important implications for voting behaviour (Duke and Edgell, 1984). First, however, we examine changes in housing supply and consumption. Housing provides a link between economic changes and changes in lifestyles and living conditions in terms of its production (on which the fortunes of a significant part of the construction industry depend) and the way in which changing patterns of provision are related to broader patterns of social change.

£ 1980 prices

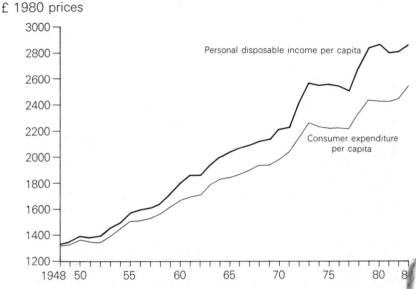

Figure 1.7   Per capita personal disposable income and consumer spending (1980 prices) 1948–1983 (Central Statistical Office, 1984, *Economic Trends Annual Supplement*).

1.4.1   Housing policies and changing patterns of housing provision and allocation

Housing is fundamentally important to people's lifestyles and living conditions. The mechanisms by which houses are produced and allocated and the different degrees and forms of State involvement in these processes are of considerable significance both to those affected by them and to governments' whose electoral fortunes may depend on the outcomes. Does housing provision challenge the prevailing logic of capitalist relations of production or help reinforce their grip, via emphasizing home ownership and appeals to the 'property-owning democracy'? State-subsidized public sector housing provision may help to socialize private capital's costs of production but at the risk of calling into question the general principle of private ownership of property. Can this risk be avoided by taxation policies that discriminate in favour of owner-occupation? Such issues have been recurrent features in debates on postwar housing provision in the UK.

Scant interwar investment in many areas and the impact of the Second World War meant that the postwar period began with a severe housing crisis. Much of the housing stock was inadequate, while there was a shortage of dwelling units. The government's short-term response involved a combination of conversions, repairs and building prefabs, many of which were preserved long beyond their intended lifespan. However, housing policy never occupied a central position in the Labour government's reformist policies. Its longer-term commitment to an expanded public sector housing programme reflected a pragmatic response to severe shortages of materials and a fear, grounded in the experience of uncontrolled suburbanization in the 1930s in the Southeast, that these would be inappropriately deployed by speculative private sector builders rather than deeply held socialist convictions regarding housing policy. A series of measures was enacted enabling local authorities to expand their housing role but the increase in public sector completions was checked in 1947 in response to public expenditure restrictions. Nevertheless, by 1951 1.5 million new, mostly public sector, dwellings had been built but almost 8 million households were still in unfit dwellings, with almost 2 million sharing accommodation. Housing was to be an important issue in the 1951 General Election, with the Conservatives critical of Labour's record.

A legacy of this was a promise made at the 1950 Conservative Party conference, committing the new government to building 300,000 houses per annum. Putting pragmatism before ideological purity, the government initially turned to the public sector as the mechanism for pursuing this target, which was attained in 1953. Public sector completions never reached such levels again. Increasing the number of houses built was achieved only at the price of constructing smaller houses with fewer facilities as standards, initially far from palatial, were cut further. Once the pre-election commitment was met, emphasis was switched to the private sector, in terms of both construction and promoting owner-occupation. The net result was a fall of almost 20 percent in annual investment in new dwellings between 1954 and 1958.

The government's revised housing policy was set out in a 1953 White Paper. It identified five issues that set the agenda for the bipartisan consensus on housing policy that subsequently emerged: encouragement of private enterprise; encouragement of owner-occupation; restoration of private renting, allowing rent increases to finance repairs; specification of the main role of local authorities as slum clearance and rehousing; greater emphasis on improvements and repair. Legislation was subsequently passed to enable these five aims to be translated into action. To some extent, housing policies had their intended effects, and the proportion of owner-occupier households rose from 29 percent in 1951 to 45 percent in 1964. As private sector completions rose, those in the public sector fell as this was used as one mechanism to contain public expenditure. Public expenditure pressures, allied to rising land prices (with the abolition of betterment procedures taxes – see p. 118), led to smaller public sector houses. In other respects, though,

housing quality improved, especially after the 1959 House Purchase and
Housing Act which made it mandatory for local authorities to give grants to
provide a fixed bath or shower, washbasin, sink, WC and hot and cold
running water (Figure 1.8). However, reduced public sector completions
meant that the stock of houses for those unable to afford owner-occupation
was growing slowly. Despite accelerated slum clearance, three million
families were still living in slum conditions in 1964. One reason for this was
that private landlords used rent increases to boost profits rather than improve
dwellings. Since in practice obtaining rent increases depended on tenancy
changes, the unscrupulous activities of some inner London landlords – and of

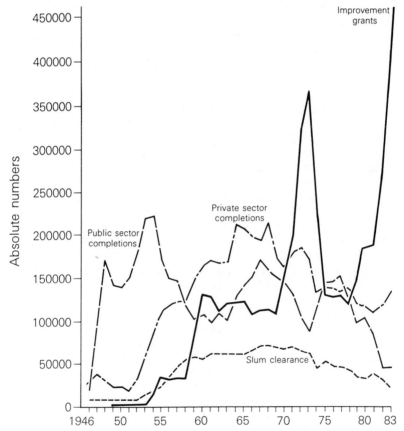

Figure 1.8 Housing completions, demolitions and improvement grants,
1946–1983 (Short, 1982; Central Statistical Office, 1984, *Social
Trends*).

one in particular – led to a new word entering the English language: Rachmanism.

This helped shape the immediate housing policy objectives of the new Labour government. It gave priority to guaranteeing security of tenure to tenants in privately rented, unfurnished accommodation and to securing fair rents. The 1965 Rent Act defined the latter as 'the likely market rent assuming no scarcity' which Short (1982, p. 55) considers a 'staggering assumption'. The government's medium-term hopes were encapsulated in the 1965 White Paper, *The Housing Programme, 1965-70*. This committed it to build 500,000 houses a year, split 50:50 between public sector rented and owner-occupied, thus putting the seal of approval on owner-occupation as the 'normal' tenure. The 'property-owning democracy' was now an acknowledged bipartisan political goal. In concrete terms, the 1967 Housing Act introduced the option mortgage and guarantee scheme, to extend owner-occupation to the lower-paid while the public sector was confirmed as providing housing for those with no other choice.

Housing completions initially increased under the Labour government (Figure 1.8), though falling well short of annual targets. These increases were bought at considerable cost, however. An increasing proportion was system-built units, often in high-rise blocks, that were soon to bring great physical and social problems. While substantially insulated from the 1964–1965 public expenditure restrictions, the housing programme increasingly came under pressure and was blown away in the storm following devaluation in 1967. Local authority targets were cut by 16,500 a year. In practice, construction slumped much more dramatically, especially after Conservative gains in the 1967–1968 local government elections, while sales to sitting tenants rose. Skilled, unionized workers were mainly owner-occupiers or, given the local authorities' 'points system' for allocation, tenants in better-quality public sector housing. Those most affected by the cuts were the unskilled and racial minorities – those lacking political clout but who could be presumed to vote Labour in any case.

In the post-devaluation period, the thrust of housing policies switched from comprehensive redevelopment to improvement. General Improvement Areas were introduced in the 1969 Housing Act to revive rundown environments around areas of physically sound housing, as part of an emerging emphasis on small-area policies for inner cities. This conveniently dovetailed with growing grassroots community pressure for rehabilitation instead of clearance, but the prime motivation was public expenditure restraint. Subsequently completions and demolitions declined while take-up of improvement grants rose sharply (see Figure 1.8). In many ways, the 1970–1974 Conservative government simply altered the emphases in these policies. Public sector completions continued to decline to a new postwar minimum in 1973 and, from 1972, council rents were pushed up to 'fair rent' levels. The emphasis on rehabilitation strengthened, with greater reliance on the private sector as the means to achieve this. From 1973 there was increasing emphasis on housing associations as the 'third arm' in housing supply, further weakening the role of local authorities. Above all, the importance attached to owner-occupation was reaffirmed and reinforced; in the words of the 1974 Housing White Paper this was seen as satisfying '... a deep and natural desire on the part of the householder'.

The Labour government's 1974 Housing Act further confirmed the bipartisan consensus on housing policy, with some shifts in emphasis. Commitment to the public sector was strengthened; completions again began to increase while local authority rents were cut on average by 25 percent in real terms between 1973 and 1978 (Short, 1982, p. 62). However, public sector housing was sacrificed in the recurrent expenditure cuts from 1975. The emphasis on rehabilitation increased, with a more direct attack on the worst housing via Housing Action Areas: yet, by 1976 over two million households were still either sharing or in unfit accommodation. Decisively, though, housing policy continued to be shaped by the prioritization of owner-occupation as the 'naturally' preferred tenure, as the 1977 Housing Policy Review confirmed. By 1976 55 percent of households were owner-occupiers and any attempt to tamper with the tax relief on mortgages invited annihilation at the polls. As Ball (1983) notes, '... the subsidies have made it politically' possible to avoid fundamental reform of the housing system...' (p. 10). This was especially so in the 1970s when house prices rose more rapidly than the average rate of retail prices and owner-occupation provided a measure of protection against inflation. Nevertheless, in understanding the emphasis on policies to support owner-occupation, it is vital to acknowledge that they do not simply benefit the owner-occupier. Indeed, Ball (1983) suggests that 'The only beneficiaries of the current form of owner-occupation are those private interests who dominate it: land owners, building societies and speculative housebuilders (plus a few of the more wealthy owner-occupiers)' (p. 12).

From 1979 existing tendencies in housing policy were strongly reinforced by the Conservative government. Even so, private sector completions fell as a result of the deflationary effects of economic policy, while house prices fell in real terms between 1980 and 1982. Public sector completions slumped more dramatically as a result of public expenditure cuts (see Table 1.4) while rents were sharply increased. Large (up to 50 percent initially) discounts were also offered to sitting tenants, to whom local authorities were now compelled to sell if the tenants wished to buy their homes. Some 300,000 public sector houses, mainly better-quality ones, were sold between 1979 and 1983 and the public sector stock increasingly became a rump of poor-quality housing. In an attempt to stimulate provision of privately rented accommodation, many regulations were removed but with little beneficial impact.

The considerable alterations that occurred in tenure patterns (Table 1.5) were associated with a growing proportion of income spent on housing (Table 1.7) and increasing social differentiation in terms of which type of people lived in which type of housing. The mechanisms through which this sorting occurred were public sector allocation policies (Gray, 1976) and the play of market forces, decisively mediated via building society policies on mortgage lending (Boddy, 1976, 1980) and the role of estate agents and others active in the housing market (Williams, 1976). There are definite links between employment and occupational status and the types of housing in which people live (Table 1.6). Government housing policies have had a divisive effect on this: for those on low or no wage incomes, the unskilled and the unemployed, local authority housing has become the only option. The drive to improve standards in this sector has been systematically abandoned but rent levels have risen sharply in relation to average earnings (Ball, 1983, p. 5). Black people remain disproportionately concentrated in privately rented accommodation and the worst housing, as racial discrimination has compounded the effects of market and public sector allocation: over 20 percent of households with a coloured head shared or lacked a bath in 1976, for example. It is against this background that the question was being posed in the early 1980s as to whether there was 'a new housing crisis' (Fleming and Nellis, 1982). While less than 5 percent of dwellings were overcrowded, or lacked an inside WC or use of a bath or shower, there were still over 1.5 million dwellings lacking one basic amenity and 1 million that were unfit or needing £3000 or more of repairs. The number of unfit houses has risen even further since 1979. An increasing polarization in housing conditions has been occurring, and given the central importance of housing to living conditions, this is a profound comment on the nature of UK society in the early 1980s.

Table 1.5   Housing stock in Great Britain by tenure, 1938–1981

	Percentages			
	1938	1961	1971	1981
Owner-occupied	32.0	42.7	50.5	55.5
Rented from local authorities and new towns	10.0	26.8	30.6	31.2
Rented from private landlords, housing associations, etc.	58.0	30.5	18.9	13.1
Total	100.0	100.0	100.0	100.0

Sources: Bowers (1982); Ball (1983).

Table 1.6   Tenure profiles of heads of households in Great Britain, 1977

| | Percentage in each tenure | | | | |
| | Owner-occupiers | | Tenants | | |
	Outright owners	Mortgagors	Local authority	Unfurnished private	Furnished private
Colour of head of household					
White	23.0	27.7	33.9	13.0	2.4
Coloured	15.1	34.6	22.4	12.7	15.3
Socioeconomic group:					
Economically active heads					
Professional and managerial	19.3	61.8	8.1	8.1	2.7
Intermediate and junior non-manual	17.1	44.8	21.0	11.6	5.5
Skilled manual, etc.	13.9	35.7	38.2	10.4	1.8
Semi-skilled manual, etc.	14.4	21.8	45.1	15.2	3.5
Unskilled	14.5	12.6	55.7	13.6	3.6
Economically inactive heads	38.8	3.3	41.1	14.7	2.1
Head of household's income per annum:					
Economically active heads					
Up to £1500	20.5	8.3	35.1	25.5	10.6
£1500 but under £3000	14.9	21.6	43.2	15.5	4.7
£3000 but under £4000	13.1	40.8	33.2	10.2	2.7
£4000 and over	14.0	62.4	15.3	7.1	1.2
Economically inactive heads					
Up to £1500	32.1	2.1	47.9	16.0	1.9
£1500 but under £3000	44.9	4.0	37.1	10.8	3.1
£3000 and over	73.2	11.4	8.1	6.5	0.8
Age of head of household					
Under 25	0.6	31.3	21.4	21.2	25.5
25–29	3.1	49.1	24.9	13.7	9.2
30–44	7.5	53.9	27.2	9.5	1.9
45–64	26.2	24.9	37.7	10.2	1.1
65–74	42.4	3.0	38.5	15.5	0.5
75+	43.8	0.9	37.3	17.1	1.0
All households	23.0	28.5	33.4	12.3	2.9

Source: Central Statistical Office (1978, p.148).

1.4.2   *Private consumption patterns and some of their implications*

There have been pronounced changes in private consumption patterns over the postwar period, associated with marked alterations to lifestyles inside and outside the home. Two recurrent, interrelated themes run through these: a tendency for goods and services purchased outside the home to replace those formerly produced by unpaid labour within the family and networks of friends; and increasing polarization of activities between those centred on the home and the nuclear family and those based outside the home and centred on the 'traditional' community.

Table 1.7   Household expenditure in the UK, 1953–1983

	Percentages of total expenditure				
	1953–1954	1960	1970	1980	1983
Housing	8.9	9.3	12.6	15.0	16.8
of which					
Rent,* rates, etc.	7.2	7.3	10.7	12.8	14.5
Fuel, light and power	5.2	5.9	6.3	5.6	6.5
Food	34.9	30.5	25.7	22.7	20.7
Alcoholic drink	3.0	3.2	4.5	4.8	4.9
Tobacco	7.0	5.9	4.8	3.0	3.0
Clothing and footwear	11.1	10.3	9.2	8.1	7.0
Durable household goods	7.1	6.4	6.5	7.0	7.2
Other goods	7.8	7.5	7.7	8.4	8.0
Transport and vehicles	6.9	12.2	13.7	14.6	14.7
of which					
Net purchases of motor vehicles, etc.	1.1	5.5	4.8	5.4	5.1
Maintenance and running of motor vehicles	1.8	3.3	5.8	6.5	7.2
Services	8.1	8.9	9.0	10.8	11.3

* Includes notional rent for owner-occupiers.

Source: Hogg (1985).

Consumer expenditure has risen greatly since 1945 (see Figure 1.7) and the items on which expenditure has grown or declined most rapidly reveal much about changing lifestyles. Even so, expenditure on food remains the single largest item (see Table 1.7), though falling sharply as a percentage of total expenditure. Furthermore, there have been significant changes in the pattern of food consumption, with changing diets having implications for personal health. Consumption of dairy products, meat, fresh fruit and vegetables has grown while that of fish, potatoes, bread and sugar has declined, providing evidence of a more affluent and, in some respects, healthier population. There is a temptation to translate these aggregate trends into steak and salad, followed by fresh fruit, and washed down with a glass of wine replacing fried fish and chips, bread and butter and a mug of sugary tea as a 'typical' meal. While valid for some, low incomes (or the lack of a wage income) rule out such possibilities for many (see Central Statistical Office, 1978, Table 1.10).

More generally, there has been a tendency for family lifestyles to become increasingly privatized and centred around the nuclear family and the home; this is partly because of the effects of migration breaking up the extended family within a locality. The home has retained, maybe enhanced, its importance as a socialization mechanism through which children learn to comprehend and interpret the world around them. This is related to the rapid diffusion of television sets (Figure 1.9) to the 1983 saturation level of 98 percent household ownership and, more recently, of videos. At the same time cinema attendances plummeted from 26 million a week in 1951 to 2 million in 1977. By the mid-1970s persons aged five years or more on average watched television between 16 and 20 hours a week, depending on the season of the year. The implications of virtually universal household possession of televisions extend far beyond the production and consumption of popular culture, important though this is (Clarke, 1984). It allows advertising campaigns directed at creating truly national markets, thereby eroding regional distinctiveness in consumption patterns. Moreover, television is influential in creating and disseminating news. For example, in 1985 television transmitted vivid images of riot police at Brixton, Handsworth and Tottenham, and of children dying of starvation in Ethiopia, and has the capacity to shape the agenda of issues for public attention. Much of the style of politics and political debate has also been redefined to cope with or take advantage of TV presentation. At the same time, the influence of the older news media – magazines, newspapers and radio – has declined, at least relatively.

There has also been a great extension in the purchase and use of labour-saving equipment in the home: by 1983 95 percent of households had a vacuum cleaner, 94 percent a refrigerator, 80 percent a washing machine, 77

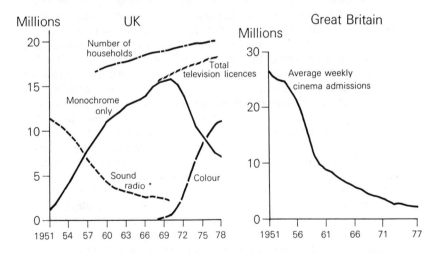

* Abolished on 1st February 1971

Figure 1.9 The growth of TV licences and decline in cinema attendance, 1951–1978 (Central Statistical Office, 1977, *Social Trends*).

percent a telephone, and 57 percent a deep freeze (Hogg, 1985). Replacing unpaid domestic labour with machines produced as commodities has been closely linked to the growth of paid employment among married women. The resultant demands made on their time have necessitated this substitution while their wages often provide the means of purchase. The increased number of working married women has also led to some redefinition of the domestic division of labour in the household (Pahl, 1984) and, more generally, of the position and status of women, but it is important not to overexaggerate the extent of this. Similarly there is a tendency towards an increase in the 'self-service' economy based on the purchase of machines and tools which allow services, formerly purchased, to be carried out by household members, although again the importance of this should not be overestimated.

While there have been changes in lifestyles within the home, there have been equally important ones in people's mobility and contact with the wider world. The most significant change for many has been new forms of relationships with people and places, predicated on rising affluence, personal mobility and, at least until 1973, the assumption of cheap petrol forever. Rising household car-ownership levels have been a central element in this, although they rose much more slowly after 1973 (from 54 to 59 percent a decade later). Paralleling this, public transport patronage has declined, partly because services have been cut back as supply and demand have fallen in a vicious downward spiral that has left some rural areas devoid of public transport (see Chapter 4.5). It is important to distinguish rising household car-ownership levels from increased personal mobility for all, however (Hillman et al., 1973). Often married women and children are deprived of the household's single car which the male household head takes to work. This can severely constrain a married woman seeking work as well as women's and children's access to a whole range of services. To compound matters, assumptions of virtually universal household car ownership have become central to many land-use plans so that urban environments have been designed to accommodate access by car. The location of food retail outlets, for example, has changed markedly with a great decline in the number of corner shops and the concentration of facilities in major town centre developments (often as part of chain stores such as Marks and Spencer or British Home Stores), or in hypermarkets on green-field sites at the edges of urban areas. Such locational changes reflect both land-use planning regulations and the speculative development activities of property companies. The new patterns may be convenient for car-owning households, especially those possessing deep freezes, but are inconvenient for those without access to a car. In the mid-1970s, for example, 40 percent of households lived more than 45 minutes' walk from a chain store (Department of Transport, 1976).

Increasing affluence and mobility have also affected patterns of leisure and recreation outside the home. Eating in restaurants, especially by those on higher incomes, has become more commonplace (Central Statistical Office, 1978, Table 7.10). Partly reflecting the impact of New Commonwealth immigrants and of UK citizens holidaying abroad, the range of foods consumed in different national types of restaurant has also increased considerably. Outdoor activities have also altered: membership of cycling clubs has fallen while that of camping and caravan organizations has risen (Table 1.8). There has also been an expansion in other organizations related to activities such as sailing in which participation presupposes considerable residual disposable income (after basic needs have been met), as well as access to private transport. Even so, membership of such organizations affects only a small proportion of the population. For many, household car ownership has simply provided the capacity to reach a much greater variety of locations – perhaps to visit friends and relatives, or to escape from the city to the fresh air of the countryside or coast. Nevertheless, many are denied the pleasures that car ownership permits; for them, a more home-based and TV-centred pattern of leisure is more a matter of necessity than choice.

The combination of paid holidays and rising real wages has enabled many more people to holiday away from home, in other parts of the UK and abroad. The growth in holidaying has also been quite closely linked to that in car

Table 1.8 Outdoor activities: membership of selected organizations in the UK, 1950–1977

	000s					
	1950	1960	1965	1970	1975	1977
Camping						
Camping Club of Great Britain	14	52	92	110	157	175
Caravan Club	11	44	41	84	174	180
Walking, climbing and riding						
Youth Hostels Association						
(including Scottish YHA)	247	219	265	274	317	320
The Pony Club	20	30	29	33	46	50
Water sports						
Royal Yachting Association	1	11	22	31	36	52
Cycling						
British Cycling Federation	67	21	15	11	11	14
Cyclists Touring Club	54	26	22	19	–	29
Miscellaneous						
National Trust (including NT for						
Scotland)	26	118	186	263	609	700
British Field Sports Society	27	20	18	21	43	55

Source: Central Statistical Office (1978, p. 184).

ownership. In 1961 almost 50 percent of holidays taken within Britain and 75 percent of those taken abroad were in hotels; by 1977 the comparable figures were 25 percent and rather less than 60 percent (Central Statistical Office, 1978, Chart 12.2), signifying a growth in camping and caravaning holidays. Holidaying abroad annually is still limited to a minority of the population, however, and UK residents spend more on tourism in the UK than abroad (Sandles, 1985). In the 1950s the increasing number of holidays reflected a growth in the number of people taking a holiday – by 1961 about 55 percent of adults took at least one holiday a year. Since then the large minority of people not taking an annual holiday has fluctuated around 45 percent while the numbers taking two or more holidays a year had grown to about 20 percent by the mid-1970s. A slightly shorter summer holiday was often combined with a winter skiing holiday and it was this trend that largely accounted for the 5.5 percent annual real increase in household expenditure abroad over the decade 1973–1983 (Hogg, 1985). It is also evidence of increased social polarization in the UK.

Despite the fact that most holidays continue to be taken within the UK, it is the growth of mass tourism abroad via package holidays which perhaps most sharply reveals the increased mobility and changed lifestyles of the affluent postwar UK, or at least of some members of this society. The package holiday industry has been an important area of growth in the national economy and helped to lower the costs of foreign holidays, enabling more of the working class to afford them as some of the gains of scale economies and bulk buying have been passed on to the consumer. In the 1960s such holidays were directed towards Spain and other Mediterranean countries but in the 1970s more exotic, non-European destinations began to feature increasingly in holiday companies' brochures. The experiences of different cultures, diets and drinks, albeit a selective one, had its impact back in the UK, for example in the proliferation of Greek and Italian restaurants.

1.4.3   Welfare provision and collective consumption

Public sector provision of education and health care was central to the postwar social-democratic Welfare State. Private sector provision of these as services to be bought and sold in the marketplace was not abolished, however. Indeed the conception of the National Health Service (NHS) was significantly and of necessity modified to accommodate the private practice interests of consultants (Bevan, 1952, pp. 98–121). The location of the line demarcating the private from the public sector has been an issue for political debate, no more so than in the early 1980s, as the general pressures to curb public expenditure increases (Figure 1.10) were reflected in increasing pressures to privatize hospital care and subcontract services such as catering and cleaning from the NHS to the private sector.

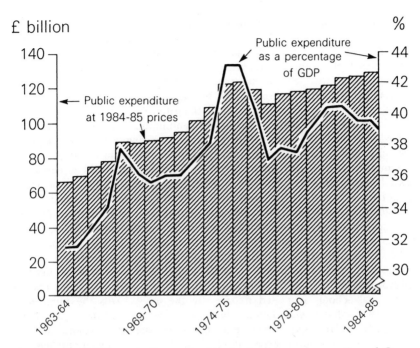

Figure 1.10 Public expenditure: absolute levels and as a proportion of Gross Domestic Product, 1963–1985 (Froud, 1985).

Increased equality of opportunity via expanded public sector education was also important in the conception of post-war society that developed in the early 1940s. Improved educational standards may have corresponded to some of capital's requirements for a more numerate and literate workforce but it is too simplistic to reduce enhanced provision to this alone. Public expenditure on education has increased considerably, both relatively and absolutely, especially prior to the mid-1970s (Blackstone, 1980; see also Table 1.4). Since then it has been cut because of public expenditure restrictions and demographic change (Townsend, 1980). Even so, over the postwar period there has been considerable expansion in public expenditure on and provision of education; whether this has resulted in greater equality of opportunity is another matter, however.

The 1944 Education Act guaranteed free secondary education for all and defined the basic framework for education in England and Wales, while specifying the division between grammar and secondary modern schools and technical colleges. Similar legislation was passed for Northern Ireland and Scotland. It was essentially permissive, specifying criteria to be met but allowing local authorities to adapt policies to meet local requirements or political priorities. Continuing Church influence, via aided and controlled schools, has added to this diversity. Consequently, it is important to remember that '… the geographical area in which children are located may well influence their educational opportunities as well as their educational achievements' (Burgess, 1984, p. 67; see also Chapter 3.5.2).

Important changes have been made in the pattern of primary and secondary provision since 1944 and, for example, the minimum school-leaving age was raised to 16 in 1972. Perhaps the most significant change has been the move to comprehensive secondary education which began in the 1950s. When the Labour government announced its intention to encourage local authorities to switch to comprehensives in the mid-1960s, less than 10 percent of public sector secondary education was provided on this basis. By 1978, despite often considerable opposition in Conservative-controlled local authorities, this had increased to 85 percent in England and Wales, rather more in Scotland and considerably less in Northern Ireland where selectivity remains dominant. The shift accelerated the trend towards bigger secondary schools: the average number of pupils rose from 363 in 1950, to 469 in 1960 and 698 in 1970 (Ambrose, 1977, p. 105). While initially the numbers of schools rose as individual schools increased in size, by the early 1970s the number of secondary schools was falling, increasing average journeys to school, especially in rural areas. Travel between different sites of the same school was also increasing as public expenditure restraints led to many comprehensives being 'cobbled together' on a split-site basis from existing schools rather than being purpose built on a single site.

The 1960s also saw important policy changes concerning pre-primary and tertiary provision. The latter expanded tremendously, partly because of a need to boost teacher training to cope with increasing numbers of schoolchildren and to cut pupil–teacher ratios. More generally, it reflected the Wilson government's acceptance of the 1964 Robbins Report recommendation that places should be provided for all those willing and able to take them, leading to a 'one-off' rapid expansion of universities and newly created polytechnics in the late 1960s and early 1970s. This acceptance reflected both a commitment to expanded access to further education as an end in itself, and a belief that it would help accelerate national economic growth by providing the highly qualified personnel necessary to bring about technological transformation of the economy. By the late 1970s and 1980s this belief, grounded in a confusion between necessary and sufficient conditions, had been revealed as erroneous. This played no small part in generating mounting pressures, focused in the 1970s on local authority colleges and in the 1980s on polytechnics and universities, simultaneously to cut and restructure further education in order to provide certain sorts of skilled labour.

The 1960s also saw growing pressures on the provision of pre-primary education and the 1967 Plowden Report strongly argued the case for nursery education. Educational arguments coincided with growing demands for such provision because of the increasing numbers of married women in the wage-labour force. By the late 1970s over 50 percent of all four-year-olds and 15 percent of three-year-olds in England and Wales were in State-maintained nursery schools; in Scotland there were less, in Northern Ireland rather more. While this represented a great increase over a decade, a majority of pre-primary age children remained outside the State sector; restrictions on public expenditure could increase this further. As a result, more alternative provision has developed. Childminding, often on an 'informal' basis as one aspect of the 'black economy', has grown as working-class mothers in particular have sought to combine getting a wage with caring for children. Playgroups have also expanded, predominantly organized on a voluntary basis by and for middle-class women (Burgess, 1984, p. 73).

What conclusions can one draw about the expansion of public sector education? In general, inequalities in access to education have been reproduced within the public sector – to say nothing of those between it and the private sector, left substantially intact and *de facto* subsidized (by tax relief on school fees). The educational system has played an important role in socializing children into a view of the world that accepts and reproduces inequalities in terms of class, gender and race: 'the evidence shows a consistent tendency for pupils in particular social categories to perform less well than others' (Burgess, 1984, p. 83). The process begins, even if unintentionally, as a result of the way primary schools differentiate between their pupils in transmitting the basic curriculum. Indeed, the structure of the teaching profession in primary schools creates expectations of a basic gender differentiation. Most (75 percent) of the teachers are female but half of the minority of men are heads or deputy heads (Department of Education and Science, 1980). These imbalances are reproduced or magnified in secondary schools. There are clear biases in subjects studied: girls are far less likely to take physical sciences, more likely to take arts or social sciences. There are also important differences in performance beyond 'O' Levels, with girls progressively falling behind boys. Race is also important. West Indians tend to underachieve but Asian children often do better than their white contemporaries, regarding educational qualifications as a route to better employment and upward social mobility. The social class inequalities found in primary schools tend to be magnified at secondary level. Many more working-class children leave school at the minimum age of 16 and this is reflected in the lower proportion with formal qualifications of 'O' Level (or equivalent), 'A' Level or a degree.

In 1979 over 80 percent of boys and 70 percent of girls did not proceed into any form of further or higher education. This difference between the sexes mainly reflects the intake of girls into secretarial and nursing courses, which itself reveals much about the social and economic position of women. Fewer girls take degree courses, however. The pattern of gender differentiation of subjects established in secondary schools continues as do inequalities in access according to gender (Edwards and Roberts, 1980), race and class (Burgess, 1984). The situation may have improved from that noted in the Robbins Report where those born in 1940–1941 whose fathers had a professional background had a 33 times greater chance of entering higher education than those whose fathers were semi-skilled or unskilled manual workers, but considerable inequalities remain. The greatly enhanced expenditure on sixth-form and further education in the 1960s in practice largely benefited middle-class children, effectively countering attempts to spend more on those types of education and in those areas (for example, via Educational Priority Area policies; see Chapter 3.5.2) that would benefit members of the working class: '... in this sense society did not "positively discriminate" in the sixties, it did the reverse' (Glennester, 1972). Even the most direct attack on inequalities in access to higher education, via the creation of the Open University, brought about no radical changes.

This has broader ramifications, for there is considerable evidence that educational experiences and qualifications influence lifechances (Brown, 1984). As Blackstone (1980, p. 227) remarks, for many years it was argued that equality of opportunity should be a central educational goal but it is now realized that this is unrealizable without first achieving a greater degree of equality in society itself. Equality of opportunity can no longer be realistically seen as the principal mechanism through which to move to a more meritocratic society, let alone an egalitarian one.

If many of the intentions underlying increased public sector provision of education have been largely unrealized, what then of health care? The establishment of a National Health Service (NHS) in 1948, breaking the connection between ability to pay and access to health care, perhaps more than anything else epitomized the intention to create a more egalitarian, humane society. As Aneurin Bevan (1952), political architect of the NHS, pointed out: '... a free Health Service is a triumphant example of the superiority of collective action and public initiative applied to a segment of society where commercial principles are at their worst' (p. 109). In practice, the NHS took over and funded an existing pattern of health care provision. Established dentists' and family doctors' practices became contracted to it to provide primary care, retaining considerable autonomy over the location and hours of their surgeries and the number of NHS patients they accept. Such decisions can and do have important implications for patients' access to these facilities — and so to the rest of the health care hierarchy. A crucial trend has been the emergence of group practices, with family doctors working as members of coordinated primary health care teams and home nurses, midwives and health visitors working from purpose-built health centres (Ambrose, 1977, p. 106). For example, between 1961 and 1976 there was a 5 percent increase in the number of GPs but a 250 percent increase in practices with more than five doctors. While such centralization brings various benefits, it also creates accessibility problems (see Chapters 3.5 and 4.6).

The difficulties in achieving the NHS's aims are most sharply revealed in the context of hospital planning. Because of the type of service it provides, the NHS is a labour-intensive operation and resources for new capital investment have always been scarce. In the late 1940s, major investment was immediately required to build new hospitals and modernize old ones. Beveridge's (1942) optimistic assertion that providing a free health service would cut demand for it by virtue of creating a healthier population had also been revealed as erroneous – hardly surprisingly, in the aftermath of the interwar recession and six years of war. However, these requirements were overridden by the priority given to keeping public expenditure in check and NHS expenditure was less than 4.0 percent of GNP (Abel Smith and Titmuss, 1956, p. 60). This tension between competing political objectives reached a climax in 1951 when Bevan and Harold Wilson resigned from the government over the decision to impose charges on some NHS appliances. This broke the principle of an NHS financed solely from general taxation and free at the point of utilization, creating a precedent of enormous significance.

The change of government in 1951 reinforced pressures to contain NHS spending, which fell to less than 3.5 percent of GDP; NHS capital expenditure also fell as a share of total fixed investment, partly because of the prioritization of housing and education. As the pace of public sector house construction subsequently slackened, increased hospital investment came to be seen as a way of containing revenue costs, especially the growing NHS wage bill. By the late 1950s both major political parties were committed to a large hospital construction programme. Against this background, the Hospital Plan was prepared (Ministry of Health, 1962) and this remains the most significant attempt to rationalize the hospital system. Its basic proposition was that hospitals should have at least 600–800 beds, serving populations of 100,000–150,000. This would require a considerable reduction in the number of hospitals, and the closure of over 700 non-psychiatric units while building 90 new ones and expanding 134 existing ones. The reasons for and implications of this were explained as follows: 'the district general hospital offers the most practicable method of placing the full range of hospital facilities at the disposal of patients ... this consideration far outweighs the disadvantage of longer travel for some patients and their visitors' (Ministry of Health, 1962, p. 13). Such hospitals would provide a higher standard of service while cutting running costs.

Shortly after the Plan's publication, it became clear that its full implementation would be problematic, requiring £500 million of public expenditure over the first decade. In fact it has only been partially and selectively implemented with only a fraction of the intended number of hospitals being closed, mainly in response to pressures on public expenditure. Pressures to cut costs led to proposals for further concentration of provision in hospitals of 1200–1800 beds (Central Health Services Council, 1969). While not formally adopted, they influenced thinking on hospital sizes in an upward direction but reaction against them was also an important stimulus to the idea of smaller community hospitals, especially for rural areas. Despite continuous pressure on public spending, investment in hospitals rose to a peak in 1972–1973 (Department of Health and Social Security, 1979). Nevertheless, between 1960 and the early 1980s the number of hospitals fell from 3000 to 2650 (Dawson, 1982).

The rate of increase of public expenditure on health then slowed dramatically (Townsend, 1980, p. 11) and new hospital starts virtually ceased by the mid-1970s. This was because of commitments to hospitals already under construction and rising revenue costs. The constraints tightened further after the introduction of cash limits in 1976, which cut the volume of services provided. Provision of NHS hospital beds per 1000 population, having risen from under four in 1960 to over ten, then fell to under eight by 1980. Furthermore, charges for NHS services rose sharply: prescription charges rose by 1000 percent from 20p to £2.00 between 1979 and 1984, for example.

Despite the restrictions imposed since the mid-1970s, public expenditure on health care has grown massively since 1948. But what have been the effects on access to such care? The most authoritative and comprehensive documentation of relevant evidence is contained in the Black Report (Townsend and Davidson, 1982). It reveals that considerable inequalities remain in access to health care, health standards and life expectancy: '... those belonging to the manual classes make smaller use of the health care system in a number of different respects, yet need it more' (p. 16); '... the poorer occupational groups continue to consult their General Practitioners less than do those in richer groups when indicators of their greater need are taken into reckoning' (p. 24). The Black Report spelled out the reasons for this: 'Class differentials in the use of various services ... derive from the interaction of social and ecological factors. Differences in sheer availability and, at least to some extent, in the quality of care available in different *localities* provide one channel by which social inequality permeates the NHS. Reduced provision implies greater journeys, longer waiting lists, longer waiting times, difficulties of obtaining an appointment, shortage of space and so on. A second channel is provided by the structuring of health care *institutions* in accordance with the values, assumptions and preferences of the sophisticated middle class "consumer". Inadequate attention may be paid to the different problems and needs of those who are less able to express themselves in acceptable terms and who suffer from lack of command over resources of both time and money' (cited in Townsend and Davidson, 1982, p. 89 – emphases in original). Such differences help explain the continuing 'marked class gradient in standards of health care'. The ultimate expression of this is that while morbidity rates for those aged 35 years and over in the top two socioeconomic groups declined steadily over the two decades to the early 1970s, those for the unskilled and semi-skilled manual categories changed little or even increased. But as Townsend and Davidson (1982, pp. 5–6) stress, much of the problem lies outside the scope of the NHS: a complex of social and economic factors affect health and 'all favour the better-off'.

Considerable progress has been made in raising absolute standards of health care for most of the population as a result of postwar Welfare State policies. However, by the end of the 1970s levels of expenditure and standards of provision lagged behind those of many other European Community countries (Hudson et al., 1984, pp. 132–137). Furthermore, Welfare State policies have sometimes had a regressive distributional impact within the UK and great inequalities remain – both within the public sector and between it and the private sector. What is at stake is the priority accorded to education and health by the nation. The evidence in the mid-1980s suggests that this priority will become even less important, with further reductions in the quantity and quality of services provided. Increasing emphasis is being placed on the recommodification of educational and health services, rather than on their provision as of right through the public sector. Considerable pressures exist to encourage the growth of private medicine as a result of company policies (via perks such as BUPA membership for senior personnel) and State policies (via tax reliefs, hidden subsidies to private medicine and lengthening NHS queues).

1.5   The changing shape of national politics

Postwar politics at the national level in the UK have been dominated by the party political contest between Conservative and Labour; this dominance has been reflected in preceding sections, in relation to the formulation and implementation of economic and housing policies, for example. The dominance of the two major parties, in terms of votes cast in general elections, was particularly marked in the 1950s (Table 1.9). From 1964 new variations were added to this basic theme and more diversified voting behaviour became apparent. This became most pronounced during the 1983 General Election, when over 30 percent of votes cast were for 'other parties'.

There have been several elements in this growing diversification. From the mid-1960s support for the Liberal Party began to recover to around its 1950

Table 1.9   Voting behaviour in postwar General Elections

	Percentage vote for		
	Conservatives	Labour	Others
1945	39.8	47.8	13.4
1950	43.5	46.1	10.4
1951	48.0	48.8	3.2
1955	49.7	46.4	3.9
1959	49.4	43.8	6.8
1964	43.4	44.1	12.5
1966	41.9	47.9	10.2
1970	46.4	43.0	10.6
1974 (February)	37.9	37.1	25.0
1974 (October)	35.8	39.2	25.0
1979	43.9	36.9	19.2
1983	42.0	27.6	30.4

Sources: Jacques (1983); Harris (1984).

level. This was partly because of a protest vote against the main parties but to a degree reflected a growing incorporation of 'green' and community politics into the Liberal Party. At about the same time, rooted initially as a protest against the failures of the Labour Party to cope with problems of economic decline in Scotland and Wales, support for the Scottish and Welsh Nationalist Parties expanded. At the same time the character of nationalist politics began to alter as their old basis in cultural and linguistic distinctiveness became combined with, and to a degree subservient to, a more economically and politically oriented neonationalism, especially in Scotland (Nairn, 1976; see also Chapter 2.5). The re-emergence of 'the troubles' in Northern Ireland (Farrell, 1980) added another dimension to the political debate on national unity as the future of Northern Ireland as part of the UK or of a united Ireland once again became a central issue. However, both Conservative and Labour governments adhered to a bipartisan approach that centred on a commitment to the majority Protestant community that the province would remain in the UK. The alternative view that it should become part of a United Ireland was made clear as the Provisional IRA took direct action onto the streets of England as well as Northern Ireland, culminating in the attempt to blow up the Prime Minister at the Conservative Party Conference in Brighton in 1984.

The lines of party political debate were further complicated by the defection of prominent right-wing members of the Labour Party. They finally openly rejected Labour Party-style socialism and formed the core of the Social Democratic Party (SDP) in 1981, alongside an initially more radical group within the new party. The SDP soon became conjoined in an uneasy Alliance with the Liberal Party in a much-publicized attempt to redefine the centrist option in UK politics. Finally, the late 1970s witnessed a resurgence of support for the politics of the far Right and for organizations such as the National Front. Although such groups failed to gain representation in Parliament, their politics to a degree found an outlet through right-wing Conservative MPs who were fervent supporters of law and order and of greater control on immigration (see p. 133). Later some supporters of the National Front and British National Party became prominent in growing violence on the terraces of football stadiums.

Despite this drift away from the major parties in electoral support, no party other than Conservative or Labour has formed a government since 1945, although the Liberals had a brief exposure to governmental powers and responsibilities in the 1970s in the short-lived and ill-fated 'Lib–Lab' pact, as James Callaghan's government desperately attempted to cling to power. Given the character of the UK's 'first past the post' electoral system, increasing support for minority parties has not been reflected in seats in Parliament. For this reason, there has been considerable support for electoral reform and the introduction of a system of proportional representation from the Liberals and, more recently, the SDP. In contrast, the Conservative and Labour Parties (excepting some on the Left of the Labour Party) generally remain committed to the present system, apparently united by the belief that each of them will emerge victorious from a general election. The victory of the Conservatives in June 1983, when 42 percent of the vote produced a majority of 144 in Parliament, helps explain why these different views prevail. There was also a distinct geographical pattern of electoral support and of members returned to Parliament that is crucial in understanding the outcome (see Chapter 2.5).

There have also been important political changes outside the immediate forum of party political debate and parliamentary politics. One of these has already been touched on: the growing visible role of trade unions in national political life, formally complementing the representation of capital's interests via organizations such as the CBI. This was encouraged by the Labour government, following the emergence of tripartite corporatism in the early 1960s. As Harold Wilson (1974) remarked: 'The TUC has arrived. It is an estate of the realm, as real, as potent, as essentially part of the fabric of our national life, as any of the historic Estates' (p. 674). This appearance of growing power and involvement in the politics of national economic policy formation and implementation raised problems for the trade unions, however. In particular, it threatened to drive a wedge between trade union leaders and rank-and-file members as the inclusion of the former into the corporate structures of the State came into conflict with their more traditional role of seeking to improve the wages – and more and more to preserve the jobs – of their members. The problems that this posed were exacerbated by the changing gender composition of the workforce, with male trade union leaders increasingly representing female members. These contradictions were initially most clearly revealed in the ambiguities in the position of the trade unions regarding incomes policies as these became a central plank of the economic policies of Conservative and Labour governments alike from the mid-1960s. The divisions between union leaders and their rank-and-file members were more easily disguised when opposing Edward Heath's Conservative government than in the final years of the preceding Labour one. They were subsequently contained in the initial years of the following Wilson/Callaghan administrations, but re-emerged sharply in the 1978–1979 'winter of discontent'.

The miners' strikes of 1972 and 1974 and those of the public sector unions in 1978–1979 were significant in shaping the analyses of the Conservative government after 1979 as to the root cause of the UK's industrial decline. They led to policies to dismantle trade union power, which found their most coherent (to date) expression in the calculated provocation of the National Union of Mineworkers (NUM) into a strike in 1984–1985 in circumstances that virtually guaranteed victory for the government. The destruction of the political muscle of major trade unions is central to the Thatcher government's conception of the social market economy, but it is arguably based on a fundamental confusion between the appearances and realities of trade union power between 1974 and 1979. While senior trade union leaders were much consulted by government in this period, economic policy was not shaped to suit the interests of their members (Coates, 1980, pp. 53–85). Nevertheless, trade unions were increasingly to be excluded from the corporatist structures of power and their role redefined narrowly in terms of 'apolitical' industrial relations issues alone.

Another major change in recent years has been the growth of one-issue politics, cutting across existing party lines. A variety of pressure groups has developed around issues such as conservation and environmental protection, ranging from campaigns against airports and motorways to those against major housing developments in green belts and against the environmental impacts of open-cast coal mining and pollutant industries. Such campaigns have typically had a strong middle-class representation, leading to conflicts between their claims to preserve the environment (as a locus for consumption) and the aims of those wishing to create jobs in areas of high unemployment (see Chapter 4.7). There is evidence that this situation may be changing, perhaps because generalization of mass unemployment to most parts of the UK has led to more people questioning the wisdom of accepting jobs at any environmental or social cost. The recent (1984) successful campaign to prevent the dumping of nuclear waste under Billingham on Teesside and the refusal in 1985 of Livingstone New Town Development Corporation to allow

Union Carbide to establish a chemical plant there (in the wake of the Bhopal disaster in India) are two recent examples that point in this direction. Although the environmental movements have not, as yet, had the same general political impact as in Western Europe – compared with the 'Greens' in West Germany, for example – their emergence was nonetheless important. Not least, it has revealed divisions within existing political parties and opened up new opportunities for political alliances in defence of communities and the environment. For example, opposition to open-cast coal mining has revealed conflicts between 'old' and 'new' Conservatives; between those with interests in the rural areas, articulated through organizations such as the Council for the Preservation of Rural England and traditional Tory landowners, and the New Right supporters of cheap open-cast coal. Conservative opponents of open-cast mining have at the same time begun to explore the possibilities of alliances with 'green' organizations such as Friends of the Earth and with coal-mining communities concerned to preserve jobs in deep mines, in unholy alliances of blue, green and red.

The Billingham example touches on a much wider issue: the revitalized campaign against both civilian use of nuclear power for electricity generation and military deployment of nuclear weapons. The latter is exemplified in the resurgence of the Campaign for Nuclear Disarmament (CND) and its message of 'protest and survive' (Thompson and Smith, 1980) but is symbolized above all in the women's peace camp at Greenham Common in Berkshire, the site of the first American cruise missiles to be deployed in the UK. This has vividly caught the news headlines and polarized opinions between those for and against the nuclear option. It says much about the changing political and social climate of the UK that the major opposition to cruise missiles was a women's protest, even if that protest was ultimately unsuccessful.

TWO

The Regional Dimension

2.1 Introduction

In this chapter we examine regional variations in economic, political and social aspects of life in the United Kingdom, mainly defined in terms of the boundaries of planning regions. Using data for such regions has both advantages and disadvantages: the advantages of available data, the disadvantages that these regions are designed more for administrative convenience than for their relevance to analyses of uneven regional development (Massey, 1978). However, as Sayer (1984) points out, while these regions '... cut across many structures and causal groups in the "chaotic" fashion', nevertheless 'chaotic or not, it is to such objects that people respond. For example, governments respond to "regional development" even though regions are "chaotic" groups' (p. 227). And one could add to this that one reason why governments respond to the perceived needs of these chaotically conceived regions is that people express attachment to, and identify with, all or parts of them. Politics and political constituencies are also organized on a territorial basis that finds a regional expression. This is perhaps most clearly seen in the cross-party lobbies associated with nationalist sentiment in Scotland and Wales but is by no means confined to these: for example, Labour MPs from the North have for many years formed a regional lobby. The Regional Planning Councils, established in the 1960s as appointed advisory bodies in the context of proposals for coordinated regional and national planning as part of the National Plan, were in part a response to such pressures, as were the Scottish and Welsh Development Agencies set up in 1975. Such institutions fall far short of being a regional tier of government, however, and in contrast to many other advanced capitalist states (see Hudson and Lewis, 1982), the regional dimension to government has been and remains absent in the UK. Proposals were made in the 1960s in relation to the debate on local government reform that would effectively have created this. They were not taken up by central government, partly because of pressures from established local government organizations and partly because of the strong centralizing tendencies within the UK state.

2.2 Regional variations in economic activities, employment and population

2.2.1 *Regional change and national full employment policies, 1944-1962*

The regional effects of the wartime economy and the period of postwar reconstruction, at least until the late 1950s, were paradoxical. While the regional unemployment problems of the interwar years were largely abolished, regional economies were frozen around patterns established in preceding phases of capitalist development. These patterns were intimately related to the UK's international political and economic role and the paradox lay in the fact that the particular forms of regional specialization had, correctly, been seen as a prime reason for the sharp inter-regional differences that emerged in the interwar years.

At the start of the 1950s people and jobs were concentrated in the Southeast, the Midlands, the Northwest and Yorkshire and Humberside, with employment in most regions concentrated into manufacturing and service activities (Table 2.1 and Figure 2.1). In a few regions, agriculture, forestry or fishing was an important source of employment; even so, while almost 20 percent of employment in East Anglia was in these activities, over much of southern Italy and western France at this time over 50 percent of jobs were in this sector (Hudson et al., 1984, pp. 54-55). This difference is indicative of the extent to which even the peripheral, formerly agricultural, regions of the UK had by this time been more fully incorporated into the spheres of capitalist industry. This had taken place in two main ways: the beginnings of the penetration of capitalist relations of production into agriculture itself (see Chapter 4.2) and an expulsion of labour from agriculture leading to people migrating not only to other activities but from rural to urban areas, often on an inter-regional basis.

There were also other important differences in patterns of economic activities and employment between regions that reflected the trajectory of capitalist development in the UK. In several regions mining and quarrying remained an important source of male employment – predominantly after 1947 in the newly nationalized coal industry; this was indicative of the genesis of industrial capitalism on the coalfields within the UK. Manufacturing employment was particularly important in the Midlands (especially the West Midlands), the Northwest and Yorkshire and Humberside, especially in the major conurbations of these regions (see Chapter 3.2), while East Anglia and the Southwest remained relatively unindustrialized. Within manufacturing there were important differences in terms of which industries were located in which regions (Table 2.2). These can be related to the evolution of capitalist industry in the UK which, broadly speaking, occurred in two phases. The first, in the 19th century, had been closely associated with the coalfields, as

Table 2.1 Regional populations and components of population change, 1951–1981

Region	1951	1951–1961 Average annual change (000s)		1961	1961–1971 Average annual change (000s)		1971	1971–1981 Average annual change (000s)		1981
		Natural	Migration		Natural	Migration		Natural	Migration	
Northern	3,127	19.3	− 8.0	3,246	17.4	− 8.1	3,293	2.0	− 6.5	3,097
Yorkshire & Humberside	4,509	19.5	− 9.6	4,631	26.6	− 6.5	4,811	3.5	− 3.8	4,854
Northwest	6,417	23.5	− 12.4	6,545	34.0	− 9.4	6,747	2.2	− 21.1	6,406
East Midlands	2,896	15.8	+ 3.9	3,108	22.2	+ 7.4	3,380	7.0	+ 10.4	3,807
West Midlands	4,426	27.6	+ 4.7	4,761	39.6	+ 3.5	5,121	13.0	− 10.3	5,136
Southeast	15,216	66.4	+ 43.8	16,346	99.6	− 3.6	17,289	27.4	− 47.5	16,729
Greater London	8,206	33.3	− 61.1	7,977	44.7	− 97.4	7,441	7.7	− 83.4	6,696
Outer Metropolitan Area	3,509	24.2	+ 77.5	4,521	41.3	+ 44.4	5,345	19.6	+ 35.9	10,033
Outer South East	3,502	8.9	+ 27.3	3,848	13.3	+ 49.9	4,502			
East Anglia	1,388	6.5	+ 2.7	1,489	8.4	+ 13.5	1,686	3.7	+ 15.9	1,865
Southwest	3,247	10.5	+ 9.9	3,436	15.0	+ 22.4	3,792	− 3.5	+ 28.1	4,326
Wales	2,589	8.4	− 4.9	2,635	9.8	+ 0.5	2,723	0.2	+ 5.7	2,791
Scotland	5,103	33.9	− 28.2	5,184	35.4	− 36.4	5,230	1.8	− 13.0	5,117
Northern Ireland	1,373	14.6	− 8.9	1,427	17.2	− 6.5	1,534	10.2	− 10.5	1,547
UK	50,291	246.0	+ 7.0	52,807	326.3	− 23.7	55,610	66.7	− 31.2	55,921

Source: Lawton (1982).

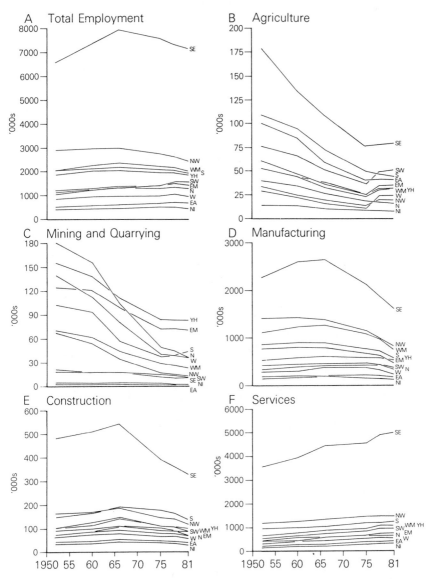

Figure 2.1 Regional employment change, by sector, 1952–1981 (Fothergill and Gudgin, 1978; Department of Employment, *Employment Gazette*, February 1983; Central Statistical Office, 1984, *Annual Abstract of Statistics*).

Table 2.2 Distribution of manufacturing and service employment between SIC Order Groups within regions (as % of total regional employment in manufacturing and services, respectively), 1952–1981

	South-east	East Anglia	South-west	West Midlands	East Midlands	Yorks. & Humberside	North-west	Northern	Scotland	Wales	N. Ireland	UK
1952, Manufacturing												
Food, drink and tobacco	9.3	22.6	15.0	5.6	6.7	8.0	7.6	8.2	12.3	7.2	9.6	8.8
Chemicals, etc.	7.4	2.4	3.6	2.0	4.1	4.4	8.4	10.8	4.9	7.3	0.8	5.9
Metal manufacture	2.0	1.1	2.1	13.3	6.7	12.3	2.9	14.4	8.8	30.4	0.3	7.2
Mechanical engineering	12.3	17.8	13.3	12.1	14.3	14.1	10.8	13.2	14.1	6.4	6.2	12.3
Instrument engineering	3.1	0.6	0.9	0.7	1.4	0.6	0.7	0.3	1.4	0.1	0.7	1.5
Electrical engineering	12.2	7.6	3.5	8.8	3.7	2.6	7.6	7.4	2.5	5.6	1.0	7.4
Shipbuilding, etc.	2.8	1.3	8.8	0.0	0.0	1.5	3.2	15.0	10.2	2.5	13.0	3.4
Vehicles	10.0	9.7	18.0	18.4	8.7	5.5	6.2	3.5	5.3	8.0	4.4	9.3
Other metal goods	5.3	1.1	1.9	16.4	2.9	7.7	3.5	3.1	3.7	6.6	1.6	6.1
Textiles	2.0	3.3	4.0	3.3	21.3	24.5	25.5	3.3	15.4	5.3	37.9	12.1
Leather, etc.	1.0	0.9	1.1	0.7	1.0	0.8	0.9	0.7	0.6	0.7	0.3	0.9
Clothing and footwear	7.8	13.7	6.9	2.0	16.9	7.6	7.9	6.9	4.4	5.2	15.7	7.4
Bricks, pottery, glass, etc.	3.4	4.4	3.7	8.9	3.8	3.4	3.2	4.7	3.4	4.6	2.3	4.3
Timber, furniture, etc.	5.7	6.0	5.6	1.9	2.7	2.7	2.8	3.6	4.1	3.0	3.0	3.8
Paper, printing, publishing	11.2	6.0	9.0	2.4	3.8	3.4	5.1	3.1	6.8	2.7	2.9	6.2
Other manufacturing	4.3	1.5	2.8	3.4	1.8	1.0	3.5	1.8	2.1	3.3	0.6	3.0
Total	99.8	100.0	100.2	99.9	99.8	99.9	99.8	100.0	100.0	98.9	100.3	99.6
1952, Services												
Transport and communications	18.3	13.8	18.2	20.1	18.8	20.9	22.5	21.0	20.3	22.9	16.0	19.6
Distribution	23.6	29.8	27.1	27.3	28.3	29.0	27.4	27.3	29.1	24.5	30.7	26.2
Insurance, banking and finance	7.4	2.6	2.6	3.3	2.5	3.0	4.9	2.5	3.2	2.6	2.9	4.9
Professional services	15.1	21.4	17.9	18.3	19.1	17.6	15.4	17.2	18.8	18.2	17.1	16.7
Miscellaneous services	21.0	18.8	18.7	16.6	15.5	17.3	18.0	17.2	16.2	16.3	15.2	18.6
Public administration and defence	14.7	13.6	15.4	14.4	15.7	12.1	11.8	14.8	12.2	15.5	18.0	14.1
Total	100.1	100.0	99.9	100.0	99.9	99.9	100.0	100.0	99.8	100.0	99.9	100.1

Table 2.2 continued

	South-east	East Anglia	South-west	West Midlands	East Midlands	Yorks. & Humberside	North-west	Northern	Scotland	Wales	N. Ireland	UK
1981, Services												
Transport and communications	12.2	11.2	8.8	8.8	10.5	10.3	10.7	10.0	10.5	9.8	6.8	10.7
Distribution	19.7	22.6	20.9	22.4	23.0	22.4	21.7	21.6	19.8	18.1	15.6	20.6
Insurance, banking and finance	13.6	8.5	8.5	9.3	7.0	7.6	8.6	6.1	7.0	5.9	6.8	9.8
Professional services	25.5	27.9	28.0	27.3	29.8	28.9	28.0	28.0	30.1	31.3	35.1	28.0
Miscellaneous services	17.7	20.6	22.6	19.1	19.1	20.0	19.9	21.0	20.4	20.2	18.5	19.2
Public administration and defence	11.3	9.0	11.3	13.1	10.8	10.7	11.1	13.4	12.3	14.5	17.2	11.7
Total	100.0	99.8	100.1	100.0	100.2	99.9	100.0	100.1	100.1	99.8	100.0	100.0
1981, Manufacturing												
Food, drink and tobacco	8.2	21.4	14.0	6.2	9.7	14.1	11.9	8.3	16.7	7.7	16.8	10.6
Chemicals, etc	7.7	4.9	4.3	2.6	5.0	6.2	12.1	14.7	6.4	8.1	2.7	7.2
Metal manufacture	1.8	1.1	1.6	10.4	5.0	10.4	2.1	8.8	5.4	17.1	0.9	5.3
Mechanical engineering	12.4	15.9	15.9	12.7	14.8	13.0	11.9	13.9	13.4	8.6	6.2	12.8
Instrument engineering	4.0	3.3	3.8	0.9	1.0	1.1	1.1	1.2	3.1	1.7	0.9	2.2
Electrical engineering	17.6	8.8	9.2	11.8	7.0	3.9	9.7	10.6	8.7	12.4	6.2	11.3
Shipbuilding, etc.	1.9	1.6	5.1	0.5	0.4	1.2	0.7	11.2	7.0	0.4	7.1	2.4
Vehicles	10.0	7.7	12.1	16.2	8.7	6.5	12.1	2.9	5.4	10.6	8.8	10.1
Other metal goods	6.6	3.8	5.1	16.8	5.4	10.2	5.6	3.5	4.3	6.4	1.8	7.4
Textiles	1.0	1.1	2.2	2.1	16.5	11.4	7.7	2.9	8.5	4.3	17.7	5.6
Leather, etc.	0.4	0.5	1.1	0.5	0.8	0.4	0.5	0.3	0.4	0.0	0.0	0.5
Clothing and footwear	3.2	3.8	4.6	1.7	9.7	4.9	5.5	5.6	4.7	4.7	12.4	4.7
Bricks, pottery, glass, etc.	2.6	3.8	2.4	6.7	3.3	4.6	3.3	2.9	2.7	3.4	3.5	3.6
Timber, furniture, etc.	4.4	4.9	4.0	2.2	3.1	3.9	3.7	2.7	3.3	3.4	2.7	3.6
Paper, printing, publishing	14.0	11.0	9.4	3.6	5.6	5.5	8.1	6.2	7.8	5.1	5.3	8.5
Other manufacturing	2.9	6.0	4.9	5.3	4.1	2.8	3.9	4.1	2.3	6.0	6.2	4.3
Total	98.7	99.6	99.7	100.2	100.1	100.1	99.9	99.8	100.1	99.9	99.2	100.1

Sources: Fothergill and Gudgin (1978); Department of Employment (1981).

industries such as iron and steel, railways, shipbuilding, mechanical engineering and chemicals developed. Such industries often formed an interlocking complex in both physical terms via inputs and outputs and financial ones via interlocking shareholdings and ownerships (Carney et al., 1977). Similar structures occurred in other coalfield areas outside the UK, such as the Ruhr. The industries can predominantly be classified as department I, producing the means of production, the raw materials, machinery and transport equipment used in other industries. Basic consumer goods – department II – industries, notably clothing and textiles, also developed in some of these regions. Thus in the early 1950s regions such as Scotland, Wales, the North, Northwest and Yorkshire and Humberside specialized in some or all of these industries.

The second main phase of industrial growth took place in the 1920s and 1930s, concentrated in the Southeast and West Midlands (again predominantly in the major urban areas) and based on newer means of production and consumer goods industries such as aircraft, cars, consumer durables and so on. This diversification into new growth industries was often associated with an initial round of penetration of American capital (see Figure 2.3; Law, 1980, pp. 173–177), concentrated in and around London, as household names such as Ford and Hoover set up production facilities. Fixed capital investment in these new industries was largely absent from the older industrialized regions in the interwar years as these new industries had different locational requirements. People migrated from the older industrialized regions to the (relatively) booming Southeast and West Midlands in search of work. Even so, unemployment remained at very high levels in what became the Special Areas as the first tentative steps in regional policy emerged to try and deal with regional imbalances (Table 2.3; see also McCallum, 1979). What emerged from these two phases of industrial growth can be described as a territorial division of labour. All stages of production – from head offices to routine production – tended to be located in one region. Regions were differentiated from one another by the industries in which they specialized and by the commodities produced in and through them.

There was rather less variation between regions (although considerable variation within them – see Chapters 3 and 4) in the relative importance of service sector employment (see Table 2.2 and Figure 2.1). The more homogeneous distribution reflects two influences. The location of many consumer service activities depended on the distribution of population and purchasing power while, by the early 1950s, the setting of national norms for educational and health provision in the State sector began to have an impact. The enhanced importance of services in the Southwest reflects the significance there of a particular type of consumer service – tourism. There is rather more evidence of regional differentiation in producer services, linked to the ways in which different regions were tied into the international and

Table 2.3 Major legislative and related changes affecting regional policy

Date	Item	Comments
1934	Special Areas (Development and Improvement) Act	Designated four special areas; marks beginning of 'work to workers' policy
1940	Publication of the Royal Commission on the Distribution of the Industrial Population, Cmnd 6153 (The Barlow Report)	'... a landmark on the development of thought on the regional problem in Britain' (McCrone, 1969, p. 104)
1944	White Paper on Employment Policy (Cmnd 6527)	The basis of the postwar commitment to full employment
1945	Distribution of Industry Act	Defined Development Areas and the assistance available within them
1946	New Towns Act	
1947	Town and Country Planning Act	Introduced Industrial Development Certificates
1958	Distribution of Industry (Industrial Finance) Act	Supplemented the 1945 Act; made locations outside Development Areas eligible for assistance
1960	Local Employment Act	Replaced Development Areas with Development Districts, defined on the basis of local unemployment rates
1963	White Papers on North East England (Cmnd 2206) and Central Scotland (Cmnd 2188)	Indicative of an emerging new approach to regional and national planning
	Major reports from the NEDC (1963a, b)	Further developed the relationships between national and regional planning
	Local Employment and Finance Acts	Strengthened regional policy financial incentives
	Location of Offices Bureau set up	Advisory role only; became more concerned with suburbanization of offices from London than dispersal to peripheral regions

Table 2.3   continued

Date	Item	Comments
1964	Department of Economic Affairs and Regional Economic Planning Councils and Boards set up	
1965	Control of Office and Industrial Development Act	Introduced Office Development Permits
	The National Plan	Echoed and developed the approach of the 1963 National Economic Development Council reports
	Highlands and Islands Development Board established	A new initiative in policy towards rural areas
1966	Industrial Development Act	Reinstated Development Areas. Significantly strengthened investment allowances and grants, nationally and in the new Development Areas
1967	Regional Employment Premium introduced	A wages subsidy to companies in Development Areas
	Special Development Areas set up	A response to the localized effects of accelerating the rundown of the coal industry
1969	Publication of the Hunt Committee Report on the Intermediate Areas (Cmnd 3998)	A response to the gap in aid levels between Development Areas and Special Development Areas and non-assisted areas
1970	Local Employment Act	Designated Intermediate Areas
1972	Industry Act	Introduced Regional Development Grants and selective regional and industrial assistance
1974	Labour government announced its intention to use government office dispersal as a major regional policy tool	

Table 2.3 continued

Date	Item	Comments
1975	Industry Act	Established National Enterprise Board
	Scottish and Welsh Development Agencies set up	New institutions, partly in response to nationalist pressure
1976	Budget (December) abolished Regional Employment Premium	'... the most drastic single cut in regional expenditure ever' (McCallum, 1979, p. 29)
1977	Reversal in role of Location of Offices Bureau: now to bring offices back into London	'... the end of office development control as an effective instrument of regional policy' (McCallum, 1979, p. 30)
	For the first time since 1966, Assisted Areas were downgraded	
1978	Inner Urban Areas Act	Evidence of switch from regional to urban policy
1979	Major cuts in regional policy announced by new Conservative government	Projected 38 per cent cut in regional aid over three years; Industrial Development Certificates abolished. Location of Offices Bureau and Regional Economic Planning Councils abolished
1984	Further major cuts in regional policy announced	

imperial economies. The importance of transport and communications in many old industrial areas reflected the growth of rail and water transport activities, often specifically related to importing and exporting raw materials. What stands out, however, is the importance of the Southeast, with a tremendous concentration of employment in insurance, banking and finance because of the City of London's position as a centre of international finance capital and of the Empire. This serves sharply to differentiate the Southeast (or, more precisely, parts of it) qualitatively from other regions. The pre-eminence of the Southeast in high-level control activities is reinforced by the concentration of national government activities; over 50 percent of all such activities were located there. Other regions, particularly Northern Ireland, may have had a greater share of their service sector employment in public administration and defence but the key central government functions remained concentrated in London and the Southeast.

How did these regional patterns of employment and economic activity subsequently alter? Changes in the 1950s and early 1960s actually reproduced them; total employment grew in all regions, though at varying rates, and registered unemployment remained at very low levels in most regions, while a distinct North–South differentiation emerged in net in- or out-migration. The simplest way to disentangle the processes underlying these developments is to consider employment change on a sectoral basis (see Figure 2.1).

Agricultural employment fell sharply in all regions between 1952 and 1960. What differentiates the regions is the rate of decline. This can be related to existing variations in types of agriculture and the organizational structure of agriculture, which influenced the pace of introduction of new methods of farming, new forms of machinery and new types of fertilizers and seeds. Indeed, despite the profound changes that affected agriculture over the next 30 years, the basic pattern of regional differentiation in agriculture persisted. Consequently Newby (1977) could point out that 'It is an over-simplification to regard the North and West solely in terms of small livestock farms and the South and East in terms of large scale arable agriculture, but as a broad generalization this distinction holds' (p. 82). At the same time as labour demand in agriculture was declining, that in the manufacturing and service sectors was growing vigorously in the 1950s.

Mining and quarrying employment fell in all regions in which it was significant in the immediate postwar years, mainly due to a gentle employment rundown by the National Coal Board. Even so, in the period 1947–1958 great priority was attached to maximizing coal output. At the time of nationalization 95 percent of primary energy requirements were met by coal and this had changed little by the second half of the 1950s. The *Plan for Coal* (National Coal Board, 1950) aimed significantly to cut the costs of winning coal – and so the price of electricity – but implementing this reconstruction programme took longer than anticipated (see p. 17). Consequently, the NCB, supported by the government, sought to maximize output from existing collieries. The government also wished to hold down the price of coal, however, often refusing to sanction price rises requested by the NCB. A necessary corollary of this approach was holding down miners' wages and, to ensure that miners did not desert the pits en masse as a result, the NCB successfully argued that new, higher-waged male-employing industry should not be introduced into coalfield areas (Hudson, 1985). Consequently, even during the period of 'strong' regional policy (1945–1947) following the passage of the Distribution of Industry Act (see Table 2.3), when some 50 percent of new industrial investment was steered to the Development Areas (Figure 2.2), new male-employing manufacturing was steered away from the coalfields. Even so, the prevalence of shift-work in coal mines and steelworks prevented many married women taking paid work. This was one reason why considerable inter-regional differences in female activity rates persisted in the 1950s.

After 1947 the Labour government sacrificed its commitment to regional policy because of more pressing national economic policy objectives (see p. 13). This *de facto* rundown and the non-implementation of regional policy were intensified in the 1950s by the Conservative government which, by the end of the decade, was suggesting that regional problems had been solved and Development Areas were replaced by smaller Development Districts in 1960. Although expenditure on regional policy rose somewhat in the late 1950s and early 1960s (McCrone, 1969), this was essentially on an *ad hoc* basis to deal with specific local unemployment problems that emerged as the rundown of coal-mining jobs accelerated once cheap imported oil was substituted for coal in electricity generation. At the same time, shipbuilding jobs contracted sharply in the face of increasingly fierce international competition. In addition, there were areas in which textiles employment had already fallen earlier in the 1950s as a result of international competition, significantly reducing waged employment for women in localities in the Northwest and Northern Ireland.

More generally, though, manufacturing employment grew in this period and the 'traditional' manufacturing industries in the old industrial areas joined with the NCB in opposing the introduction of alternative male-employing manufacturing. For them, this was a boom period as postwar reconstruction, allied to the Korean War, boosted demand for the commodities they produced in a climate of mild international competition (see p. 2–4). Output, profitability and employment increased but, in general, there was an absence of fixed capital investment in new technologies and expanded capacity. Instead, increased output and employment reflected fuller working of existing capacity (see Hudson, 1984). It was only towards the end of the period that a major programme of new fixed capital investment in vehicle production occurred in Merseyside and Scotland – a harbinger of the broader trend of production relocation to peripheral regions in the 1960s. Even so, very modest increases in total manufacturing employment were recorded in several regions while symptoms of deindustrialization were evident in the decline of manufacturing jobs in Northern Ireland between 1952 and 1966. In contrast, in the newer industries located in the Southeast and Midlands, employment and output increases were associated with capacity expansion. Indeed, the growing labour demands associated with this were one reason for considerable net in-migration to these regions. Nevertheless, while the greatest absolute increases in manufacturing employment were in the Southeast and Midlands, the greatest relative growth was in those regions that were least industrialized at the start of the postwar period: East Anglia and the Southwest. This was indicative of the way

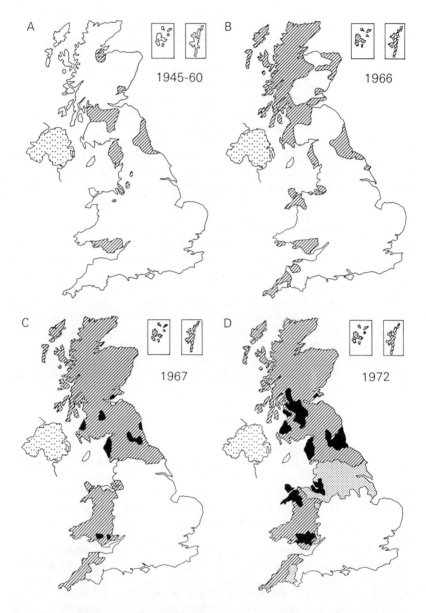

Figure 2.2   Regional policy assisted areas in the postwar period (McCrone, 1969; Regional Studies Association, 1983).

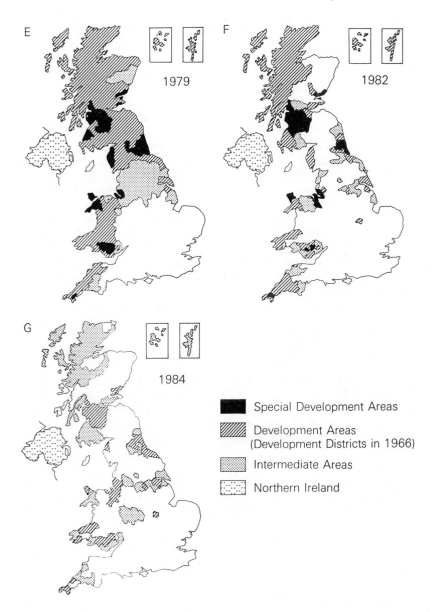

E   1979

F   1982

G   1984

■ Special Development Areas

▨ Development Areas
(Development Districts in 1966)

▦ Intermediate Areas

⬚ Northern Ireland

industry was springing up in these regions or relocating from the Southeast into adjacent regions where there were relatively large reserves of labour within agriculture. In the 1940s and 1950s there were some examples of complete transfers of production from the Southeast to these regions (for example, Bush Radio's move to Plymouth in the late 1940s) as well as movement of branch plants.

The other major source of change in employment was the services sector. The greatest absolute growth was in the Southeast, in part linked to the boom in speculative office building released by removal of betterment levies in 1954, but the highest rate of growth was in East Anglia. Different regional growth rates were related to differing rates of population change, variations in income and purchasing power and to a levelling-up in standards of public sector service provision. Service sector growth was particularly associated with rising female activity rates and a growing proportion of women, especially married women taking part-time jobs in the labour force. Nevertheless, continuing high levels of male employment in coal mines and steelworks in areas where the cultural tradition defined the woman's place as in the home helped reproduce regional inequalities in female activity rates during the 1950s.

While total employment grew in all regions, the sectoral pattern of changes varied considerably. In general, employment grew more rapidly in southern than in northern regions but, with the exception of Northern Ireland, full employment conditions prevailed, being maintained by age- and gender-selective migration. In this sense, especially for a time in the 1950s, a pattern of regional employment and population changes was established that seemed consistent with the national goal of maintaining full employment. Then, towards the end of the 1950s, this started to break up. Localized intraregional employment losses from coal mining and shipbuilding began to occur while inflationary pressures generated in the Southeast threatened to become more generalized throughout the economy. Although very much a two-industry, two-region (Northeast England and Clydeside) crisis, rising unemployment raised memories of the 1930s and led to calls for new policies to tackle problems of national growth and regional imbalance. These evolved into a broader alternative approach to regional policy and planning.

2.2.2   *Regional change and modernization policies, 1962–1975*

Around 1962 national economic policy began to emphasize modernization and faster output growth as the route to full employment (see p. 19). Central to this was a concern to eliminate regional differentiation as a mechanism for allowing faster, non-inflationary growth in national output while simultaneously solving the regional problem. Attaining the latter objective involved transforming the internal environments of the problem regions via increased public expenditure on infrastructure as well as enhanced financial incentives to mobile companies. In fact the 1960s actually witnessed a deepening of national (see p. 20–4) and regional problems, both qualitatively and quantitatively, as private capital and nationalized industries were restructured in pursuit of increased competitiveness, efficiency and profits. New and qualitatively different spatial divisions of labour were becoming superimposed on the degenerating old territorial one.

Once again, the easiest way to examine the processes involved is to consider change by sector (see Figure 2.1). Agricultural employment continued to fall, generally more sharply than in the 1950s and becoming more severe through the 1960s: there were losses of around 20 percent before 1966, 30 percent after this date. The highest rates of decline were in those regions with relatively large employment in agriculture in 1960, as the shift to more capital-intensive methods increased.

Mining and quarrying employment fell at an accelerating pace, reaching a peak towards the end of the 1960s, primarily because of NCB policies. Employment losses were most severe after 1966 and were regionally uneven. These variations reflected the NCB's aims of cutting both total coal output and unit costs of production. Consequently employment reductions were most pronounced in older coalfields such as the Northeast, South Wales and Scotland in contrast to areas in the Midlands, such as Nottingham, and parts of Yorkshire. New investment was concentrated in these latter areas where there were thicker coal seams and greater opportunities for cheaper, more mechanized production methods.

The regionally differentiated rundown of coal mining posed considerable political problems for the 1964–1970 Labour government. Cutting unit energy costs was a central element in Labour's National Plan (see p. 20). This, along with parallel restructuring of other basic industries such as the railways and steel (partly renationalized in 1967), was seen as an essential step in cutting the energy and input costs of manufacturing in the UK, thereby increasing international competitiveness. But a corollary of this was a substantial rundown in areas that were traditional heartlands of electoral support for the Labour Party. The price of buying the acquiescence of the National Union of Mineworkers and Labour supporters in running down the coal industry – which was carried out virtually without strike action against closures (T. Hall, 1980) – was commitment to a stronger regional policy to introduce alternative male manufacturing jobs in such areas. Indeed, successfully reindustrializing coalfield areas was seen as the acid test of the National Plan's intention of achieving balanced regional and national growth. While the Plan was soon abandoned, the commitment to a stronger regional policy remained, embodied first in the 1966 Industrial Development Act and, soon after, in the creation of Special Development Areas and the introduction of the Regional Employment Premium (see Table 2.3). While some new manufacturing plants were introduced into the declining coalfield areas, the reindustrialization intentions were at best realized only partially and temporarily.

More generally, important quantitative and qualitative changes were taking place in the regional distribution of manufacturing employment (see Figure 2.1). Employment fell between 1960 and 1966 in the Northwest, Northern Ireland, Scotland and Wales and elsewhere grew much more slowly than in the 1950s. Between 1966 and 1975 jobs in manufacturing fell in all regions except the North, the Southwest and Wales, in which they increased marginally, and East Anglia, where they grew sharply. The greatest absolute and relative declines were in the Southeast, West Midlands and Northwest. How is this pattern to be understood?

The evening-out in the inter-regional distribution of manufacturing employment has been interpreted as reflecting the effects of a strengthened regional policy (for example Moore and Rhodes, 1973). Following a brief interlude in 1970–1972, interventionist regional and industrial policies were further strengthened by the Conservative government's Industry Act 1972, increasing the differential attraction of investing in the Development and Special Development Areas (see Table 2.3). Nevertheless, it is oversimplistic to attribute a given number of jobs to a 'regional policy effect'. Regional policy measures certainly had some effect in changing the regional geography of manufacturing employment but this has to be understood in relation to changes both within the structure of private companies and in the policies within the public sector, particularly those of the NCB. It also has to be considered in relation to changes in the international economic order and division of labour. As individual companies grew, the scale of production increased and transport and communication technologies advanced, it became both possible and necessary to reorganize production. The production process could be split up between locations so as to match the requirements of different stages with the attributes of different areas. It is important to remember, however, that many manufacturing companies remained essentially small, one-plant organizations, unable to respond to regionally differentiated production possibilities in this way. Even so, such companies were increasingly facing competition on an international scale and often became tied into wider international patterns of production via subcontracting to multiplant companies.

The rapid growth of manufacturing employment in East Anglia and the slower growth in the Southwest after 1966 can be related more to physical planning proposals to disperse manufacturing activity to regions where there were still some reserves of labour in agriculture rather than to the effects of regional policy. In the North and Wales between 1966 and 1975 the stability in total manufacturing employment conceals changes in its composition. Male employment in the older manufacturing industries was declining, being replaced by jobs in branch plants in other industries, often filled by women. While regional planning and policy measures had a hand in this, the massive labour reserves, both male and female, being recreated in these and other regions by NCB policies were a much more significant factor for many companies. As miners lost their jobs, the constraints on their wives taking paid jobs outside the home weakened.

It is important not to overgeneralize about 'the branch plant economy', since branch plants were integrated into broader corporate structures in a variety of ways. However, while they represented a diversification of the types of industries in these regions, they were homogeneous in terms of types of labour process and stages in the overall production process; most branches provided mainly semi-skilled or unskilled assembly work. Moreover, these changes were indicative of fundamental alterations in the intranational and international divisions of labour. Regions such as the North and Wales, with substantial pools of unemployed workers, became the locations in which companies relocated routine unskilled or deskilled work processes – locations that Lipietz (1980) refers to as type 3 regions.[1] Initially, this new role was mainly cast within the context of an intranational restructuring of capital as companies such as Courtaulds, GEC and Plessey set up plants there (Figure 2.4). Increasingly these branch plants were owned by foreign-based multinationals, however (Figure 2.3). Peripheral regions became 'global outposts' (Austrin and Beynon, 1980) as companies such as Philips, Rohm and Haas and Timex set up branch plants and the context changed to the role of these areas in a new international division of labour. These changes led a number of commentators, political and academic (such as Firn, 1975), to regard the introduction of new industries not as a solution to the regional problem but rather as a new dimension of it.

The decisive reason why these peripheral regions experienced an absolute and relative increase in manufacturing employment is that it was increasingly profitable to produce there (Hudson, 1984). Conversely, the sharp fall in manufacturing employment in the Southeast, West Midlands and Northwest, on a scale that implies capacity reductions and disinvestment, suggests a precipitate collapse of manufacturing profitability. This reflected the technological backwardness, by international standards, of much manufacturing capacity, coupled with inflationary pressures on costs transmitted through land and labour markets in the aftermath of the 1962–1964 'dash for growth' (see p. 19). These were most severely felt in the Southeast and Midlands, one symptom being the continued growth of construction employment up to 1966. Closing capacity in these regions did not necessarily mean a switch to Development Areas, however. Often it was linked to investment overseas or out of manufacturing into more lucrative activities such as property speculation in the Southeast. A considerable speculative property boom developed in London, collapsing in the early

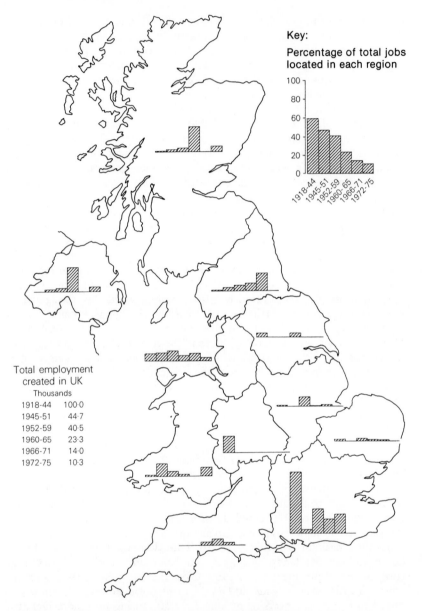

Key:

Percentage of total jobs located in each region

Total employment created in UK

Thousands

1918-44	100·0
1945-51	44·7
1952-59	40·5
1960-65	23·3
1966-71	14·0
1972-75	10·3

Figure 2.3   Regional distribution of employment in foreign-owned manufacturing plants in the UK, 1918–1975 (Law, 1980).

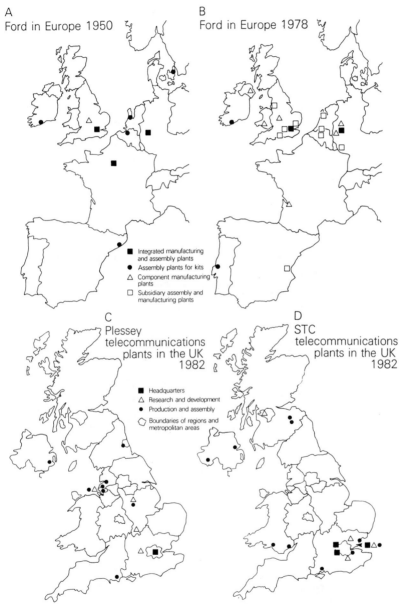

A
Ford in Europe 1950

B
Ford in Europe 1978

■ Integrated manufacturing
   and assembly plants
● Assembly plants for kits
△ Component manufacturing
   plants
□ Subsidiary assembly and
   manufacturing plants

C
Plessey
telecommunications
plants in the UK
1982

D
STC
telecommunications
plants in the UK
1982

■ Headquarters
△ Research and development
● Production and assembly
⬡ Boundaries of regions and
   metropolitan areas

Figure 2.4 The 'new spatial division of labour': telecommunications equipment in
the UK and cars in Europe (adapted from Bloomfield, 1981; Meegan,
1982).

Table 2.4 Regional variations in female employment, 1966–1981

	South-east	East Anglia	South-west	West Midlands	East Midlands	Yorks. & Humberside	North-west	Northern	Scotland	Wales	N. Ireland	UK
Females as % of total												
1966	37.7	34.6	35.1	35.3	34.9	35.1	37.8	32.4	36.7	31.8	37.3	40.4
1975	41.3	39.5	40.2	39.0	39.7	39.3	41.2	38.8	41.3	38.1	40.1	42.6
1981	43.1	41.2	42.7	41.6	41.8	41.3	43.6	42.1	43.7	41.6	NA	
Part-time as % of female												
1975	39.7	43.8	43.3	40.0	39.7	43.3	38.7	38.3	34.3	36.6	NA	39.6
1981	40.1	43.3	46.5	42.3	41.8	44.9	42.2	43.0	38.7	40.5	NA	41.7
Female part-time as % of total part-time												
1975	81.9	82.3	82.9	84.8	82.7	85.6	85.7	85.8	84.2	84.2	NA	83.6
1981	81.8	82.3	82.3	85.6	84.1	86.9	88.3	87.6	84.9	85.8	NA	84.1

Source: Central Statistical Office (1981, 1983).

1970s with reverberations that ran through the national banking system. To follow through Lipietz's (1980) schematic interpretation, type 2 regions such as the West Midlands retained those manufacturing activities requiring specialized skilled labour only available locally. The Southeast emerged, or reinforced its position, as the type 1 region within the UK in which head offices, R and D, and related high-technology manufacturing activities were increasingly to be found. A qualitative differentiation thus emerged in the types of activities found in different regions (see Figure 2.4) and manufacturing employment increasingly depended on corporate decisions regarding investment and disinvestment. This qualitative differentiation was also underpinned by State policies, not only in the reduction of production costs via regional policy measures in Assisted Areas, but also because of concentration of government research facilities and industrial subsidies for R and D in the Southeast and, to a degree, the Southwest. This growing differentiation within the manufacturing sector reinforced the Southeast's pre-eminent position in terms of control functions and related jobs within nationally and internationally oriented service sector activities.

It is important to remember, however, that many consumer activities remain locally tied, by virtue of both their market and/or size and type of operation. For example, small independent firms still held over 40 percent of the grocery market in the late 1970s even though their share of it fell by 15 percent during the decade, as supermarket chains increased in importance (Massey, 1983a, p. 178). Service sector employment grew absolutely and relatively in all regions, though at varying rates, so by 1975 there were considerable variations in the tertiarization of regional economies. After 1966 the Southeast experienced the slowest rate of growth in service sector employment. As in manufacturing, though, the Southeast's dominance in high-level control and decision-making functions increased, partly because of the growing dominance of private sector services by bigger companies. In both private and public sectors, routine clerical functions were dispersed to other regions, partly in response to regional policy aspirations and partly as a result of commercial calculations. This was generally a limited spatial decentralization, especially of private sector services to the adjacent regions of East Anglia and the Southwest or from Central London to suburban locations or other towns in the Southeast (see also Chapter 4.3.2). Long-distance inter-regional movement of large numbers of jobs was limited, being mainly confined to the public sector.

The expansion of service sector jobs was linked to changing proportions of male and female employment and growth in part-time work. While male employment fell in all regions, female activity increased, though at different rates. Nevertheless, there was remarkably little regional variation in the proportion of women in the wage labour force and this variability tended to decrease between 1966 and 1975 (see Table 2.4). Increasingly, the growth of female employment involved married women taking part-time service sector jobs. Therefore, marked inter-regional variations in female employment in wage labour that existed at the start of the postwar period had been substantially eliminated as a consequence of the changing sectoral pattern of employment. These new jobs were not in any preordained sense 'women's work'; rather, within the prevailing cultural and social definitions of male and female work, women were much more likely to accept them. This often resulted in two-income households in the Southeast but in the North, Northwest, Scotland or Wales it was as likely to result in women becoming the major household wage-earner as men lost their jobs in coal mines, steelworks or shipyards.

The changing pattern of labour demand also had implications for inter-regional migration and unemployment rates. While the total number of employees in employment fell in several regions, unemployment rates initially remained low but differences began to widen as unemployment grew in several regions in the 1960s, particularly in the North, Northern Ireland, Scotland and Wales. By 1975 the unemployment rate in several other regions was approaching that of Wales, if not Northern Ireland. These unemployment differentials persisted despite continuing out-migration from those regions most severely affected by unemployment. Continuing in-migration into regions with low unemployment is indicative of tight labour market conditions (which this helped to alleviate) and, to some extent, migration for reasons other than work, such as retirement (Law and Warnes, 1976). Thus, in a phase that was to see the end of State commitment to a vigorous regional policy, the economic situation in the 'old' problem regions was deteriorating. In addition, the map of problem regions was itself beginning to alter – most notably with the apparent relegation of the West Midlands from the league of prosperous regions to that of problem ones.

2.2.3 Regional change and disinflation policies, 1975–1983

The decisive change in emphasis in central government's national economic policy from seeking to maintain full employment via modernization of the economy and faster output growth to seeking to control inflation (see p. 24–5) had regionally differentiated effects. These were revealed in progressive reductions of expenditure on, and restructuring of, regional policy (see Table 2.3) (Regional Studies Association, 1983) but they were simply the most obvious manifestation of the uneven regional impact of this major policy alteration. A corollary of this, as central government withdrew from regional policy, was a burgeoning set of related small-firm and small-area initiatives by agencies such as local authorities (Cochrane, 1983) and the British Steel Corporation (BSC), leading to the designation of Enterprise Zones and Freeports (Anderson, 1983; see also Chapter 3.6.2).

After 1975, following the UK's entry into the EEC and adoption of the Common Agricultural Policy, new crops began to appear, notably the distinctive vivid yellow flowers of oilseed rape in many arable areas. The decline of agricultural employment slowed and, in some regions, was reversed. While the absolute magnitudes of increase were quite small, the relative increases were often quite spectacular, especially in the Southwest and Wales (although this partly reflected a redefinition of agricultural employment to include part-time, seasonal and casual workers). More generally, the shake-out of labour from agriculture prior to 1975 was such that a point had been reached at which, with existing technologies, the rate of further labour shedding had to slow.

The rate of employment decline in mining and quarrying eased in all regions between 1975 and 1978, and in the East Midlands employment rose. This largely reflected the extent to which the NCB had cut its labour forces prior to 1975 and the new role in national energy supply that coal apparently was to play following the 1973–1974 oil price rises. Even so, the tripartite *Plan for Coal* (National Coal Board, 1974), agreed between the NCB, the NUM and the new Labour government in the wake of the 1974 miners' strike, implied continuing differentiation between major coal-mining regions. The Plan was premised on coal competing in the market with other energy sources. Consequently, older coalfields such as the Northeast, Northwest, South Wales and Scotland would receive relatively little new investment while parts of the Yorkshire and Nottinghamshire coalfields would be the recipients of major new investment to modernize existing collieries and sink new ones. After the 1979 election, with the new Conservative government's hardened attitudes towards the nationalized industries and its commitment to nuclear power, coal-mining losses accelerated again in all regions, although the least severe cuts were in Yorkshire and the East Midlands. While employment in mining and quarrying in Scotland rose between 1978 and 1981, this was because of growing activity and foreign investment linked to North Sea oil (Mackay, 1979; Figure 2.5), which more than offset coal-mining job losses. The differential decline of employment between coalfields continued after 1981 (Hudson and Sadler, 1985), one effect of which was the 1984–1985 miners' strike (Beynon, 1985).

Manufacturing employment fell in all regions except the East Midlands and Southwest between 1975 and 1978. The decline in the Development Areas resulted from two different sorts of influences: the limited extent and character of restructuring of their traditional industries, and the collapse of the new growth industries of the 1960s. In so far as there had been a degree of restructuring in the traditional industries in these regions, it had generally been too feeble compared to the pace of restructuring internationally. In shipbuilding and steel the job losses were directly mediated by the State as shipbuilding was nationalized in 1977 (Hudson, 1985). The British Steel

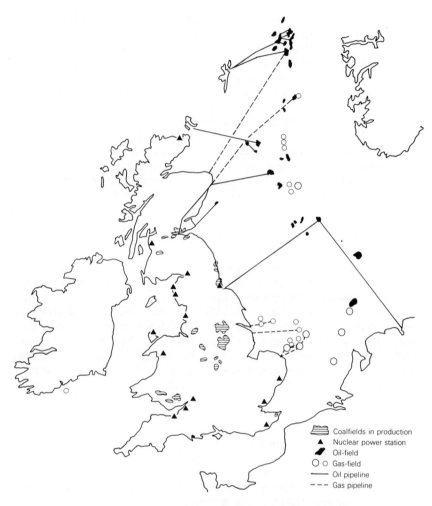

Figure 2.5   The location of primary energy sources within the UK.

Corporation's ambitious 1973 *Ten Year Development Programme*, which centred on major capacity expansion at Llanwern and Port Talbot, Ravenscraig, Scunthorpe and Teesside, was abandoned – *de facto* in 1976, *de jure* in 1978 (Bryer et al., 1982). Retrenchment replaced expansion plans and severe job losses followed – though the 1973 Plan itself assumed that considerable job losses would in any case occur.

While the pace of job losses was slowed by the Labour government because of anticipated social costs, after 1979 the new Conservative government had a very different attitude, eagerly embracing the European Community's restructuring proposals summarized in the so-called 'Davignon Plan'. The nationalized steel industry, with a history of regional chauvinism and fragmented trade unions, was selected as an example with which to demonstrate the new government's policies towards nationalized industries – its commitment to cut the public sector and break trade union power. Massive regionally concentrated job losses followed with little effective opposition from those affected by them (Hudson and Sadler, 1983). Shipbuilding employment was similarly cut.

At the same time as employment in 'old' manufacturing industries declined, that in 'new growth industries' introduced in the 1960s also began to fall, revealing the limited extent and fragility of the reindustrialization that had taken place. Companies responded to intensified competition by cutting jobs or closing branch plants. This was partly related to a tendency to relocate production abroad as more newly industrializing countries came into competition with UK peripheral regions for scarce new investment. Cutbacks in regional policy assistance, especially abolition of the Regional Employment Premium in 1976 at a time when other countries were offering very attractive incentive packages, reduced the relative attraction of the Assisted Areas in the UK. With the removal of exchange controls in 1979 (see p. 11), the tendency to switch production abroad strengthened and manufacturing job losses in the Assisted Areas accelerated sharply. Although Scotland and Wales had been granted development agencies in 1975 as part of the attempt to defuse nationalist ambitions (see p. 102), manufacturing job losses were no less severe there than in other peripheral regions. In some respects, however, the promotional activities of these agencies were important. Through attracting new Japanese and USA-based capital to invest in activities such as micro-electronics, they helped insert these areas into the new international division of labour in a manner that was not happening in other peripheral regions.

The processes of change affecting private sector manufacturing in the Development Areas were by no means confined there. Their impact was felt to varying degrees in other regions. Perhaps the most significant feature is the continuing decline of manufacturing employment in the Southeast and West Midlands between 1975 and 1978, particularly in the latter as the car industry contracted rapidly. This led to job losses and plant closures in numerous subcontracting companies supplying components, although the pace of decline was slowed by substantial State financial support for British Leyland (Coates, 1980, pp. 116–128). Between 1978 and 1981 all regions experienced falling manufacturing employment on a scale that indicates net disinvestment and capacity closures in most of them. Even so, the cutbacks of the 1978–1981 period were relatively least severe in the Southeast, Southwest and

East Anglia – 'the South' was increasingly differentiated from the rest in this as in other respects.

In so far as a sunshine belt of 'high-technology' micro-electronics industry based on new small firms is to be found in the UK, it is located in places like Cambridge – now advertising that 50 'high-tech' companies have located in its Science Park (*Financial Times*, 18 July 1985) – and the M4 corridor and around the M25 London orbital motorway. A recent survey of electronics firms considering relocating revealed that almost 30 percent would prefer a site in the Southeast, almost 15 percent in the Southwest, 11 percent in Wales and 7 percent in Scotland, but less than 4 percent expressed a preference for the Northern region and only 2 percent for Northern Ireland: 'there is a great danger of a North–South divide where the South will receive the majority of the investment and the North, at best, will display only pockets of electronic activity' (Electronics Location File, 1985). Because of past patterns of social and economic development, the most favourable preconditions for the successful implementation of government policies to encourage the formation of small professional service and manufacturing firms are also to be found in the South (Marquand, 1979). The take-up of government support for small 'high-tech' firms is concentrated in the South, and this concentration is also underpinned, directly and indirectly, by State expenditure on defence aviation and space and nuclear programmes, for many small companies subcontract from major government establishments in the region. Provision of major international airports at Heathrow and Gatwick has also been important, in conjunction with motorway developments, especially in maintaining the Southeast's more general importance in the international economy. The decision taken in 1985 to develop a third major airport at Stansted can only reinforce the Southeast's attraction within the UK for such manufacturing and service activities.

There was a much more variable pattern of employment change in the services sector than in manufacturing between 1975 and 1978. Service employment fell in the North and in Scotland, mainly because public expenditure restrictions reduced growth in education and health care, while in the private sector there were downward multipliers because of previous job losses in mining and manufacturing. In the Southeast, Southwest and Wales service sector employment increased more rapidly than in the previous decade, however. This faster growth reflected the expansion of tourist activities and population growth, both as a result of natural increase and in-migration, often for retirement. In addition, following entry into the EEC in 1973 and the rapid changes that began to affect international financial markets in the wake of the 1973–1974 oil crisis, the Southeast reinforced its pivotal position in the international financial system.

After 1978 the government made increasingly ambitious attempts to control public expenditure and its economic policies had a severe deflationary impact on the manufacturing sector. Consequently, service sector employment growth rates fell dramatically and, in several regions, employment fell (see Figure 2.1). Nevertheless, service sector employment became relatively more important in all regions because of job losses in manufacturing and mining.

Changes in the pattern of employment within the service sector over the preceding three decades have tended to affect all regions in a similar manner (see Table 2.2). The relationship between the distribution of many service sector activities and that of people and purchasing power led to comparatively little inter-regional variation. Expansion of the Welfare State, though first checked and then to a degree reversed after 1975, nevertheless resulted in professional and scientific services accounting for at least one-quarter of all service sector jobs in every region. It is the more peripheral regions that remain most heavily dependent on public service jobs, however, and so most vulnerable to further public expenditure restrictions. The most extreme example is Northern Ireland, whose exaggerated dependence on public sector employment (public administration, defence) bears comparison to 'clientelist' regions in Southern Europe, such as the Mezzogiorno (Pugliese, 1985).

Regional variations in service sector employment are related to the UK's changing position in the international political and economic order. The continuing prominence of the City of London in the international financial sector is reflected in the Southeast's dominance of producer services, especially insurance, banking and finance. The relative importance of regional employment in transport and communications also reflects such changes. The growth of London's airports is particularly important in the Southeast and they have generated a considerable number of jobs, both directly and indirectly (for example, in tourist hotels and in numerous firms supplying the airports). Furthermore, modifications in the direction and composition of the UK's international trade, especially after entry to the European Community (see pp. 7–8), coupled with changes in marine transport technology (such as containerization), have led to seaport changes. Employment has declined relatively less in the Southeast and East Anglia, as ports such as Felixstowe and Harwich have grown, than in other regions where ports were tied into the old international division of labour and links with the Empire.

As a result of sectoral changes in labour demand, female activity rates and the proportion of waged employment taken by women continued to rise, as did the tendency for part-time to replace full-time jobs, in all regions. Inter-regional differences in the prevalence of part-time female employment nevertheless widened between 1975 and 1981 as part-time work increased more rapidly in those regions most severely hit by recession or in those, such as the Southwest, where activities such as tourism were important (see Table 2.4). Such regional changes in the types of labour demand were undoubtedly important but perhaps the most significant point is that, between 1978 and 1981, the total number of employees in employment fell in all regions, albeit at different rates. Decline was least severe in 'the South' and most severe in the Northern region (see Figure 2.1) These job losses coincided with a period of growing labour supply because of demographic factors and a stabilization of male activity rates in several regions so that job losses were no longer compensated for by men dropping out of the labour force; therefore, unemployment rates rose sharply. Although inter-regional differences in unemployment rates narrowed for a short time in the mid-1970s because the impacts of the post-1974 recession on jobs were first experienced in the Southeast and West Midlands, a distinct differentiation then emerged between 'the South' and the rest. The West Midlands, in this respect, was now firmly part of the problematic periphery rather than of the affluent economic core. This led to increasing calls from within the West Midlands for preferential government assistance.

By the early 1980s, then, the map of regional differentiation in economic structures, employment patterns and unemployment rates had altered dramatically from that of the early 1950s as the impact of the UK's changing position in the international political and economic order was experienced in different ways in different regions. The absolute and relative decline in mining and manufacturing and the growth in services had significantly altered the economic fortunes of, and prospects for, different regions. Although the sharp inter-regional polarization in manufacturing employment patterns that characterized the interwar period had substantially narrowed (see Table 2.2), perhaps the single most dramatic indicator of these changes was the combination of mass national unemployment and sharp inter-regional variations in unemployment rates. This made the early 1980s appear uncomfortably like the 1920s and 1930s.

2.3   Regional variations in public expenditure

The postwar expansion of the UK public sector resulted in regionally differentiated effects of public expenditure taking on immense significance in relation both to regional economic change and to living conditions and lifestyles (which we consider in the next section). These were not necessarily intended effects, for many public expenditure programmes lack an explicitly regional dimension. The significance of this emerged in the early 1960s, with proposals for regionally selective public expenditure increases as a key mechanism for achieving balanced regional and national growth. In the absence of regionally disaggregated expenditure data, it was impossible to say whether such objectives were being realized. Regionally disaggregated data for regionally relevant expenditure were eventually compiled through the Public Expenditure Survey Committee (PESC) system, although published only from 1969 (see Short, 1981). 'Regionally relevant' excludes important areas of public expenditure that are defined as national programmes, the benefits of which cannot be attributed to any particular region, however; for example, defence, overseas services and prisons (see Table 1.4). Such expenditure does nevertheless have varying impacts in different regions.

The variations in regionally relevant public expenditure are nonetheless revealing and, in general, fairly stable over the period under consideration, at least in aggregate (Short, 1981). Northern Ireland in particular, as well as the Northern region, Scotland and Wales, all have per capita expenditures well above the national average (Table 2.5). By 1978 Northern Ireland and Scotland exceeded national average per capita expenditure on almost every PESC programme, evidence of the extent to which they were dependent on State decisions as to the level and composition of expenditure over a very wide spectrum of social and economic life. Much the same conclusion could be drawn for the Northern region and Wales, particularly as regards the economy. Public expenditure via regional policies is used to restructure production while income transfers via social security and unemployment benefits maintain a minimum level of consumption for those thrown out of work or unable to get a job after leaving school. To a considerable extent, these could be regarded as a group of State-managed peripheral regions, particularly vulnerable to progressively severe restrictions on public expenditure from the mid-1970s but especially after 1979. Public expenditure by the UK government in these regions has been supplemented by European Community expenditures from its Regional Development Fund, Social Fund and the European Investment Bank but the sums involved are small (Hudson et al., 1984, pp. 8–16) and likely to decrease further following enlargement of the Community to take in Portugal and Spain.

At the other extreme most remaining regions have per capita expenditures consistently below the national average on all or almost all PESC categories. By 1978, for example, the Midlands had below average expenditures on all programmes. This was one reason for the growing demands from the West Midlands for greater injection of public expenditure as its economy slumped sharply, incomes fell and unemployment rose.

In many ways the most surprising data are those for the Southeast. Apart from the group of four 'problem regions' identified above, the Southeast is the only region where total per capita public expenditure exceeds the national average and it has by far the greatest volume of public spending within it. Furthermore, the available evidence (Short, 1981) suggests that changing priorities in public expenditure from the mid-1970s have further discriminated in favour of the Southeast. By 1978 per capita spending in the region fell below the national average on only three headings: agriculture, etc.; trade, industry and employment; and social security – a revealing combination. Above-average spending on the remaining programmes has

Table 2.5 Regional variations in regionally relevant public expenditure per capita, 1977–1978

	Northern	Yorks. & Humberside	East Midlands	East Anglia	South-east	South-west	West Midlands	North-west	Wales	Scotland	N. Ireland	£ per capita current prices UK
	Index: UK = 100											
Agriculture, fisheries and forestry	107.3	75.6	75.6	115.0	61.1	100.0	69.9	60.6	142.5	229.5	382.4	19.3
Trade, industry and employment	219.1	87.2	67.1	30.0	46.5	55.1	78.6	118.5	192.2	179.4	334.2	38.3
Roads and transport	116.8	99.4	65.5	94.9	107.7	70.0	76.2	88.9	124.7	136.2	120.6	47.0
Housing	109.0	76.1	84.3	77.7	125.6	55.3	94.6	89.1	73.7	117.4	118.5	94.2
Other environmental services	125.5	86.6	72.2	88.1	103.1	69.9	84.5	97.7	111.3	156.9	112.8	47.8
Law, order and protective services	87.2	88.1	79.8	75.0	110.2	86.9	80.7	93.5	82.1	89.8	329.5	35.2
Education and libraries, science and arts	96.6	97.6	90.6	90.2	105.2	82.4	87.3	97.7	103.0	119.3	112.2	155.6
Health and personal social service	94.5	90.6	86.5	86.0	107.7	93.2	85.0	98.9	98.6	118.7	119.2	147.2
Social security	109.7	102.6	92.0	87.1	92.9	103.3	92.8	109.6	116.1	105.9	109.5	241.0
Total	109.7	93.3	85.1	84.4	100.8	85.1	87.4	99.8	108.5	122.2	141.6	826.2

Source: Short (1981).

considerable implications for living conditions. The large increase in expenditure on roads and transport is mainly due to new motorway investment. At the same time, in-migration to the Southeast has led to pressures for increased public expenditure on housing, schools and hospitals. The recent switch to increasingly privatized provision of housing, education and health care has only reinforced the already advantageous position of the Southeast. Such changes have been important in sustaining an environment that is attractive to those involved in high-level decision-making, or emergent entrepreneurs in 'high-tech' industries. Senior civil servants have consistently and successfully defeated attempts to move their jobs from London and important reasons for this are the environment and living conditions available in the Southeast and which their salaries enable them to enjoy. These are substantially sustained by public expenditure policies which, deliberately or inadvertently, discriminate in favour of the Southeast. While not part of formal regional policy, their regionally discriminating effects are of considerably greater significance.

Growing polarization between the Southeast and other regions is underpinned by State expenditure patterns. If private capital is more successful – in terms of profitability as well as in providing jobs – in the Southeast than in other regions, this is in no small measure due to the disproportionate volumes of public expenditure pumped into it. This is a conclusion with profound implications for any attempt seriously to tackle 'the regional problem' in the UK.

2.4   Regional variations in living conditions and lifestyles

Lifestyles and living conditions vary considerably between regions. Some aspects of these differences are discussed in this section, broadly following the structure used in examining the national level (see p. 30) but focusing more on recent inter-regional variations than exploring their historical development. Given the link between living conditions and monetary incomes in capitalist societies, the considerable inter- and intraregional variations in household incomes and their sources are significant (Table 2.6). Although prices, especially of housing, vary markedly between and within regions, income variations are still the best single indicator of spatial variations in living conditions.

In view of the preceding discussion of changing regional economic and population patterns, these variations in average income and intraregional income distribution are not entirely unexpected. For example, retirement migration to the Southwest is reflected in the region having the highest percentage of household incomes deriving from pensions, annuities and investments. The concentration of administrators, managers and professionals in the Southeast results in both higher average incomes and the

Table 2.6   Regional variations in occupational groupings of heads of households and incomes, 1980–1981

	Northern	Yorks. & Humberside	East Midlands	East Anglia	South-east	South-west	West Midlands	North-west	Scotland	Wales	N. Ireland	UK
Average weekly household income, 1980–1981 (£)	140	135	149	152	183	149	155	155	147	144	123	158
% households with income less than £80	32.7	35.0	27.0	25.1	18.0	28.8	26.4	29.1	29.3	32.2	38.9	27.5
% households with income of £200 or more	21.0	21.1	22.2	28.2	35.8	24.2	28.1	28.3	23.1	23.2	17.4	27.9
Status of head of household, 1980–1981												
% professional and technical	5.9	4.5	6.9	8.9	11.7	8.1	8.4	6.8	6.4	5.6	2.6	8.1
% administrative and managerial	6.6	5.7	7.3	9.8	11.2	7.0	8.7	7.8	6.5	6.4	3.0	8.3
% manual	40.8	42.4	40.9	38.2	29.5	30.0	42.2	38.1	40.5	35.3	39.8	36.1
% retired and unoccupied	33.4	33.9	29.2	26.1	27.8	36.3	24.8	32.7	29.5	37.9	39.0	30.0

Source: Central Statistical Office (1983).

highest proportion of weekly incomes over £200 in the early 1980s. This prevalence of very high incomes is important in providing demand for various luxury goods in the region, as well as helping to drive up house prices. Yet, at the same time, more than one in five households had an income of less than £80 per week, while even in the prosperous Southeast almost 10 percent of household income was in the form of social security payments. Even so, the general effect of recession in the 1970s and early 1980s has been to increase the income gap between the Southeast and the remaining regions as unemployment and poverty have become more generalized in the latter. The greatest concentrations of poverty and low household incomes remain in Northern Ireland, however. Almost one household in eight has a weekly income of less than £35 while some 22 percent of household income comes from social security payments but, even there, one household in six has a weekly income of £200 or more.

In the next two sections we examine the implications of such income differences for housing and private consumption patterns within regions, looking at how households spend their incomes. Subsequently, variations in welfare and collective consumption are considered to see whether State welfare expenditure helps to compensate for inequalities in income levels and in private consumption between regions.

2.4.1 *Regional housing conditions*

Housing issues are considered in some detail in Chapters 3 and 4 and here we confine ourselves to a few remarks about variations at the regional level. By the late 1970s, regional variations in housing conditions had in certain respects been virtually eliminated. The application of national standards concerning the provision of basic amenities, allied in part to changing tenure patterns, resulted in very few houses in any region lacking amenities such as a hot water supply, an inside toilet or a bath or shower. Changing forms of domestic heating had been one reason for the declining demand for coal but while many houses still lacked central heating in the early 1980s, especially in Northern Ireland (63.6 percent), there was comparatively little variation between the other regions (46.9 percent in Scotland to 34.4 percent in the Northern region).

In other respects, there are considerable inter-regional variations in the conditions, quality and type of housing, and in some ways these had widened during the 1970s and early 1980s. One indication of these was differences in tenure patterns (Figure 2.6). Public sector renting tends to increase with decreasing household incomes, the regions with the highest shares of houses in this category tending to be those with below-average incomes and above-average per capita public expenditure on housing. Above-average expenditure in the Southeast is, however, more a result of inflated land and

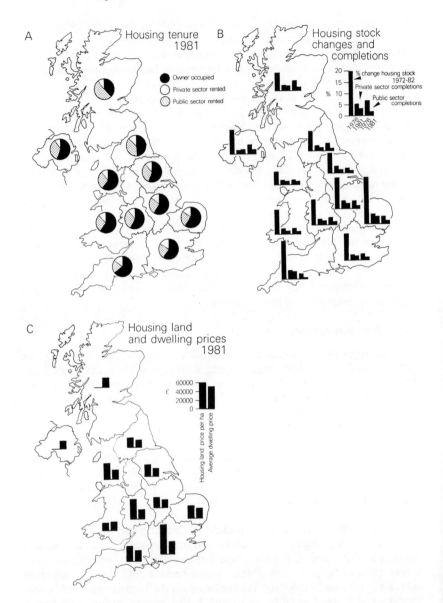

Figure 2.6 Regional variations in housing conditions, 1972–1981 (Central Statistical Office, 1983, *Regional Trends*).

house-building prices (Figure 2.6) than of a high percentage of public sector housing. Private sector renting remains most common in the Southeast (especially London – see Chapter 3.3) while regional variations in owner-occupation tend to be inversely related to those in public sector renting. These tenure variations have implications not only for quality of housing provision but more generally for social class composition and lifestyles.

They take on added significance when put in the context of changes in population and the housing stock over the preceding decade (Figure 2.6). While national population rose by only 1 percent, the regional distribution of population was altering, primarily because of differential rates of in- and out-migration. There was a much faster growth (11 percent) in the national stock of dwellings over the same period, related partly to changing age structure and household composition but also to regional population changes and migration patterns. This, coupled with the changing balance of public and private sector completions, helped to produce considerable regional variations in the housing stock.

Housing stock increased most rapidly in East Anglia, the East Midlands and the Southwest although by far the greatest net increment to the housing stock occurred in the Southeast (over 700,000) and West Midlands (almost 200,000). As the balance increasingly tilted from the public sector to the private sector as the main mechanism for financing construction at a time when completions in both sectors had fallen, additions to the housing stock became increasingly concentrated in this group of regions, which offered the best opportunities for profitable construction. These regions were either experiencing net in-migration, related to employment or retirement, or were those in which average incomes and house prices were highest. Although housing land prices were considerably higher in the Southeast (especially), Southwest and West Midlands, the greater capacity to purchase houses made them more attractive to house-building companies, reinforcing the concentration of new housing within them.

New housing did not necessarily mean better-quality housing, however, as construction companies tended to compensate for soaring land prices by erecting smaller, flimsier dwellings (Hall et al., 1973). The demand for very expensive larger and/or for higher-quality dwellings, on which profit margins are greater, further enhanced the attraction of these areas to the construction companies. A recent issue of *The Sunday Times* (14 July 1985) contained advertisements from Wates for three-bedroomed maisonettes at Morgans Walk in Battersea Bridge Road, London, for £175,000 and upwards; from Hampton and Sons for two–four-bedroom apartments from £230,000 and a five-bedroomed house for £570,000 on the bank of the Thames, a few minutes' journey from London's West End. All are examples of the upmarket new housing that can be built and sold in the Southeast, especially near central London. In part, the booming demand for upmarket houses in areas of

London such as Hyde Park, Pimlico, Chelsea, Kensington and Belgravia, is related to the buying of property by non-UK citizens and to the expansion of overseas banks and financial services companies in London (Gray, 1985). London's role in the international financial system thus has significant effects on the housing market.

There are, then, qualitative and quantitative regional variations in housing conditions and provision. Gray (1985) has suggested that 'Britain now has not one housing market but two. The first is in London and the South East ... the second is the rest of the country, where there is higher unemployment and where people are reluctant to move house or trade up-market if there is any possibility that their job might be threatened'. The regional variations have great significance for those without a job who wish to adopt the advice given by Norman Tebbit, a former Secretary of State for Employment in Margaret Thatcher's government, to 'get on their bikes' to search for work. Variations in tenure patterns and house prices, when added to the problem of exchanging local authority houses (at a time when the public sector stock has been squeezed), present considerable objective barriers to inter-regional migration. Gray (1985) suggests that differential rates of increase in house prices in the 1980s have aggravated the already wide gap in the cost of housing in the North and South to the point where it is 'becoming prohibitively expensive' for a family to come south to look for work. Such barriers sharply reveal the futility of attempting to solve regional unemployment problems via inter-regional migration. This, after all, was one reason why central government sought in the first place to create a regional policy in the 1930s and new ways of tackling regional problems via linked regional and national planning in the 1960s.

2.4.2   Regional private consumption patterns

The average level of individual and household consumption varies with both income and purchasing power and price levels, as well as with cultural differences that influence purchasing decisions. Not surprisingly, given marked regional variations in housing tenure patterns and house prices, average expenditure on housing varies considerably between regions (Figure 2.7). The highest levels of expenditure, absolutely and relatively, are in the Southeast. This is because of higher price levels for a given house type: for example, a pre- 1919 terraced house costs, on average, £15,650 in Yorkshire, but £47,620 in London (Gray, 1985). There is also generally better-quality housing in the private sector in the Southeast as more households are able to dispose of a larger proportion of their higher than average incomes on housing. Absolute spending on housing varies much more between regions than does housing expenditure as a proportion of household income as higher incomes are reflected in higher house prices. The lowest levels of spending on

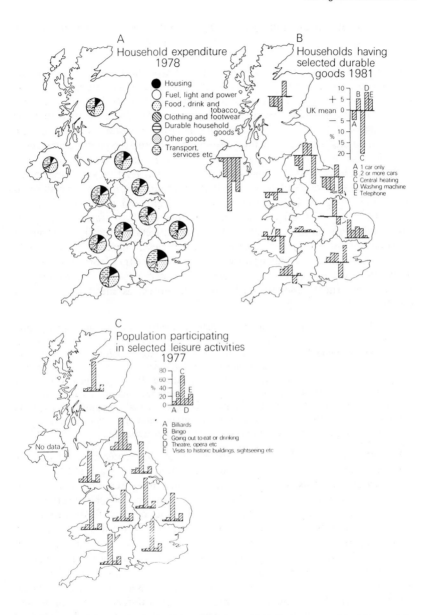

Figure 2.7 Regional variations in the ownership of consumer durables and in leisure patterns (Central Statistical Office, 1983, *Regional Trends*).

housing, absolutely and relatively, are found in those regions in which private sector prices are lowest and renting from the public sector is the most prominent mode of tenure.

Compared to housing, the absolute and relative variation between regions in other categories of household expenditure is much less pronounced. This is particularly so in the case of basic items such as foodstuffs, fuel, light and power and clothing and footwear. In a sense, expenditure on such items is both unavoidable and relatively income inelastic. Beyond a certain income level which enables the need for these items to be met, expenditure on them rises at a much slower rate than income increases. In so far as it does vary, such expenditure tends to be absolutely highest but relatively smallest in the more affluent regions and vice versa. Perhaps the most important exception to this general pattern is expenditure on fuel, light and power in Northern Ireland. This partly reflects the lack of indigenous fossil fuels there (gas is produced from imported coal) and it also reflects politically determined decisions about energy price levels. Nevertheless, there are considerable regional variations in expenditure patterns within these broad categories which, for example, give some credence to the stereotypes of a culturally and socially constructed North–South divide in tastes, as identified by Allen (1976).

> They (Northerners) prefer things that make immediate sense; plain, homely fare, without suspicious sounding ingredients, fussy additions or fancy names ... Northerners tended to turn up their noses at the more esoteric combinations – chicken and ham, sardine and anchovy — and plumped, almost infallibly for 'no-nonsense', tried and trusted flavours: ham, salmon, beef - or even plainly and simply 'meat'. The Northerner would prefer to feel that what he eats does him good – the South is the land of mixtures, of experimental mingling – jelly and blancmange together as a single dish, for example - and of subtler flavours: saltier bacon, more pungent types of cheese, more bitter marmalade ...

In fact, regional differences in the types of food consumed seem more complex than just the simple North–South dichotomy suggested by Allen. One reason for this is that major national food retailing chains and department stores (Fine Fare, Marks and Spencer, Sainsbury, etc.) have played an important part in diffusing various types of 'new' foods throughout all regions, or at least in their major urban centres. Nevertheless, the limited data available suggest that consumption of fresh fruit, meat and green vegetables is higher in the South, not least because the latter are generally cheaper in season. More eggs, bacon and ham, bread, cakes, biscuits, sugar and tea are consumed in the North, Scotland and Wales (Central Statistical Office, 1981). These dietary variations reflect differences in income and expenditure but also attitudes as to what constitutes a proper diet, lending some support to Allen's views on regional tastes. Variations such as the greater emphasis on high-calorie foods in the North, for example, have a material basis in the heavy manual work once prevalent there and also have implications for health and health care provision. A similar point can be made with regard to regional variations in expenditure on alcohol and tobacco. This tends to be greatest in those areas which formed the centres of the first round of capitalist industrialization in the UK. A male-oriented culture developed there, centred around workplace relations in which club and pub occupied a central role. While women and children remained at home, men would congregate outside the house consuming alcohol and tobacco; this was one way of creating an alternative to the rigours, often the dangers, of the workplace. The process was by no means uniform, however. It was itself subject to cultural variations, notably in areas such as Wales where the grip of Methodism was marked. Even though the industries that were central to the emergence of this sort of working-class culture have since declined considerably (see p. 71), their heritage is still visible as certain aspects of the associated lifestyle persist.

Inter-regional differences in expenditure on food, drink, tobacco and clothing are less pronounced than those on household durables, other goods and transport, vehicles, etc. Spending on these tends to be highest, both absolutely and relatively, in regions where average incomes are higher and where more households have sufficient disposable income available after meeting more basic needs such as housing and food. Not that these are luxury goods; rather in some regions a greater proportion of households cannot afford what are, by now, widely regarded as essential elements of everyday life. While over 90 percent of households in all regions owned a television set by the early 1980s, emphasizing the significance of this as a medium for the nationwide dissemination of news and views, ownership rates for other consumer durables are more variable (see Figure 2.7). Even so, there is still a quite widespread diffusion of basic labour-saving devices: in the region with the lowest average income almost 70 percent of households own a washing machine and 85 percent a refrigerator. Almost 60 percent of households in Northern Ireland had a telephone, certainly less than in the Southeast (80 percent), but nevertheless indicating widespread adoption. There are undoubtedly much greater regional variations in the ownership of more sophisticated consumer durables such as video recorders, deep freezes and microwave ovens. Nevertheless the great majority of households owning more basic labour-saving devices is suggestive of important changes in the distribution of domestic labour within the home, related both as cause and effect to the levelling-up in activity rates for married women (see Table 2.4). In this sense 'modernization' of household lifestyles went hand-in-hand with attempts to 'modernize' regional economies and employment patterns.

The remaining area in which there are marked inter-regional variations in expenditure patterns is transport. Expenditure on transport is highest, absolutely and relatively, in the Southeast and other above-average income regions. One reason for this is the greater amounts spent on commuting in the Southeast, especially to London. Expenditure variations are to a degree positively reflected in household car-ownership rates. These rates increase with average incomes but, even in Northern Ireland, almost 54 percent of households have a car. The lowest ownership levels are in the North where one household in two has a car. Car-ownership rates also depend on the cost and level of provision of public transport. The highest rates are found in East Anglia and the Southwest, both regions in which there have been rural areas wholly lacking public transport for over a decade (Department of the Environment, 1972; see also Chapter 4.5.2). For many people in such areas, having a car is a matter of necessity.

It is important not to confuse household car ownership with personal mobility (Hillman et al., 1973). Not all people in car-owning households are able to drive, for example. In most households with one car, it will be used for weekday commuting to work by the husband; his wife and children remain dependent on some other mode of transport on these days. A minority, though an increasing one, of households have two or more cars and the pattern of regional variability on this dimension is much more closely correlated with income levels. This does not necessarily simply reflect a greater ability and willingness to buy and maintain two cars, however. Regions with above-average incomes are those where the proportion of households with very high incomes is greatest. It is such high-income earners (senior managers and executives, for example) who are most likely to receive a car as a 'perk' with their job. Again, the greater incidence of two or more car households in the Southeast is both a result of the higher proportion of married women in well-paid full-time jobs and a factor that enables such women to search more widely for employment.

The greater mobility which access to a car permits also finds expression in regional variations in leisure activities outside the home. Rising incomes, coupled with established patterns of social life as well as increased mobility, resulted in at least 60 percent of households going out for a meal or drink at least once in four weeks (see Figure 2.7). The relatively low proportion in the Southeast is indicative perhaps of the effects of generally longer commuting journeys and a greater tendency to privatized and home-centred patterns of eating, drinking and entertaining. In contrast, the North has a long tradition of social life centred around pubs and clubs outside the home. In other respects the combination of higher incomes and definitions of culture in the Southeast leads to more people visiting historic buildings or the opera; such activities find less favour in regions such as the North, Scotland and Wales, where bingo, billiards and snooker are more popular. Again the suggestions of a North–South divide, to which Allen (1976) refers – or more accurately a core-periphery one – are to some extent evident.

There are also variations in taking holidays (Table 2.7). In all regions many households did not spend even one night away from home but, in general, these were distributed proportionately among the regions. The relatively small numbers of holiday-makers originating from East Anglia and the Southwest is partly due to the numbers of people who have moved there on retirement; indeed, because of its climate and natural environment, many holiday-makers from other regions are attracted to the Southwest. The comparatively low numbers of holiday-makers from other regions such as the North are linked to lower average incomes, with more expensive foreign holidays being particularly sensitive to income levels. The outstanding feature is the disproportionate number of people from the Southeast taking holidays abroad, perhaps indicative of a greater spirit of adventure (cf Allen's remarks, p. 92) but more decisively related to disposable income. This in turn helps support the thriving private service sector in the Southeast – travel agents, tour operators and so on prosper there. Yet again there is a reciprocal relationship between regional economic performance and individual lifestyles which helps reproduce and widen the gap between 'the South' and the rest of the UK.

It seems that the Southeast is the locus of highly mobile, affluent groups whose lifestyle within the UK is very much home based (especially with the cult of dinner party catering – a further new growth in service activity there) but for whom overseas holidays are an important part of recreation outside the home. At the same time there are 'imitation' effects in lifestyles which selectively penetrate all regions, reflected in the growth of new types of bars and restaurants, health clubs and saunas as these have diffused from the

Table 2.7 Holiday makers and non-holiday makers in Great Britain, 1979

	% Adult population	% no. of holidays	% holidays in Britain (1 + nights)	% holidays abroad (4 + nights)
North	7	8	5	5
Yorkshire & Humberside	8	6	11	9
East Midlands	6	5	8	5
East Anglia	4	5	4	3
Southeast	31	29	29	40
Southwest	8	9	8	5
West Midlands	10	11	12	8
Northwest	12	12	12	11
Wales	5	6	5	5
Scotland	9	9	8	9
Great Britain	100	100	100	100

Source: Central Statistical Office (1981).

Southeast. Nevertheless, a regional dimension to lifestyles remains prominent.

2.4.3   Regional welfare and collective consumption

A central objective of the postwar Welfare State was to narrow, and ideally eliminate, variations in access to education and health care – including regional differences. In this section we explore how far these laudably egalitarian aims have been achieved.

Prior to 1948, hospital services were provided in a variety of ways – by charities, municipalities, private capital and, in some cases such as isolation hospitals, by government. One result was great variation, both between and within regions, in the extent and form of hospital provision. When the NHS was established, it inherited this spatially uneven pattern of provision, which stood in stark contrast to its stated aims of providing equal access and provision across the country. The emphases on centralizing hospital facilities in pursuit of efficiency, especially since the 1962 Hospital Plan, have, if anything, increased intra-regional variations (Chapter 3.5.2) while raising overall levels of provision. Furthermore, considerable inter-regional inequalities have persisted.

Fourteen Regional Health Boards were set up in 1948, covering England and Wales. Broadly speaking, the lowest levels of hospital provision were in the North and West. From the early 1950s to 1970, the relative positions of the major health board regions remained the same with the London Metropolitan Hospital Board, the highest spender, spending twice as much per capita as Sheffield (the lowest). This primarily reflected the basis on which NHS funding was established in 1948: 'last year's allocation plus a standard rate of growth'. This perpetuated rather than reversed the regional inequalities originally built into the system. In 1974, when the NHS underwent its first major reorganization, the extent of both inter- and intraregional variations in resource allocation became apparent as data were produced for the 90 new Area Health Authorities as well as the Regional Health Authorities (RHAs) (as the Boards were renamed). To try and deal with these inequalities the Resource Allocation Working Party (RAWP) was set up to establish 'a method of securing as soon as possible a pattern of distribution responsive objectively, equitably and efficiently to relative need'. The RAWP defined 'need' for hospital resources by 'weighting' the population to take into account the variation in individuals' needs for health care because of age and location (Smith, 1979, pp. 272–274). The RAWP also considered variations in capital stock among RHAs (Table 2.8). In general terms, this suggested a great need for and underprovision of resources in the North of England, so the RAWP suggested transferring funds overall from the South and East to the North and West, and within RHAs from over-

Table 2.8   Variations in hospital provision in English Regional Health Authorities

English Regional Health Authorities	Weighted pop. - crude pop.	1975 Shortfall (-) or excess (+) of capital stock (£ pr capita)	RAWP* Target change	Change achieved by 1982–1983	1978 Beds in hospitals per 1000 population
Northern	1.02	−4.13	15.2	10.23	8.3
Yorkshire	1.03	−5.72	6.1	2.53	8.5
Trent	0.95	−7.72	15.3	9.80	7.1
East Anglia	0.94	+5.74	7.8	2.18	7.1
NW Thames	0.97	+16.28	−12.8	0.48	8.3
NE Thames	1.00	+13.54	−11.8	3.57	8.2
SE Thames	1.07	+0.84	−10.8	−2.91	8.2
SW Thames	1.09	+8.27	−5.5	0.15	9.1
Wessex	0.98	−11.48	9.0	3.63	7.1
Oxford	0.88	+11.24	−6.0	−7.60	6.1
South Western	0.96	−1.16	6.9	2.63	8.2
West Midlands	0.95	−6.75	8.7	4.87	7.2
Mersey	1.04	+17.53	5.2	4.58	9.2
North Western	1.09	−16.54	16.9	11.50	7.7
Wales	NA	NA	NA	NA	8.6
Scotland	NA	NA	NA	NA	11.4
Northern Ireland	NA	NA	NA	NA	11.1

* RAWP = Resource Allocation Working Party.

Source: Townsend and Davidson (1982).

resourced urban areas to suburban and rural ones. These latter proposals provoked considerable hostility (Woods, 1982) which, along with central government restrictions on NHS spending, have meant that the proposed inter-regional resource reallocations had not been achieved by the early 1980s. Whether they can be remains a moot point.

At the start of the 1980s there were still considerable regional variations in levels of provision of, and access to, medical facilities, both at primary (general practitioners, etc.) and secondary (hospitals) levels. Variations at subregional level are more marked still (Townsend and Davidson, 1982, pp. 86–87). Despite national norms, there are considerable variations in the numbers of doctors and dentists per capita; generally, list sizes are greater in the North than in the South. Although this does not necessarily imply corresponding differences in the quality of health care, these data nonetheless suggest variability in ease of access to dental and medical facilities. Similarly there are considerable variations in the numbers of NHS hospital beds per capita; the highest levels of provision are in the South of England, the lowest in Northern Ireland and Scotland. The growing number of private hospitals, concentrated in the more affluent Southeast, is exacerbating existing inequalities in NHS provision: there are 20 times the number of private hospital beds in the Southeast than there are in the Northeast even on a per capita basis (Mohan, 1984b).

Differential provision of medical facilities is at least related to variations in health conditions and death rates, even if they do not cause these. Research at St Thomas' Hospital Community Medicine Department (*The Sunday Times*, 27 March 1983) suggests that in areas of England and Wales that are less well provided for with health care services, people die unnecessarily. There are over 20,000 deaths annually for which treatment is medically possible but is unavailable. Just over half of these are perinatal deaths (of babies under four weeks of age). Regionally, the areas with the highest probabilities of death tend to be the old industrial areas of the North and West and those with the lowest probabilities tend to be predominantly in the Southeast; the former tend to be areas with relatively poor provision of medical facilities but the latter are relatively well provided for (Figure 2.8). The correlation is far from perfect, however, suggesting that more than just levels of medical care provision is involved, while there are also urban–rural differences. Even so, nine of the ten areas in England with the highest standardized death rates are located in the Northeast and Northwest; the only one in the Southeast is the inner-London borough of Tower Hamlets (Townsend and Davidson, 1982, pp. 165–167). In this sense, the region and locality in which you live may literally be a life and death matter.

While not a matter of such gravity, regional variations in educational provision and participation can also have a profound effect on lifechances (Figure 2.9). Such variations begin at the pre-school stage although, in contrast to many other aspects of regional variation, provision for the under-fives in State-maintained schools tends to be lower in the South than in the North of England, Northern Ireland and Wales. This is very much related to party political control of local authorities and the highest levels of provision tend to be in regions where local authorities are Labour controlled. The contrast between participation rates in Greater London (48.6 percent) and the rest of the Southeast (23.0 percent) similarly reflects differences in party political control. State provision of facilities for the under-fives has been important in enabling married women with pre-school age children to take a waged job in regions such as the North. On the other hand, provision for the under-fives outside the State sector is greater in the higher-income South, tending to counterbalance the underprovision within the State sector there.

There is less regional variation in primary and secondary provision within the State sector, largely because of the existence of national norms, at least in England and Wales. The number of pupils per teacher varies little between regions: 20.3 in Scotland, 21.6 in the North and 23.7 in the East Midlands at primary level, and 14.4 in Scotland, 16.2 in the Northwest and 17.4 in the Southwest at secondary level (Central Statistical Office, 1981). On the other hand, almost half of all private school places in the UK are located in the

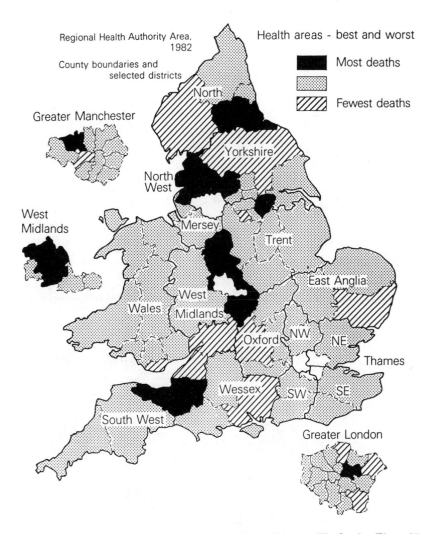

Figure 2.8 Regional variations in mortality and health care (*The Sunday Times*, 27 March 1983).

Southeast. The concentration is not simply a reflection of regional variations in the ability to pay for education; it also highlights the persistence within the educational system of public schools, which play a crucial role in reproducing the class structure of UK society.

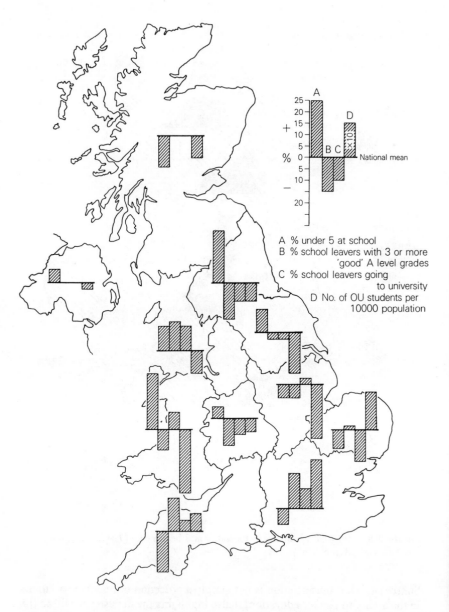

Figure 2.9 Education: regional variations in resources and achievements (Central Statistical Office, 1983, *Regional Trends*).

Despite nominally equal levels of provision within the State sector, there are considerable variations in average levels of attainment. Children in the South are more likely to do well in examinations, stay on beyond the minimum school-leaving age and go on to higher or further education (Figure 2.9). Furthermore, participation in Open University courses is highest in the Southeast, East Anglia and the Southwest. While the Open University provides a second chance for those who missed out on a university education first time round, differences in income and social class composition result in regional inequalities in those participating in higher education through it. More generally, participation in further education is linked to variations in the social and occupational composition of regions and, in so far as this influences employment opportunities, helps to reproduce this composition.

One important objective of creating the postwar Welfare State was to eliminate differences in access to, and levels of provision of, education and health services. Important regional differences remain, despite – or in some cases because of – the particular way in which State policies for education and health care were designed and implemented. Substantial cutbacks in State spending on these basic services, as part of a redefinition of the Welfare State and a shift to privatization, can only widen regional variations.

2.5 Regional variations in politics

It is a salutary experience to contrast the geographies of the 1945 and 1983 General Elections. In 1945 the Labour Party gained widespread electoral support from a variety of social groups and regions, attracted by the vision in its election manifesto of a more egalitarian, humane and socially just society. In 1983, following four years of divisive policies at home and the Falklands/Malvinas venture abroad, the General Election result revived the vision of Disraeli's 'two nations'. Although in part attributable to the emergence of the Liberal–Social Democratic Alliance as a 'third force' in national party politics, the geography of the 1983 General Election revealed sharp regional polarization in support for the Conservative and Labour Parties. The geography of voting revealed quite precisely who had gained and who had lost from four years of Thatcherism. Although Margaret Thatcher's Conservative Party won only 42 percent of the votes nationally, their regional concentration south of a line from the Severn to the Wash, coupled with the Alliance splitting the non-Conservative vote, resulted in a massive parliamentary majority of 142. To put this another way, outside of London the Labour Party won virtually no seats south of the Severn–Wash line while well over 80 percent of Labour MPs were returned for constituencies to the north of it. While a particularly sharply defined regional division, the same basic North–South, Conservative–Labour divide has been visible in UK politics throughout the postwar period. Indeed, the consensus between 'one-nation' Tories cast in the mould of Harold Macmillan and Labour social democrats on the need for government regional intervention reflected a shared perception of this divide and a shared awareness of the need to address the problems it posed.

Even so, if the UK's electoral geography involved a division between a Conservative south and Labour north (recognizing important rural–urban differentiations within both), this basic pattern was challenged on an explicitly territorial basis from the 1960s. Following the partition of Northern Ireland and Eire in 1922 (Farrell, 1980, pp. 21–65), nationalism had been an issue of recurrent importance in political debates in the UK but, in the 1960s, the re-emergence of 'the troubles' in Northern Ireland and the reawakening of nationalist sentiment in Scotland and Wales thrust it to the forefront of these debates. Scottish and Welsh nationalism raised fears of what Nairn (1976) was later to refer to as 'the break-up of Britain', and this had important effects (see, for example, Crossman, 1976). There had long been a tradition of cultural nationalism in both Scotland and Wales but in the 1960s, especially in Scotland, this re-emerged and became transformed into a more politically and economically oriented neonationalism. This posed a particular danger to the Labour government of the 1960s. Not only did it pose a constitutional threat but it also threatened areas of traditional Labour hegemony and political support.

One reason for the transformation and resurgence of nationalism was the perceived failure of Labour's modernization policies to deal adequately with the economic and social problems of these areas. In addition, in Scotland the discovery of North Sea oil and the coining of the slogan 'It's Scotland's oil' seemed to suggest that the resources were available for an autonomous Scotland to tackle its problems more effectively than a parliament in Westminster. Consequently, demands for more autonomy became stronger in Scotland than in Wales. Electoral and more general support for the Scottish Nationalist Party (SNP) and Plaid Cymru began to grow, peaking in the 1974 October Election when the SNP captured over 30 percent of the vote in Scotland and returned 11 MPs to Westminster (Smith and Brown, 1983). The level of electoral support subsequently fell, not least because the contradictions of parties based on cross-class alliances began to emerge at the point of trying to agree on policies and objectives. In addition, in Scotland it became clear that it would not be 'Scotland's oil'. Nevertheless, before all this became apparent, the fears of the 1974–1979 Labour government led to the establishment of the Scottish and Welsh Development Agencies in an attempt to defuse demands for greater political autonomy.

This tactic of granting a greater degree of administrative autonomy seemed to succeed as referenda for assemblies in Scotland and Wales resulted in rejection by their populations, decisively in Wales though much less emphatically in Scotland. In addition, unintentionally though predictably, it led to demands from several English regions for parallel agencies. This brought the question of a more general regional devolution of power to greater prominence in political debates about how best to tackle regional problems, not least as regional devolution was increasingly the order of the day over much of Western Europe (Hudson and Lewis, 1982).

While the rise and fall of regionalist and nationalist politics had some important effects, and for a time threatened profoundly to alter the party political map, ultimately their effects were more or less contained within the two-party system. The major exception to this was in Northern Ireland. Here the complex intermeshing of religion and politics led from the 1960s to the formation of a number of new political parties and political organizations, in general allied to the Catholic or Protestant churches and aiming for either a united Ireland or union with Great Britain. These were in addition to longer-established organizations such as the IRA (the Provisionals breaking away from the Officials in 1969) and the old Ulster Unionist Party. The situation in Northern Ireland threatened to move beyond control and posed a major threat to the UK State in the early 1970s so that in 1972 the Conservative government of Edward Heath suspended the powers of Northern Ireland's Parliament at Stormont and instigated direct rule from Westminster. It was a rule that would only be enforced by military and paramilitary State power. In the absence of any generally acceptable political solution the death toll rose into the thousands as a result of the activities of extremist organizations pursuing political goals via tactics of terror and violence.

Outside of Northern Ireland, it seemed for a time as if some important changes would be imprinted on the map of party political support but, by and large, the old regional division between Conservative south and Labour north, which is an integral part of the geography of capitalist development in the UK, has survived unscathed. The emergence of the SDP and the Liberal–SDP Alliance, though a national political development, carries with it potentially profound implications for regional patterns of political support but we return to this later (p. 199).

Note

1. In a series of influential publications, Lipietz (1977, 1980) has set out a schematic framework for analysing the changing intranational spatial division of labour. He categorizes regions into three types, depending on the prevailing social and environmental conditions and the type of labour-power available within them: '(1) those with a highly technological environment, with close links between business centres, innovation centres and centres of R and D and scientific teaching. "Externalities" are intense. The value of labour-power is important here; so too is the skilled part of the labour force.

(2) Those with a high proportion of skilled personnel (technicians, professional workers), which presupposes an industrial tradition corresponding at least to the stage of large scale industry, and an average value of labour power. (3) Those with reserves of labour which can be regarded as unskilled and as having a very low value of reproduction, since they are produced by the disintegration of other modes [of production] or by the decline of obsolete industries corresponding to an earlier stage of the division of labour' (Lipietz, 1980, pp. 67–68). In an attempt to increase profitability companies seek to reorganize their production processes to take advantage of the possibilities that this regional differentiation offers. While developed in the context of France – so that its use elsewhere must be undertaken with due caution – Lipietz's approach has since been adopted, extended and used in the UK (Massey, 1983a). Lipietz (for example 1984) has since extended his own analyses to the changing international division of labour.

THREE

The Urban Dimension

3.1 Introduction

The level of urbanization in the United Kingdom is one of the highest in Europe and in 1981 an estimated 89.6 percent of the population lived in urban areas (Denham, 1984). Four urban areas – Greater London, the West Midlands, Greater Manchester and West Yorkshire – each had more than one million residents and together they accounted for one-quarter of the total population. The largest 60 cities and towns – each with a population of over 100,000 – account for more than half the population of the UK. There is regional concentration of major urban areas in a zone extending from the Northwest to the Southeast (Figure 3.1), described as the UK's 'megalopolis' (Hall et al., 1973). Important outliers exist in Central Scotland, the Northeast and South Wales but there are few metropolitan areas in other regions.

The economic role of urban areas – especially of the larger cities – has changed considerably in the postwar period. In 1945 cities were still seen as dynamic centres of growth (for example by the Barlow Commission; see Table 2.3), and much postwar planning focused on the need to constrain their supposedly inexorable growth. However, by the 1960s the largest cities were experiencing considerable difficulties. Economic restructuring in that decade, already discussed in earlier chapters, undermined the employment bases of many cities, leading to the much publicized policy initiatives for the 'inner-city problem areas' in the 1970s. It was not simply that the large cities, especially their inner areas, had large job losses, but they also lost population, first to the outer suburbs and then to more distant settlements. This redistribution was socially uneven for it was the higher- and middle-income groups who moved out to the more spacious suburbs that have become synonymous with privatized, home-based consumption. In contrast, those left behind – the less skilled, the elderly, single-parent families, and black immigrants – have formed a social residuum.

The planning system also contributed to inner-city difficulties, especially as a result of urban containment and urban decentralization policies. Restrictions on development land forced up land and house prices which, in

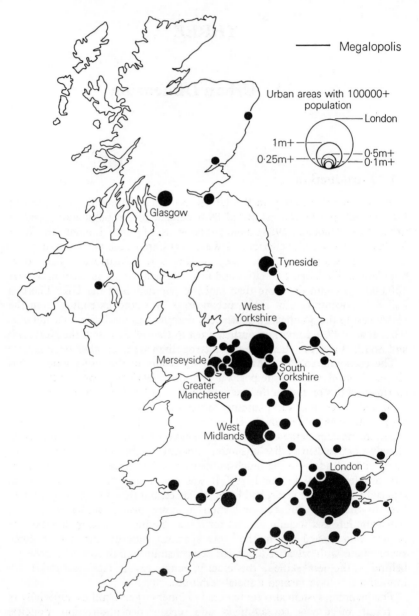

Figure 3.1 Urbanization in the UK, 1981 (Hall et al., 1973; Denham, 1984).

turn, exaggerated the difference between those with selective access to suburban houses, and those constrained to live in high-density, often high-rise urban dwellings. There has also been polarization of social classes and of ethnic and racial groups both between housing tenures and between urban locations. As a result, there are stark spatial concentrations of the poor and deprived within the larger cities, both in inner areas and, more recently, in peripheral public housing estates. Social tensions in these areas, expressed increasingly in violent confrontations (sometimes with a racial dimension), culminated in the 'hot summer' of 1981 and again in the autumn of 1985 in prolonged riots and the near collapse of law and order in such places as Toxteth and Brixton. Central government has developed a number of inner-area policies to ameliorate some of the conditions in the major cities in the 1970s and 1980s but these have proven grossly inadequate – if not appropriate – given the magnitude of the problems. Some central government policies allied to restrictions on local government expenditure have actually contributed to the economic and social problems of inner-city residents.

3.2 Restructuring of metropolitan economies

3.2.1 The collapse of manufacturing

The fortunes of the major cities diverged sharply in the 1930s: London, and to a lesser extent Birmingham, boomed while cities such as Newcastle, Glasgow and Liverpool slumped, as did their surrounding regions. After 1945 the conurbations began to experience relative job decentralization which, from the mid-1960s, became massive disinvestment and job losses, at first in the inner areas and then at the metropolitan scale. The decline was more widespread on this occasion, with manufacturing collapsing in London and Birmingham as well as in the more peripherally located cities.

Between 1959 and 1978 London lost 42.5 percent of its manufacturing jobs and the other conurbations had combined losses of 26.5 percent, while there were relative shifts to small towns and rural areas (Table 3.1). Employment decline was greatest in the early 1970s: between 1971 and 1976, the conurbations had a net job loss of 14.3 percent, while Birmingham, Liverpool and Manchester each had losses of about 20 percent, and the GLC of about 30 percent (Dicken, 1982). A clearer picture is obtained if the changes are disaggregated for inner- and outer-urban areas. The long process of inner-area decline had already commenced in the 1950s, although it accelerated later, while outer areas only started to lose manufacturing jobs in the 1960s.

Manufacturing job losses stemmed mainly from high rates of closures and low rates of openings of firms: existing firms went bankrupt or channelled investment to new areas while new firms found more profitable production conditions outside inner areas. Establishment mobility has been of less direct

Table 3.1   Manufacturing decline in urban areas in Great Britain

	% change in manufacturing employment, 1960-1978
London	−42.5
Conurbations	−26.5
Free-standing cities	−13.8
Large towns	−2.2
Small towns	+15.7
Rural areas	+38.0

Source: Hamnett (1985).

% change in manufacturing employment in the inner and outer areas of the conurbations, 1951-1976

	1951-1961	1961-1971	1971-1976
Inner areas	−7.5	−20.2	−15.0
Outer areas	+4.8	−16.5	−13.7
Conurbations	−1.6	−18.4	−14.3
Rest of Great Britain	+9.6	+8.8	−6.2

Source: Dicken (1982).

importance in restructuring but, though small in number, mobile firms are likely to be relatively dynamic. In the period 1966–1974/75, the proportion of manufacturing job losses attributable to the excess of firm closures over openings was 50 percent in Merseyside, 69 percent in London and 86 percent in Manchester while in Glasgow, in the earlier period 1958–1968, the proportion was 80 percent (Elias and Keogh, 1982). Recent evidence on London confirms that about two-thirds of all job losses in the period 1976–1980, in both inner and outer areas, were attributable to high rates of *in situ* redundancies compared to low rates of new job creation (Drake-Brockman, 1984). Coventry provides further evidence of the startling scale of job losses. Between 1975 and 1984 the city's top ten manufacturing companies had a 47 percent employment decline: some firms such as Alfred Herbert (machine tools) had closed, others such as Leyland and Talbot were operating with less than half their 1975 workforce, and none had retained more than 70 percent of earlier employment levels (*Financial Times*, 26 April 1985). Even the 'growth' areas of the early postwar years have experienced an industrial collapse.

There is no evidence that these job losses are due to a particularly unfavourable industrial composition: shift share analyses by Danson et al. (1980) of the period 1952–1976 and by Fothergill and Gudgin (1982) of the years 1959–1979, found that composition effects were actually more favourable in the conurbations than in the UK as a whole. Moreover, studies comparing the industrial composition of inner and outer areas of conurbations – such as that by Lloyd and Mason (1978) in Manchester – have also found no unduly unfavourable effects in the former. Job losses have become generalized both among industrial sectors and between inner and outer areas, as is illustrated by the pattern of redundancies in London between 1979 and 1982 (Drake-Brockman, 1984). Redundancies in the inner-London boroughs of Camden and Islington were concentrated in traditional sectors, especially paper and printing (41 percent) and clothing and footwear (11 percent), but in the outer-London boroughs of Ealing and Brent they were dominated by losses in modern 'growth' industries such as electrical engineering (28 percent) and vehicles (29 percent).

Both independent firms and multibranch enterprises are reacting to international competition by creating a new division of labour that leads to disproportionate job losses in the conurbations. Massey and Meegan's (1978) study of the electrical engineering industry in the inner areas demonstrated that 58 percent of job losses were *in situ*, while a further 31 percent were lost in the course of the transfer of production, and only 11 percent were lost to other regions. This restructuring is based on the needs of firms to reduce costs and/or cut capacity in the light of new conditions of production. For multibranch enterprises, this has often involved substitution of capital for labour and spatial separation of stages of production. Skilled labour has been made redundant in inner-city locations while production has been expanded in those regions offering flexible (and often female) cheap labour (see Chapter 2.2). The age of capital equipment in many older, inner-city plants has accelerated this change; given the need to modernize, firms with inner-city production facilities have sometimes found it more advantageous to write off rather than renew aged premises and machinery in these areas. Where new investment does occur, substitution of capital for labour leads to lower employment densities. Given the lack of space for physical expansion in these zones, this has meant a fall in employment levels. Once decline has commenced, the weakening of inter-firm linkages in these zones makes further plant closures more likely.

It has been argued by government ministers (for example, Peter Shore in his keynote speech on inner cities in 1976) that urban and regional policies have contributed to the industrial decline of the conurbations. Zoning and compulsory purchase orders (CPOs) supposedly have limited the supply of industrial premises, while regional policies encouraged job transfers to the Assisted Areas. There is evidence to support this view. On occasion, local authorities may use CPOs to acquire residential and industrial premises for redevelopment but, in a study of Manchester between 1966 and 1972, Lloyd and Mason (1978) found this had been important in only 146 out of 1129 plant closures. Regional policy measures may also have been important on occasion but Massey and Meegan (1978) found that only 11 percent of job losses stemmed from inter-regional transfers – although, of these, about two-thirds involved moves to Assisted Areas. Electrical engineering, however, is an industry for which labour conditions in the Assisted Areas have been particularly attractive and Dicken (1982) found that after 1965 intraregional rather than inter-regional transfers from the conurbations were important. Suburban locations offer favourable conditions for new investments for several reasons: there is improved access as a result of investment in the road network around, and the motorways between, the large cities, larger production sites are available, and the labour force has also decentralized in recent decades (see Chapter 3.4.1). Some firms have also sold inner-city premises in order to realize the redevelopment value of landholdings. This was particularly important in the late 1960s and early 1970s when the office boom drove up demand for, and the price of, urban land. At the same time, manufacturing profits were falling sharply, so that firms were encouraged to capitalize on the land values of inner-area industrial sites (see Ambrose and Colenutt, 1975). However, although transfers may be important in some areas or in some industries, it is the high rate of closures that lies at the root of the decline in manufacturing employment. The cutting-edge of industrial restructuring is now to be seen as clearly in metropolitan inner areas as it is in coal, steel or shipbuilding centres. Nowhere is this more vividly illustrated than in Liverpool, which earned itself the title of 'the Bermuda Triangle of British capitalism' in the 1970s (Merseyside Socialist Research Group, 1980). But industrial collapse has also become synonymous with inner-area economies in all the larger metropolitan areas.

3.2.2 Expansion of service employment

Expansion of the service sector has been discussed earlier (Chapters 1.3 and 2.2), so there is only a brief further review here. Cameron's (1980) analysis of employment change in the 1960s showed that the ratio of service jobs to total resident population in all seven conurbations (Birmingham, Glasgow, Leeds, Liverpool, London, Manchester, Newcastle) increased from 0.141 to 0.167 with London remaining dominant as its ratio increased from 0.197 to 0.220. Expansion of services has been sectorally uneven; in the conurbations, in the 1960s, the largest increases were in financial, professional and scientific services (Cameron, 1980). Other services have expanded less rapidly. There has been restructuring in retailing and other distributional activities, while employment in public administration has also grown fairly slowly.

Changes in service employment can also be analysed at a broader scale using Metropolitan Economic Labour Areas (MELAs) (Spence et al., 1982). These are large-scale, functional urban areas with, in crude terms, their 'cores' being major cities, their 'rings' including nearby local authorities which provide substantial numbers of commuters, and their 'outer rings' being the outermost reaches of their commuting hinterlands. The MELAs can be further subdivided so as to pick out those with populations over one million in 1971 (which approximate the present metropolitan counties, excepting Sheffield). At this scale, employment in the distributive trades has fallen in the cores of all MELAs but there have been gains in the rings due to growing service provision for the suburbanizing population. In contrast, financial and professional services have exhibited strong growth in virtually all urban zones. However, these aggregate data do not indicate the types of jobs created. For example, in terms of office employment, the numbers of clerical jobs have fallen while the numbers of managerial employees have increased in the cores. This reflects creation of a new spatial division of labour within some service industries.

Two major considerations are important in the absolute decentralization of service jobs. First, rising land costs and office rents (partly in consequence of urban containment policies), linked with escalating costs of clerical labour, threatened profitability and capital accumulation in the 1960s. The suburbs offered lower office rents and reserves of suitable (female) labour, while changes in telecommunications technology permitted some larger companies to decentralize more routine office functions to these lower-cost locations. In contrast, reliance of more senior office staff on direct access to clients meant that the more skilled jobs remained in the urban cores – especially in the metropolitan areas.

The second major influence on office location – leastways in London and Birmingham – was government policies for planned office dispersal. The extension of regional policy so as to incorporate office activities has already been outlined (see Table 2.3): in brief, the aim was to limit further expansion of office jobs in London (and later Birmingham) so as to ease pressures on land costs, local housing markets and urban transport (see Chapter 3.3.1). From 1965 office development permits (ODPs) were used to encourage office dispersal from London by limiting construction of new premises. However, some eight million square feet of new office space were still built in the city over the next three years, partly because developers had previously stockpiled planning permissions for new office buildings. There was, anyway, a time-lag in completing larger projects. However, ODPs were rarely refused and, by the early 1970s, were granted to about 75 percent of applicants. Moreover, most firms refused ODPs were able to stay in London – either by obtaining an ODP in a later application, or by moving into existing premises (Goddard, 1979). Therefore, instead of encouraging inter-regional office transfers, ODPs mainly contributed to increasing office costs and to short-distance intraregional decentralization, especially of more routine jobs. Far from indicating a policy failure, Pickvance (1981) sees this as fulfilment of a deliberate strategy to facilitate a double process of decentralization/centralization: routine jobs were moved out of central London, thereby permitting increased specialization in higher managerial functions and enhancing London's status as an international office centre in competition with Paris and other European capitals. Such a strategy would have been increasingly attractive to the Wilson government as international monetary crises after 1967 laid bare the declining international competitivity of the UK economy.

3.2.3 Employment and unemployment

The contrasting trends in manufacturing and service employment have been unbalanced and the growth of new jobs has not been sufficient to compensate for job losses in the major cities. In the 1950s, as the national economy continued to expand, there were employment gains in most cities. By the early 1960s growth was slowing in the 'million' cities with only 33,000 jobs gained in the period 1961–1966, compared to over 600,000 jobs in the rest of Britain.* By the later 1960s the 'million' cities were experiencing real problems with almost half a million jobs lost between 1966 and 1971: growth in the rest of urban Britain had also slowed, but remained positive. By the 1970s the mould was set and there were further losses in London, the conurbations and other large provincial cities (Table 3.2). Only the smaller towns and rural areas had employment gains in this decade, although with the onset of recession these areas also had losses in the period 1978–1981.

Employment changes were not uniformly distributed throughout urban areas (Table 3.3). In the early 1960s job losses were concentrated in the cores of the largest cities while the centres of smaller cities continued to record gains or, at worse, small losses. Restructuring had already brought about major job losses in the metropolitan areas even before a second and larger wave of redundancies occurred in the late 1970s. London and Merseyside also emerged at an early stage as cities with particularly acute economic problems. All urban zones in London lost jobs in the 1960s, testimony to massive decentralization to the outer Southeast. In Merseyside, the losses were more localized but the conurbation centre had a startling 45 percent job loss in the 1960s. These employment trends intensified in the 1970s and more large-scale job losses occurred in inner-urban areas throughout Britain.

British cities have shared fully in the national growth of unemployment since the mid-1960s and some idea of the situation in late 1984 is given in Figure 3.2. There are both regional and size elements in the distribution.

* The term 'Britain' is used deliberately when data exclude Northern Ireland.

Table 3.2 Employment changes in local labour market areas in Great Britain, 1971–1981

	000s		Change 1971–1981	
	1971	1981	Absolute (000s)	%
London	4,269	3,891	−378	−8.8
Conurbations	2,719	2,367	−352	−12.9
Provincial dominants	1,505	1,448	−57	−3.8
Cities	6,469	6,429	−40	−0.6
Towns	5,890	6,084	+194	+3.3
Rural areas	785	847	+62	+7.9
Great Britain	21,638	21,067	−571	−2.6

Source: Centre for Urban and Regional Development Studies (1984a).

Note: The CURDS definition differs from that used by Spence et al. (1982, Tables 3.2 and 3.4), especially in treating the conurbations as entities rather than as several separate urban regions. CURDS identified 20 metropolitan regions and 115 free-standing urban areas, compared to the 126 urban regions analysed by Spence et al. (1982). Neither study included Northern Ireland.

Table 3.3 Total employment changes in Metropolitan Economic Labour Areas, 1951–1971

	Percentage change		
	1951–1961	1961–1966	1966–1971
'Million' cities			
Cores	3.1	−3.2	−7.4
Rings	8.9	13.8	3.1
Outer rings	2.6	6.8	1.0
Rest of Britain			
Cores	11.2	5.8	−0.6
Rings	5.0	8.7	4.2
Outer rings	−3.3	4.9	−1.6

Source: Spence et al. (1982).

Unemployment rates are generally higher in the North than in the South of Britain, and there is also high unemployment in Belfast. However, there are also generally lower unemployment rates in smaller and free-standing cities

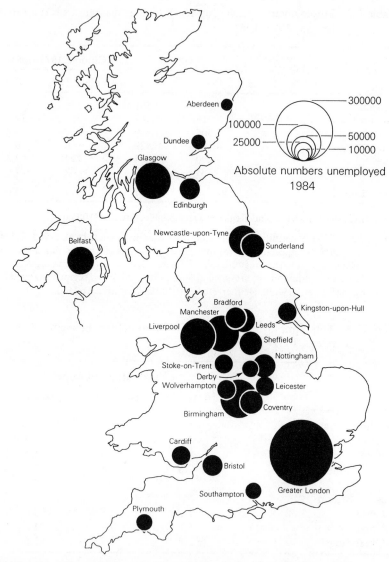

Figure 3.2   Unemployment totals in British cities, 1981 (Redfern, 1982).

such as Bristol or Nottingham than in the conurbations. Excluding Leeds, all
the travel-to-work areas within the conurbations have unemployment rates
above the national average, and some of the highest rates occur in the very
largest cities such as Liverpool, Newcastle and Glasgow. The West Midlands

also had high rates of unemployment in Birmingham, Coventry and Wolverhampton. The exception is London: despite having some of the largest job losses, the unemployment rate is well below the national average. This is partly accounted for by population decentralization and out-migration but the London figures are very deceptive, concealing some of the most extreme intra-urban variations in unemployment. Aggregate figures provide only a first indication of the problems facing the populations of the largest cities. Unemployment rates are highly variable between groups and between inner and outer areas, and we return to this theme later (Chapter 3.6).

There were no specifically urban policies to ameliorate job losses in the large cities or to encourage new investments in their inner areas before the 1980s. While there was growing concern with deprivation in inner areas from the mid-1960s, most initial policy responses were social or a mixture of social and economic initiatives (see Chapter 3.6.2). However, in 1981 the Conservative government declared a number of Enterprise Zones, many but not all of which were in the conurbations (see Figure 3.5). The stated aim was partly to regenerate the national economy, but also to create an urban economic policy to assist those cities that had experienced particularly acute employment difficulties. The 11 initial designations included the Isle of Dogs, Newcastle/Gateshead, Salford/Trafford, Liverpool (Speke), Clydebank and West Belfast – all classic cases of urban decline. The second set of designations in 1982 were made at a time of major cutbacks in the steel industry, so several steel towns such as Workington, Scunthorpe, Flint and Rotherham were included, along with metropolitan areas.

The basic idea of the Enterprise Zone stemmed from the concept of Freeports – the creation of small zones free of government restrictions and subject to relatively low taxation. The original concept was ultimately watered down, but Enterprise Zones still offer substantial advantages over ten years to firms locating in them. These include exemption from rates and development land tax, 100 percent allowances on capital expenditure for corporation and income tax purposes, exemption from industrial training levies, a simplified local planning system, and general reduction in government bureaucracy.

The Enterprise Zones were rapidly developed and, between 1981 and 1984, about one-quarter of their derelict land and buildings were brought into productive use. This development was aided by considerable pre-existing public expenditure in several of them, in sharp contrast to the free-market ideology the Zones were supposed to represent. Some 725 firms were established providing about 8000 new jobs but success rates varied. While more than 1000 jobs were established in Clydebank, Corby and Swansea, there were only 92 new jobs in Belfast. Nevertheless, some 60 percent of incoming firms were new starts and at least one commentator (Hall, 1984) considers the policy to have been a modest success.

However, the policies can be viewed more critically (see Anderson, 1983). The Zones have a noticeable 'boundary' effect, for many firms have relocated from just outside the designated area – hardly surprising as this could result in savings of £3000–11,000 per annum on rates even for medium-sized premises. The boundary also casts a negative 'shadow' effect on areas outside the Zones; for example, Norcliffe and Hoare (1982) found that demand for, and the rents of, premises in some adjacent areas were actually falling (see Chapter 3.6.2 for similar drawbacks in other area-based policies). Most Zones have also failed to attract the dynamic, innovative small firms that were seen as likely to provide a basis for future economic growth. For example, in the Manchester Zones the new firms are typical of the traditional enterprises of the region (light manufacturing, warehousing or food production) and do not include many recognizable 'growth' or 'sunrise' industries (Shutt, 1984).

Enterprise Zones have had limited economic significance but their political implications should not be ignored. Shutt (1984) argues that they have been important for the Thatcher government's attack on local authorities' autonomy. Creating the Zones in itself reduces local councils' powers within these areas, while their low rates are used as a lever to make adjacent (Labour) councils reduce their business rates. Furthermore, the system of bidding for Enterprise Zone designation divided the Labour Party: the Left and the trade unions opposed this while individual Labour councils participated in the bidding. Anderson (1983) is even more damning and sees the policy as primarily an exercise in legitimation, providing '... a "fig-leaf" to cover the Government's nakedness on the question of attempting to "solve" the problem of rising unemployment' (p. 341), while providing the first step towards converting all the UK to an 'enterprise zone', a reconstruction of 19th-century capitalism in the late 20th century.

After the lukewarm attempt at economic deregulation in the Enterprise Zones, it was probably inevitable that a second, stronger policy initiative would be launched – the Freeports (see Figure 3.5). These are entrepôt zones for processing imported materials, which would remain duty free if re-exported. It is too early as yet to evaluate their economic performance but they are likely to be subject to the same critique as Enterprise Zones.

3.3   Planning, housing and the built environment

In formulating urban policy, successive governments have had to balance consumption and production needs in attempting to create an environment suitable for both. In terms of consumption, there has been a need to accommodate the shift to more individual and privatized lifestyles for the majority of the population, mostly in suburban locations, but also a need to redevelop the fabric of older urban areas. In terms of production, the main aims of spatial policy have been to support capital accumulation in new, mostly outer-urban areas, and only with recent outbreaks of urban violence has attention been directed to the inner cities. Labour and Conservative governments have shared a bipartisan approach to most urban policy issues except, perhaps, housing tenure. All the strategies, however, have been worked out in the context of recurrent crises in the national economy.

Postwar policy was formulated against a background of massive interwar suburbanization in the South of Britain, when over four million new dwellings were constructed mostly on the outskirts of towns and cities. The new physical form of urbanization was associated with the emergence of new lifestyles and consumption patterns requiring low-density, home-based and relatively 'comfortable' surroundings. Suburbanization was based on government subsidies to private builders, encouragement of building societies which channelled the savings of the rapidly expanding white-collar salaried workers into housing development, and the availability of cheap land and labour. Mainly a new form of consumption for the middle class, it was partly extended to the working class through construction of suburban local authority estates. However, the new form of urban development embodied a major contradiction: suburbs represented the life ambitions and savings of the middle class but, at the same time, they threatened to destroy the traditional rural landscapes that made these extra-urban locations attractive. Postwar urban policy was to be dominated by this potential conflict.

The 1945-1950 Labour government laid down the foundations of postwar urban policy, creating what Mellor (1977) termed 'the British social experiment'. The guiding principle was provision of 'amenity' (mainly interpreted as green areas in New Towns, green belts, etc.), to be secured by containment of existing urban areas linked with controlled decentralization. The mechanisms for this were negative land-use planning controls and controlled housing investment. The negative powers were embodied in the 1947 Town and Country Planning Act which instituted a system of development plans and development controls, permitting local authorities to refuse permission for specific developments. Local authorities were also given some powers over land development rights. The 1942 report of the Uthwatt Committee had recommended that the development rights in land should be vested in the State. Local authorities should use compulsory purchase orders (CPOs) to acquire land at its existing use value, to be resold at full market price for its development value; the difference between these – 'betterment' – would then accrue to the State rather than the private developer. The 1947 Town and Country Planning Act was more limited in scope but did allow local authorities to impose a charge of 100 percent on the difference between the existing use and development use value of land, an effective nationalization of development rights (Ratcliffe, 1976).

Positive powers over development were not incorporated in the planning framework but in housing policy, for it was assumed that most new construction would be undertaken by the State, as initially was the case. Between 1945 and 1956 some 1.43 million local authority dwellings were built, mainly in the suburbs, thereby extending at least some aspects of new middle-class consumption patterns to rehoused working-class families. The showpieces of positive planning were the 14 New Towns initiated between 1946 and 1950, mainly to facilitate planned decentralization from London (Figure 3.3). The development corporations appointed to develop the New Towns had extensive powers to purchase land, finance housing and provide infrastructure, and illustrated the potential, but also the dangers, of positive planning. However, only a small proportion of all postwar development was in New Towns, even in the 1945–1951 period.

Conservative governments in the 1950s largely accepted this policy framework, with some important exceptions, so the postwar consensus over planning was quickly established. They pursued similar 'containment' objectives and emphasized negative development control powers but, otherwise, sought to restore more of the initiative for development to the private sector. Betterment provisions were repealed in 1953 and private transport was deregulated as postwar rationing of materials ended. With rising per capita incomes, car ownership in the United Kingdom doubled in the 1950s, reaching 5.5 million registered vehicles in 1960 – but there was no attempt to develop an integrated urban transport policy. Support for the New Towns also waned and only one additional new town – Cumbernauld – was designated during these years. Instead, the 1952 Town Development Act allowed the conurbations to make individual arrangements with smaller towns for overspill schemes. This offered a cheaper strategy for decentralization and also shifted more of the initiative for development to private construction companies in these towns.

By the late 1950s the inadequacies of existing urban policies became clear. Sustained economic growth and an unexpectedly large population boom brought considerable pressure on development land in the Midlands and Southeast, while the urban transport system failed to keep up with the growing number of private vehicles. In the 1960s modernization policies led government to assume a greater role in planning economic development and this spilled over into urban planning. New urban-regional strategies were proposed whereby economic growth and urban containment goals were to be pursued through a major programme of decentralized investment. Several large New Towns were planned so as to remove development pressure from in and around the major cities, while reducing the costs of production for manufacturing industries. Washington New Town in the Northeast is a prime example of this strategy: although it fulfilled some housing overspill requirements for Tyneside, it was primarily conceived of as an accessible and low-cost production site for the regional (and national) economy. Other New Towns designated in the early 1960s – such as Livingstone and Skelmersdale

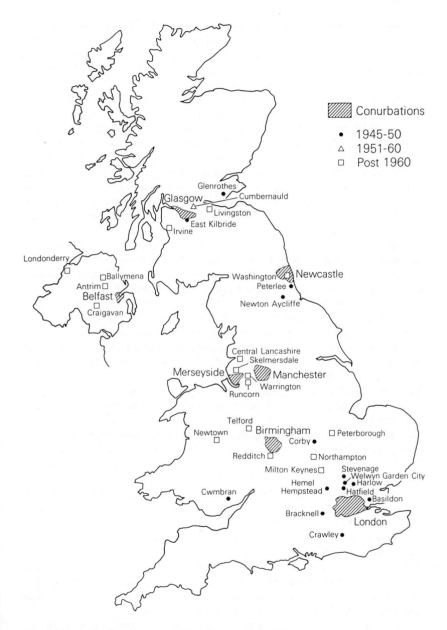

Figure 3.3 Conurbations and New Towns in the UK.

– were conceived in similar fashion (Figure 3.3). These new planning strategies did not necessarily involve New Towns and, for example, the Mathew Plan for the Belfast region suggested development of peripheral green-field industrial sites to facilitate accumulation by local and multinational capital (Byrne and Parson, 1983).

The early 1960s also saw moves towards positive urban transport policies in the face of growing circulation problems in the larger cities. A major catalyst was the 1963 Buchanan Report which assumed traffic growth in towns was unavoidable – which was true given the priority allocated to private vehicles. The Report argued it would only be possible both to protect the environment and to cater for the needs of private vehicles through large-scale remodelling of central cities including, where necessary, programmes of urban motorway construction. This became the new ethos of urban transport policy and many cities, such as Newcastle and Birmingham, undertook major urban road building schemes in the 1960s.

Labour governments in the late 1960s largely accepted the new direction of urban policy. Development pressures were greatest in the Southeast where there was a threat that growth could be 'choked-off' by rapid escalation of land and transportation costs. The South East Study in 1964 had already proposed planned dispersal from London to a series of major growth points at the outer edges of the region, in such places as Southampton, Bletchley, Northampton and Ipswich, and later regional studies made similar proposals (Hall, 1975). As a result of the economic crisis in the late 1960s and the downward revision of population predictions, none of these strategies was ever fully implemented. Three New Towns were designated in the Southeast at Northampton, Peterborough and Milton Keynes, and some New Towns such as Warrington and Irvine were designated in other regions (Figure 3.3). These were mostly (Milton Keynes is an exception) based on existing towns rather than being green-field sites, which lowered overall development costs – an increasingly important consideration for the State. In urban transport, Labour governments continued support for private vehicles and the urban road programme, convinced that opposing the car lobby would be electoral suicide (McKay and Cox, 1979). However, there were steps to improve integration of public transport, and metropolis-wide transport administrations were established in Birmingham, Manchester and Tyneside. A Labour government also set in motion the Redcliffe–Maud Commission on local government reform so as to bring administration into line with new spatial forms of social and economic organization. Finally, the 1967 Land Commission Act reintroduced the betterment levy which facilitated assembly of land banks as an instrument of positive planning; however, this was underfunded and had negligible practical importance.

Urban policy in this period provided only a loose framework for development, and much of the initiative was left to the private sector, sometimes in partnership with ambitious local authorities. This is illustrated by both retailing and office developments. In the immediate postwar years shopping centres were rebuilt in many war-damaged cities, and there were two main models for this: one incorporated car traffic, as in Plymouth, and the other was based on pedestrianized precincts, as in Coventry. However, the major period of shopping centre redevelopment was the 1960s and early 1970s, and 105 of the largest 155 cities in the UK acquired major (larger than 50,000 square feet) new shopping centres between 1965 and 1977. Property developers helped to promote these schemes as they stood to benefit from both land speculation and high rent yields in the new centres. However, they were also favoured by local authorities – Labour and Conservative – who saw them as one way to modernize their cities (see Ambrose and Colenutt, 1975, for the example of Brighton). Retailing redevelopment was also a means of maintaining the local authority's income from business rates so it is not surprising that councils in Newcastle (in Eldon Square) and Manchester (in the Arndale Centre) were prepared to cooperate with the developers. Furthermore, in Newcastle 'modernization' of the regional capital's central commercial facilities was regarded as a crucial precondition for attracting new manufacturing industry to the Northeast. Local authority planners have also generally supported retailing in central areas – thereby protecting investments in the new centres – by restricting out-of-town retailing in superstores and hypermarkets. Narrowly defined (as having over 25,000 square feet of selling space), there were still only four hypermarkets in the UK in 1980 (Dawson, 1982) – far less than in some other Western European countries – although this number has subsequently increased.

The demand for office space has been strong throughout the postwar period and, although there has been some decentralization, office employment has continued to grow in city centres. The major period of office construction was the late 1960s and early 1970s when demand was high and, more importantly, the profitability crisis in manufacturing led to financial institutions switching funds to office development. High rents and local authorities' zero rating of empty premises encouraged speculative investments in office premises for the profits from soaring property values surpassed the costs of borrowing capital, even if the development remained vacant – as in the infamous case of London's Centre Point – for several years. Many schemes were high rise and during these years the skylines of cities such as Newcastle and Bristol changed radically. Only in the late 1970s did the conservationist movement, aided by faltering growth in the market for office properties, halt the seemingly relentless colonization of city-centre skylines.

Urban policy in the 1970s has mainly been dominated by three issues: limited party political differences over the role of the State in development, a reassessment of urban transport policy and, most importantly, a shift from planned decentralization to support for inner-city areas. The party political consensus over the role of the State in development was not fundamentally challenged but the 1970–1974 Conservative government did shift even more initiative to the private sector: it withdrew from further New Town expansion, abolished the betterment levy, and opted for a faint-hearted reform of local government in 1972, which owed more to political expediency than to the needs of rational administration and planning. The 1974–1979 Labour government did little to reverse this balance with one exception, the potentially important 1975 Community Land Act. Under this Act local authorities acquired powers to purchase land at existing use value in order to accumulate land banks for future urban development; increases in land values resulting from planning permission for development were also to be taxable so as to secure the financial benefits for the community. This could have shifted much of the development initiative to the public sector but, in practice, Conservative local authorities refused to implement the Act, and the programme of land purchases was anyway grossly underfunded.

In urban transport there was a retreat from Buchananism and wholesale restructuring of the urban fabric. The years 1973–1974 were a turning point. Recently elected Labour majorities in the Greater London Council (GLC) and the new metropolitan counties began to abandon large-scale road building programmes, partly because of escalating costs but also as a result of pressure from the increasingly vociferous and well-organized anti-road traffic lobby. This lobby had been particularly effective in opposing the 1969 plan for Greater London, which had proposed extensive orbital motorways in and around the capital. The oil crisis in 1974 strengthened the lobby's case and, by the mid-1970s, the Labour government was considering greater support for urban public transport. Central Exchequer subsidies to municipalities were consolidated and extended in the new transport support grant in 1975 and there were also major investments to develop, extend and better integrate public transport systems in cities such as Glasgow, London, Liverpool and Newcastle. However, support for the private car through massive public expenditure on road repair and construction outside the major towns was not fundamentally challenged.

The 1970s also saw a major reversal in urban policies towards the larger cities. Decentralization was not completely abandoned but inner areas now came to the centre stage of politics. In 1974 the Labour government adjusted the needs element in the rate support grant so as to direct more resources to the metropolitan areas and, later, policies such as the inner-city Partnerships channelled more central resources to these zones. Ultimately, this would threaten the already limited autonomy of local authorities (see Chapter 3.7).

As part of the Labour government's economic strategy to cut public expenditure, local authority expenditure generally was squeezed in the late 1970s (see Table 1.4). As a result, local authorities had even less scope and resources for positive planning, so the incremental approach to development, which was reliant on private sector funds and initiative, continued to dominate. Since 1979, Conservative governments have further encouraged the private sector: local authorities have been instructed to release more development land, planning controls over small-scale changes to existing buildings have been relaxed, and the Community Land Act has been repealed. The government's strategy of reducing public expenditure has also led to even more restrictions on local authority autonomy and the vetoing of particular policies, such as the GLC's massive subsidization of public transport fares (see Chapter 3.7). Although the severity of these measures is unparalleled, they are a continuation of the strategy of the previous Labour administration, so that urban policy is still subject to broad political consensus.

As a result of the policies and processes discussed, a number of important changes have occurred in residential environments in the postwar UK. Land-use policies have had important implications, especially containment which has been 'extremely inegalitarian' (Pahl et al., 1983, p. 129). Labour's strategy in 1945 had been to link containment to planned decentralization, particularly to the New Towns. In many respects these have been a success: although criticized for not providing sufficient opportunities for the less skilled and suffering from some problems of social integration in the early years, most of the 32 New Towns (housing two million people) in the UK provide well-planned built environments. The towns are mostly spacious, have reasonable levels of service provision and, in comparison to older towns, are usually more self-contained in terms of providing work locally for residents. However, only a small part of urban decentralization has been accommodated in the New Towns. Most decentralization has been to modern housing estates – some public but mostly private – on the edges of existing villages, towns and cities. Short (1982) writes of the private estates that they

> ... vary in size of house and overall density, and this variation is reflected in the composition of the inhabitants. At one extreme the low-slung, low-density, well-built bungalows house those who have made it, while the smaller cheaper housing accommodates those who are still trying to make it. This post-war suburban housing is variegated enough to accommodate most of the variations in the middle-income range. (pp. 213–214)

Although physically differentiated, the suburbs have similar roles in the structure of the UK society and economy, offering tolerable living conditions compatible with a high consumption economy. Environment and lifestyle are inextricably linked for the suburbs favour familism and privatized, home-based consumption. The postwar expansion of the suburbs has been facilitated by relatively cheap land in rural areas (if not on urban fringes) and economies of scale in construction which favour development of large, new, peripheral estates rather than piecemeal redevelopment in inner-urban areas.

In addition, speculative residential development has been fuelled by the profits accruing from land development, little hampered by taxation and betterment levies. Such production conditions have been matched by buoyant demand, fuelled by the building societies, which have channelled finance to housing development while their lending policies have usually favoured purchases of new suburban dwellings. These economic conditions only weakened in the 1970s. Increased costs of capital, reductions in public expenditure, and periodic crises in the flow of funds to the building societies have together led to cutbacks in house building. There have also been reductions in the size and quality of new dwellings as the ratio of costs to real incomes has moved against the interest of purchasers, especially first-home buyers. Containment policies have contributed to this as they have usually led to a rise in land and hence house prices (Hall et al., 1973).

There has also been redevelopment of housing in inner areas. The pressure for this came not from property developers (as in the USA) but from local councils anxious to improve conditions in older urban areas. War-damaged residential areas required immediate remedies but there were also large areas of mostly early- and mid-Victorian houses lacking basic amenities or in a ruinous state of repair. Local authorities have used compulsory purchase powers to undertake large-scale schemes to demolish these 'slums' and replace them with council estates; this involved some 1.7 million dwellings between 1955 and 1973. Initially most local authority dwellings were single-family homes but, between about 1957 and 1969, there was a major shift to high-rise construction; by 1965 about 20 percent of all new public sector dwellings were in blocks of flats with more than ten storeys. In part this was due to pressure from the construction industry, keen to obtain a mass market for industrial systems building methods for high-rise towers. Given the constraints on urban land this was one way of reducing redevelopment costs. There was also pressure from within the planners' and architects' professions from protagonists of the modernist movement.

The ascendancy of high rise was, however, short lived and this had been almost totally rejected as a housing strategy by the 1980s. Public expenditure cuts led local authorities to seek cheaper housing 'solutions', so there was a shift to improving older dwellings instead of urban renewal (see Figure 1.8). Moreover, public opinion had turned sharply against high-rise housing which was seen as destroying communities, being associated with mental stress, and – after the Ronan Point disaster when a large towerblock was devastated by a gas explosion – unsafe. Many communities successfully opposed proposed clearance schemes for their areas (for example, see Dennis, 1970, on Sunderland), securing a commitment to improvement instead.

This shift in policy was facilitated by the Housing Acts of 1969 and 1974. The first of these introduced General Improvement Areas and made grants of up to 60 percent available for improvements in areas of essentially sound dwellings. As this omitted the worst housing areas, the 1974 Act introduced Housing Action Areas, in which grants were available for 75 percent or more of improvement costs and landlords could be compelled to undertake repairs. Many cities abandoned their programmes of high-rise development: in Glasgow six new high-rise dwellings were built for each new low-rise dwelling in the 1960s but, by the 1970s, large-scale redevelopment had been virtually forsaken (Pacione, 1979). Housing association activity has also been directed to the inner cities and, in the late 1970s, some 40 percent of housing association tenants lived in areas designated under the Inner Urban Areas Act.

The overall changes in housing tenure have already been outlined in Chapter 1.4.1. Compared to the national average, the major cities have higher proportions of local authority dwellings and proportionately less owner-occupation. The major exceptions are London, with a very high proportion of private renting, and cities in Scotland, the North and Midlands, which have well above-average numbers of council houses as a result of large-scale municipal rehousing programmes. There are also major differences between inner and outer areas (Table 3.4). Owner-occupation is consistently higher in the outer areas, as a result of suburbanization of higher-income groups, except in Sunderland with its dominant peripheral public housing estates (see Robson, 1969). Private renting is highly polarized, being concentrated in (older) inner areas, while the distribution of public housing varies between cities according to whether municipal policies have favoured inner-area renewal or suburban estates.

The private rented sector has become the most spatially polarized tenure, being massively concentrated in inner areas: with virtually no new dwellings being built for private renting, this tenure is rarely represented in suburban areas. Even in the older inner-urban areas, large numbers of privately rented dwellings have been sold by landlords so as to realize capital gains in a buoyant property market, particularly when faced by real or expected rent controls. This has been most widespread in areas of single-family dwellings – whether terraced or detached – and, until recently, rented flats in medium- and high-rise buildings have had limited sales potential. However, there is now – especially in inner London – a 'flat break-up market' (Hamnett and Randolph, 1984). Financial institutions have become more willing to advance mortgages on flats. In addition, many property-renting companies have chosen to disinvest from housing and channel funds into commercial property, especially at times of rapid office development. Private renting has become the residual housing category: there are small submarkets of expensive, superior-quality rented dwellings for the young or the very mobile middle classes, especially in London, but most private rented property is in large, poor-quality older houses.

In contrast, there has been a steady programme of council house building until at least 1979. The stock of council houses is, however, spatially,

Table 3.4   Socioeconomic characteristics of inner- and outer-urban areas in England and Wales, 1981

		% population change, 1971–1981	% of persons in households with a New Commonwealth or Pakistan born head	% male unemployment	% of households			
					Owner-occupied	Public rented	Private rented	With car available
Cities in metropolitan counties								
Birmingham	Inner	−17.6	36.6	25.4	44.0	34.6	21.4	38.3
	Outer	−4.5	6.1	16.6	52.9	37.8	9.4	52.2
Liverpool	Inner	−26.6	3.0	31.0	31.3	39.1	29.6	25.3
	Outer	−9.5	0.9	21.0	45.7	39.9	14.4	45.3
Sheffield	Inner	−19.5	6.8	19.0	33.7	49.6	16.7	37.0
	Outer	−1.5	1.9	12.6	47.0	45.1	7.9	51.2
Manchester	Inner	−24.5	18.3	28.3	26.3	54.4	19.3	29.9
	Outer	−13.7	3.0	17.6	40.1	44.0	15.9	43.8
Leeds	Inner	−14.6	15.2	22.2	39.8	37.2	23.0	34.9
	Outer	−7.4	2.4	13.3	48.4	42.6	9.0	49.3
Coventry	Inner	−11.1	15.8	19.8	66.2	19.2	14.6	51.8
	Outer	−3.2	4.7	17.3	66.3	25.7	8.0	61.7
Bradford	Inner	−12.7	34.8	23.9	55.8	25.8	18.4	31.9
	Outer	0.2	7.2	14.7	65.6	25.0	9.4	50.4
Wolverhampton	Inner	−8.4	34.6	24.3	40.7	43.4	15.9	44.8
	Outer	−4.2	8.0	17.4	46.2	48.5	5.3	59.0
Sunderland	Inner	−15.1	1.3	19.9	58.9	26.4	14.7	44.6
	Outer	−6.4	0.3	24.3	27.5	66.8	5.7	40.8
Newcastle-upon-Tyne	Inner	−18.0	7.1	21.7	30.5	38.9	30.5	32.4
	Outer	−11.0	1.3	20.7	35.9	52.1	12.0	36.9

		% population change, 1971–1981	% of persons in households with a New Commonwealth or Pakistan born head	% male unemployment	% of households			
					Owner-occupied	Public rented	Private rented	With car available
Other cities in the North and Midlands								
Leicester	Inner	−12.2	41.2	20.8	57.1	19.4	23.5	39.6
	Outer	6.0	10.3	13.6	46.0	44.9	9.0	53.1
Nottingham	Inner	−28.7	16.3	21.5	35.2	42.0	22.8	35.0
	Outer	4.7	3.7	13.7	38.7	54.0	7.3	49.7
Kingston-upon-Hull	Inner	−31.6	1.7	23.5	46.5	23.4	30.1	33.8
	Outer	7.6	0.5	18.3	35.2	55.2	9.7	45.6
Stoke on Trent	Inner	−7.9	3.1	14.0	61.6	26.1	12.3	48.7
	Outer	−3.1	1.5	14.1	53.6	39.2	7.2	54.7
Derby	Inner	−21.8	17.6	17.4	51.8	26.1	22.1	39.4
	Outer	9.0	5.1	8.5	61.2	31.8	6.9	62.4
Other cities in the South and West								
Bristol	Inner	−12.4	8.0	14.9	55.2	18.2	26.5	52.3
	Outer	−6.3	2.1	11.7	54.0	38.9	7.1	63.3
Cardiff	Inner	−17.1	7.5	20.9	60.9	12.4	26.7	42.8
	Outer	1.4	1.8	14.0	60.8	30.6	8.6	62.6
Plymouth	Inner	−11.8	1.9	14.2	52.9	16.3	30.8	48.9
	Outer	10.2	1.1	9.8	55.5	32.1	12.4	63.2
Southampton	Inner	−11.1	8.0	13.1	56.8	17.6	25.6	53.4
	Outer	0.9	2.1	10.7	52.6	37.9	9.5	60.9
Inner London		−17.6	18.8	14.4	27.3	42.8	29.9	41.3
Outer London		−5.0	11.7	8.0	61.9	23.2	15.0	64.0
Great Britain (average)		0.6	4.1	11.6	55.8	31.2	13.2	60.5

Source: Redfern (1982).

morphologically and socially differentiated, there being at least three types: estates of single-family dwellings, mainly in peripheral locations; high-rise tower blocks built in the 1960s and early 1970s, especially in inner areas; and areas of older housing acquired for improvement purposes or for slum clearance programmes that were subsequently abandoned.

At one extreme, local authority dwellings are among the better-quality small- to medium-sized housing built in the postwar period, especially in the case of general needs dwellings built immediately after 1945. However, at the other extreme, a Department of the Environment survey in 1974 revealed that about one-third of all housing authorities had at least one 'difficult-to-let' estate built since 1945 which, in aggregate, represented over 60,000 dwellings: these were mostly high-rise flats. Some estates have gained national notoriety, such as the one consisting of 2000 maisonettes built in the Everton district of Liverpool in the mid-1960s. Popularly known as 'the piggeries', they were effectively given to a private developer in the late 1970s as this was considered more cost effective than either demolition or improvement. Although an extreme but not unique example, there is a general category of estates which Taylor (1979) tellingly labels 'difficult-to-let, difficult-to-live-in, and difficult-to-get-out-of'. In part the problems of these estates stem from the poor quality of construction, especially in the case of high-rise blocks built in the 1960s. Moreover, low-rise estates can also be difficult to let, and the reason for this lies in local authority housing management practices. Most housing departments operate allocation and transfer policies whereby both tenants and dwellings are graded and matched: the highest ranked tenants usually get the better-quality houses, and the 'problem' families are 'dumped' in the worst-quality 'sink' estates (see Gray, 1976). The social implications of these policies are grave: allocation of dwellings becomes synonymous with allocation of status or stigma, access to jobs and services and, generally, with lifestyles and lifechances.

Council house sales have intensified since the 1980 Housing Act, making the social implications of such housing management policies even more acute. It is the better-quality and better-located dwellings that are being sold (rarely any high-rise flats), mainly to better-off tenants. Forrest and Williams (1984) write that '... we are moving towards a situation where state housing will become stigmatised welfare housing associated with the unemployed, the low paid, blacks, and other minority groups' (p. 1173).

Finally, since the mid-1950s there has been sustained expansion of owner-occupation, especially of suburban estates. Land costs and economies of scale in construction have made development of owner-occupied housing in inner areas relatively unprofitable. Instead, owner-occupied housing in these areas has mainly involved older dwellings being purchased from private landlords. Social access to owner-occupation is conditioned by class and income (see Chapter 1.4.1): for example, in 1983 only 25 percent of those with a gross weekly household income of less than £100 were owner-occupiers, compared to 88 percent of households with a weekly income over £300 (Central Statistical Office, 1985). Building societies have had an important role in expanding selective social access to mortgage finance (see Chapter 1.4.1), for their lending policies favour non-manual workers with relatively high and stable incomes. They have also been spatially selective, generally preferring new, suburban dwellings while being shy of investing in older, terraced, inner-area houses. Whereas building societies provide some three-quarters of finance for mortgages nationally, in inner areas such as Saltley, Sparkhill and Soho they provide less than 10 percent. In extreme form, this has been formalized as a policy of 'red-lining' inner areas so as to embargo all mortgage loans within these zones. Building societies consider that these areas offer poor securities on their loans and they prefer to invest in the suburbs, sometimes making block allocations of mortgages to particular new estates (Williams, 1978). This may thwart the aims of housing improvement programmes in the inner cities while, instead, actively promoting new consumption patterns in the suburbs.

Social access to particular housing tenures is selective and this has implications in terms of individuals' access to good-quality housing as well as to particular urban locations. Owner-occupation clearly offers many advantages, including a rapidly appreciating capital asset, better housing standards usually and access to sought-after, suburban locations for household consumption. Access to housing tenures is not only socially selective within each generation: Madge and Brown (1981), for example, have shown that 82 percent of young couples with both sets of parents in owner-occupation are in the same tenure, while 45 percent of those with both sets of parents living in local authority dwellings are themselves in council houses. 'Tenure classes' may not yet be hereditary, but housing is one means by which occupational inequalities are generalized into the wider social structure. The first generation who shared in the postwar expansion of owner-occupation is now aging so that an increasing number of young couples are likely to benefit financially from inheriting their parents' homes. As many are already home-owners, such inherited wealth can be used to improve housing conditions or to enhance other forms of household consumption. Therefore, there is likely to be an ever-widening gap between those whose parents are and are not owner-occupiers. However, the benefits of this tenure are not universal; in some economically depressed areas, houses are difficult to sell and prices stagnate.

Changes in housing and housing policy have had important implications for the inner areas but, even at this scale, these are not socially and spatially homogeneous. Short and Bassett (1981) identified three main types of housing neighbourhood in inner Bristol. At one extreme, a small number of Housing Action Areas include some of the very worst-quality owner-occupied and rented dwellings. The availability of improvement grants and local authority mortgages has led to significant improvements in housing conditions in these showpiece areas. At the other extreme, some neighbourhoods have been gentrified and their new middle-class residents have been able to secure building society loans. Finally, there are many intermediate areas between these two extremes and there is a gradient within these from 'fairly bad' to 'fairly good'. Conditions are worse in the 'fairly bad' zones where there are large stocks of poor-quality, private rented dwellings. Local authority mortgages are difficult to obtain while improvements grants have been concentrated in the Housing Action Areas. There is a housing 'trap' in these areas, embracing those with low incomes and/or living in private rented dwellings: they are frequently denied both residential mobility and the means of improving housing conditions *in situ*.

3.4   Population and social changes in urban areas

3.4.1   *The decentralization of people*

The out-migration of population has both followed and led decentralization of jobs and investments in the urban fabric. Between 1971 and 1981 all the largest cities lost population, but especially London, the metropolitan counties and Glasgow; the latter lost more than one-fifth of its total population in just ten years. However, population losses were widespread, being recorded in most cities. In contrast, there were population gains in most of the remainder of the country, especially in the New Towns, rural districts and smaller towns (see Chapter 4.4). These demographic shifts are continuations of earlier population trends and, for example, London's population has declined from a peak of 8.2 million in 1951 to just 6.7 million in 1981.

There has been population decentralization both in the metropolitan regions and within particular cities (Table 3.5). Losses were recorded in the cores of the largest 'million' cities as early as the 1950s but these intensified in the 1960s when the absolute losses in the centres of the largest cities outnumbered the gains in the rings and outer rings. Elsewhere in urban Britain, there were still population gains in the cores but there was also relative decentralization. Analysis by the Centre for Urban and Regional Development Studies (1984b), although using a different spatial framework, shows that these trends intensified in the 1970s. In the dominant cities of urban Britain population losses amounted to almost 10 percent of 1971 totals. Although there were gains in the outer zones, these were massively outnumbered by losses in the cores. In contrast, free-standing cities experienced only relative decentralization, with small percentage gains in the cores and large absolute and percentage gains in the outer zones. There was

Table 3.5 Population changes in metropolitan areas in Great Britain, 1951–1981

	1951–1961		1961–1971	
	Absolute (000s)	Percentage	Absolute (000s)	Percentage
'Million' cities MELAs				
Cores	−363	−3.7	−1199	−9.0
Rings	+783	+10.2	+828	+13.1
Outer rings	+101	+7.2	+220	+14.7
Rest of Britain MELAs				
Cores	+863	+6.9	+480	+3.5
Rings	+925	+16.4	+1675	+21.0
Outer rings	+144	+2.2	+568	+8.6

MELA = Metropolitan Economic Labour Area.

Source: Spence et al. (1982).

	1971–1981	
	Absolute (000s)	Percentage
Dominant LLMAs		
Cores	−1693	−9.7
Rings	+314	+8.9
Outer rings	+27	+8.5
Rural	+15	+6.2
Free-standing LLMAs		
Cores	+116	+1.2
Rings	+575	+10.6
Outer rings	+220	+10.2
Rural	+207	+9.4

LLMA = Local Labour Market Area.

Source: Centre for Urban and Regional Development Studies (1984b)

also decentralization within cities (Table 3.5) and inner-area losses exceeded 10 percent in most larger cities, and 20 percent in Liverpool and Manchester. The overall pattern then is of population being decanted from the centres of British cities: by the 1980s this had led to large absolute losses in the inner areas of most cities and to overall population losses in the largest cities.

3.4.2   Social polarization

Natural increase has played some part in these demographic changes but net migration differences mainly account for the decentralization of population. Net out-migration has partly been brought about by planned decentralization to new and expanded towns, but is mainly the outcome of housing market changes. Owner-occupiers and local authority tenants either preferred or were constrained to obtain dwellings in the suburbs or in surrounding towns and villages. Out-migration has been socially selective, being dependent on unequal social access to housing as well as on lifecycle changes, for suburbanization is associated with new household formation and familism.

In-migration has also been socially selective, and has involved three main groups. First, many young, single people prefer the lifestyles associated with inner-city residence, for social activities outside the household may be valued all ages may be constrained by both the job market (availability of unskilled service employment) and the housing market (availability of private rented dwellings) to live in inner areas. Finally, inner areas – especially in the larger cities – have traditionally been the locus of immigration.

The outcome of these differentiated migration flows has been social polarization. This has occurred at the metropolitan scale between the cores and rings of Metropolitan Economic Labour Areas (Spence et al., 1982), but is more pronounced within individual cities. As an example, consider London: the 1981 Census shows that unemployment rates were 80 percent higher, car-ownership rates were 55 percent lower and proportions of single-parent families were 95 percent higher in inner than in outer areas. It is the socially disadvantaged and semi- and unskilled manual workers who are most likely to be spatially polarized and be trapped in inner-urban areas. Selective access to housing submarkets is the key to such spatial segregation (see Table 1.6). In the 1960s and 1970s owner-occupation was extended to skilled manual workers and, as a result, local authority housing has increasingly become the preserve of semi- and unskilled manual workers and the unemployed: these accounted for only 40 percent of all local authority tenants in 1961, but this proportion had risen to 56 percent by 1981 (Hamnett, 1984). Given the spatial redistribution of housing tenures in the same period (see Chapter 3.3.3), social polarization is likely to follow.

Belfast provides the most notorious example of social polarization. The root of this segregation is socioeconomic but there are also cleavages within the working class in Belfast along religious lines. The segregation of the two communities is longstanding, but tends to increase at times of 'troubles', such as at the present time. With the flare-up of violence in the years 1969–1972, the percentage of the population living in streets where more than 90 percent of the residents were either Catholics or Protestants, increased from 67 to 77 percent and, in all, some 6000 families moved from 'frontier' zones or from areas where they were minority groups (Boal, 1982). Belfast is a unique and extreme case of polarization in the UK but social class, ethnic and racial polarization is widespread.

3.4.3 Immigration and racial polarization

There have been several phases of immigration in the postwar period in response to the demand for labour in the British economy, with immigrants moving into the major urban areas. Traditional Irish immigration continued throughout the 1950s but was supplemented from other sources. In the period 1946–1951 some 460,000 European immigrants, including refugees and 'European Voluntary Workers', came in response to immediate labour shortages. In the 1950s, there was immigration from the New Commonwealth, especially the West Indies, India and Pakistan (Castles et al., 1984).

With the economic downturn in the late 1950s, racial conflict surfaced in UK cities, climaxing in notorious 'riots' in Notting Hill and Nottingham. These were focused on economic issues – 'taking our jobs' – as well as on social ones – 'taking our houses, filling our schools and living off the dole'. Some politicians made campaign issues of these events, notably Conservative MP Hornsby-Smith who remarked that '... they come in by air and, at once, begin to draw National Assistance'. Racism weakened working-class unity and it was initially opposed by the Labour Party which, for example, voted against the immigration restrictions proposed in the 1962 Commonwealth Immigration Act. However, in 1964 Labour lost the safe Smethwick seat in a by-election to the Conservative Peter Griffith, who campaigned strongly on immigration issues. The following year, faced with growing popular opposition to immigration (at a time when unemployment was also rising), the Labour Party itself took steps to further reduce immigration. This established a broad political consensus on immigration, which included the introduction of further restrictions on immigrants under the 1968 and 1971 Immigration Acts; respectively, these introduced patriality conditions on immigration and reduced the right of entry of dependents. The 1981 Nationality Act, which deprived the UK-born children of immigrants of the rights of automatic citizenship, has weakened this consensus, being opposed by the Labour Party. Immigrants – essentially coloured ones – in the 1960s and 1970s have been a focus of the attentions of extreme right-wing groups such as the National Front and the National Party. Not least, this is because black people in the UK have made the transition from immigrant community to settled population at the same time as the postwar economic boom came to an end. The rising tide of violence and discrimination against them is well documented in the national press, and there are an estimated 7000 racially motivated attacks each year in the UK (Doherty, 1983).

Since 1945 immigrants have become an important element in the population of many cities but their distribution is, however, spatially very uneven. There is a regional element with New Commonwealth immigrants being more important in London, Yorkshire and the Midlands and, in absolute terms, about one-half of all New Commonwealth immigrants are resident in just two cities – London and Birmingham. There is also a strong tendency for immigrants to be concentrated in inner-urban areas, especially in Birmingham, Bradford and Wolverhampton where they form more than one-third of the local population (see Table 3.4).

The extent of immigrants' segregation in London has been measured by Lee (1977): West Indians were far more segregated from native whites than were the Irish. This is rather a crude level of analysis and most segregation occurs at the level of immigrants from particular West Indian islands. There is also evidence of segregation of different religious groups from India, Pakistan and Bangladesh. Levels of segregation are not static and West Indian segregation in, for example, London, Birmingham, Cardiff, Oxford and Nottingham, decreased during the 1960s, while that of Asian immigrants increased (Peach and Shah, 1980). While segregation decreased, the levels of concentration (as a percentage of local population) of immigrants in some areas increased, if only because of the impact of continuing (chain-migration) immigration in the 1960s. It is not yet clear whether these trends continued into the 1970s, not least because of the lack of adequate information in the 1981 Census.

The segregation of black immigrants stems from several considerations but its root lies primarily in their occupational role as 'replacement' labour. Immigrants provided a cheap and flexible source of labour in the 1950s and 1960s but they were employed primarily in the service industries, public transport and 'dirty' manufacturing jobs, especially textiles and some branches of chemicals and metal goods production (Doherty, 1983). Vacancies for these types of jobs were often found in the older inner areas of the larger cities, especially as the out-migration of the UK-born population created localized labour shortages. Their contemporary occupational role is little changed: only 16 percent of whites compared to 35 percent of West Indians and 40 percent of Asians have semi- or unskilled manual jobs (C. Brown, 1984). Women workers were similarly differentiated and 21 percent of Asian women (compared to 4 percent of whites) were employed in textiles. As these are precisely the types of jobs which declined rapidly in the 1970s, by 1982 the unemployment rate among blacks was about double that for whites; for males it was 13 percent for whites, 25 percent for West Indians and 20 percent for Asians.

Segregation of the black population could be anticipated simply on the basis of their jobs, high unemployment levels and relatively low incomes. But Lee (1977) estimated that, statistically, only about 50 percent of the segregation of

West Indians could be apportioned to their socioeconomic characteristics. Other factors also need to be taken into account, especially the workings of the housing market. Until the early 1970s, at least, immigrant groups were disproportionately concentrated in the private rented sector. Poor access to home ownership stems partly from building societies' reluctance to lend to those with low incomes and manual jobs and partly from discrimination by estate agents (Lee, 1977).

Black people have also been excluded from local authority dwellings because, until recently, many housing departments operated residential qualifications that tended to exclude (newly arrived) immigrants. Furthermore, it has been argued that, given the desire (of some immigrants) to return eventually to their countries of origin, they may prefer to maximize their savings and hence choose not to pay the higher costs of better-quality accommodation. However, the idea of return is a myth that has certainly not been a reality since immigration laws made re-entry more difficult. In summary, many immigrants have only been able to obtain access to private rented accommodation, a tenure which is highly concentrated in inner areas. There is discrimination even within this tenure and they have often had to rely on immigrant landlords for accommodation (Rex, 1973), which further contributes to segregation. Finally, it must be acknowledged that segregation is partly a product of immigrants' 'preferences': concentration offers local community support in the face of a hostile majority community, helps to preserve cultural identity and provides access to ethnic shops, restaurants and social facilities.

Why then has the segregation of immigrants actually decreased in the 1960s and 1970s? The changes can hardly be ascribed to improved employment prospects: net mobility between manual and non-manual occupations was only 3 percent for blacks between 1974 and 1982 (C. Brown, 1984) and this was more than cancelled out by rising unemployment. Instead, the reasons for desegregation lie in the housing market. Between 1961 and 1971, the proportion of West Indians in private rented accommodation fell from 74 to 40 percent as this sector declined nationally (Peach and Shah, 1980). As a result, West Indians were 'squeezed' into local authority and owner-occupied dwellings, which necessarily reduced spatial clustering.

Asians have also been able to gain better access to local authority housing. In Blackburn, between 1968 and 1972, no more than one Asian household in any one year was allocated a council tenancy but, by 1978, this had reached 56 (Robinson, 1980). In part this was due to the arrival of better-educated Ugandan Asians who were better able to understand the housing system, but there was also a general easing of access conditions for all black immigrants. However, this makes only a limited contribution to desegregation for, wherever possible, rehoused immigrants preferred a tenancy in an inner-area estate so as to remain near the centres of the Asian community.

3.5   Urban services and collective consumption

3.5.1   *Access to services*

Assembly of a suitable labour force in particular locations requires provision of housing and a range of services. While market forces can supply some of these, especially retailing and many personal and professional services, historically they have failed to provide certain key services – including health and education – that are essential for maintaining a skilled and healthy labour force. The need for collective service provision has increased with the growing participation of married women in the paid labour force (see Table 1.2), who have roles to perform as workers, mothers and housewives. MacKenzie and Rose (1983) write that:

> To perform and reconcile all these roles, women need access to a wide variety of resources: flexible child care, shops and services with late opening hours, schools which provide lunch-time meals and supervision after school and vacation care for school-age children, and networks which care for elderly and disabled household members and provide help in emergencies. Women with all these roles also need flexible and frequent public transport, and flexible working hours in both the domestic sphere and wage workplace. (pp. 183–184)

It is not only women who require access to such essential collective services – so do the elderly, the unemployed, male single parents and many other social groups. However, there are marked variations between local authorities in terms of provision of collective urban services (Pinch, 1979); this depends on local political control, traditional patterns of expenditure and methods of central resource allocation.

Access to services also depends on personal circumstances including income, mobility and residential location. Income may be the most important consideration for it allows recourse to the private sector as an alternative to public provision; for example, about 6 percent of schoolchildren are educated privately. Mobility is also important and, although public transport has been maintained relatively well in urban areas (especially compared to rural areas), access to a car or cars can be critical. Ownership of one car will usually provide greater ease of journey to work for the household head and better access to shopping and recreation at weekends for all the family. Ownership of two or more cars offers weekday advantages for working mothers, allowing them to drop and collect children at schools or child-minders, and for non-working mothers to engage in a much wider range of social activities. Access to a car depends on income, age and gender but also varies locationally, with car-access rates being lower in inner- than in outer-urban areas. In inner Birmingham, Liverpool, Manchester and London, car-ownership rates range between 25 and 41 percent, while those in their outer areas range between 44 and 64 percent (see Table 3.4). In the past, 'inner city dwellers were compensated for their relative lack of car-ownership by the density of public transport and the relatively short distances they needed to ride on it in order to reach jobs, shops, schools, doctors and a host of other services' (P. Hall, 1980, p. 169). Now there is growing suburbanization of services and the start of out-of-town retailing, but public transport remains city-centre orientated, thus leading to further disadvantages for inner-city, car-less residents.

The remainder of this section considers two particularly important urban public services – health care and education.

3.5.2 Education and health services in urban areas

There is a strong relationship between social class and quality of education (see Chapter 1.4.3) but there are also important intra- and interurban variations in educational provision for all age groups (Table 3.6). Educational provision for the under-fives, arguably a key to early achievement as well as an important aid to working mothers, is especially variable. Most urban areas (Strathclyde being the exception) have well above-average provision in terms of both nursery facilities and numbers of under-fives in schools, with Tyne and Wear, London and Merseyside scoring particularly well. At the next two stages of education – primary and secondary schools – there are more statutory requirements and, therefore, relatively little deviation from national means in pupil–teacher ratios. However, there is considerable variation in pupils' achievements although, generally, children living in urban areas perform less well than the national average. Strathclyde and Belfast have remarkably polarized patterns: well above-average proportions with no graded exam results but also well above-average with one or more 'A' Level.

The polarization of achievement rates is suggestive of deep divisions in local school structures but can also be understood in terms of varied social and environmental conditions within cities (Herbert, 1976). This link was asserted in the influential 1967 Plowden Report, which considered that children living in deprived areas were doubly handicapped by virtue of a poor learning environment at both home and school. The Plowden and the Halsey Reports emphasized that children living in such areas suffered from a number of disadvantages: poor communications between school and local community, schooling appearing to parents to be irrelevant to the needs of the child, high staff turnover, rapid population shifts leading to high turnover of pupils and disruptive classroom behaviour, and a poor learning context at home. The difficulties were further exaggerated in some deprived areas – especially inner areas – by the use of old school buildings, often in disrepair and poorly suited to modern educational needs. The 'neighbourhood' effect was clearly illustrated in Robson's (1969) study of parental attitudes to education in Sunderland: differences between areas were greater than between classes.

Table 3.6   Education in the major urban areas of the United Kingdom, 1982

	Day nursery places (per 1000 population under-five)	Children under five in education (%)	Pupil/teacher ratio		% of school-leavers		
			Primary school	Secondary school	With no graded results	With five or more 'O' Levels (no 'A' Levels)	With one or more 'A' Level
Tyne and Wear	19.5	69	20.4	15.6	12.1	9.1	12.0
South Yorkshire	5.6	63	21.7	16.6	11.3	8.1	10.8
West Yorkshire	17.0	51	22.5	17.9	14.3	9.1	14.8
Greater London	42.6	50	20.1	15.1	16.0	8.2	14.2
West Midlands	22.6	58	22.5	16.3	13.2	8.9	12.3
Greater Manchester	27.2	56	22.9	15.9	13.0	10.1	11.3
Merseyside	29.0	59	22.2	16.4	14.2	7.8	14.4
Strathclyde	13.0	35	21.6	15.0	31.1	6.7	29.1
Belfast	–	–	21.4	15.0	26.7	8.6	26.2
England	17.7	40	22.5	16.6	11.2	9.9	14.1

Source: Central Statistical Office (1984).

In response to these difficulties, the Plowden Report recommended the designation of Educational Priority Areas (EPAs) in which there would be additional funds for improving school buildings and special allowances for teachers in 'especially difficult' schools. Some 150 schools came to be covered by such designations, mostly in inner-urban areas. Individual schools and their pupils did benefit from the EPA programme but only limited resources were available, equivalent to about 1 percent of the total educational budget. Even this was reduced in real terms following public expenditure cuts from the late 1970s. Another limitation was that EPAs included only a small proportion of all disadvantaged schoolchildren: for example, EPAs in inner London had 13 percent of all the area's schoolchildren but only 20 percent of the disadvantaged. Educational handicaps are too widely distributed in urban society for the piecemeal approach of EPAs to be effective. As Jessel (1978) states, education deprivation embraces '... a wide variety of multiply-deprived districts: not just in city centres, but in economically declining urban areas, in redevelopment housing estates and in some rural areas' (p. 56).

There are also spatial variations in levels of personal health within cities (Giggs, 1979), stemming from both physical and social conditions. Physical living conditions tend to be worse in the inner areas and, for example, a study by Wood et al. (1974) of pollution in Greater Manchester found that levels were consistently highest in the centre, around Salford, and lowest in the suburbs in the Pennines and Cheshire. The health implications are clear given that there is an association between some forms of air pollution and the incidence of respiratory diseases. Socially related illnesses have a less distinctive spatial distribution and, for example, there are relatively high incidences of mental disorders in both inner areas and modern housing estates. These are related to income, occupation, age, family circumstances and a host of other considerations that do not accord with any simple environmental association.

There has been a broad consensus regarding health care delivery and, in particular, the role of the National Health Service (see Chapter 1.4.3). In terms of primary health care – the GP level – the major reorganization has been concentration into group practices and health centres at the expense of individual practices. A more comprehensive service is available within each practice, but there has also been a spatial concentration of surgeries which means that physical accessibility has deteriorated for some households, especially those lacking private transport, in both inner areas and peripheral estates.

In a study of urban West Glamorgan Phillips (1981) showed that, generally, there was no clear evidence that the rate of utilization of health services varied between social classes or between car and non-car owners (although needs may have varied). However, working-class households were generally less able to utilize the health services effectively: they were less confident in consultations and seemed to get less satisfaction from these than did middle-class families. They were also less effective in obtaining more than the most basic health services and rarely made use of preventive health care. The actual spatial pattern of surgery attendance was not directly related to social class but households with cars were more likely to attend surgeries other than those nearest their home. This is partly due to continuing attendance at surgeries near to a previous family residence but it also indicates the greater choice available to car owners. Inner-area working-class residents are often especially disadvantaged. In inner London, although GPs' lists were relatively small, health care provision suffered from the prevalence of older, poorly equipped premises and from the large proportion of doctors' time spent in private practice (Eyles and Woods, 1983). This was especially serious given the large numbers of local residents with special needs including the elderly, immigrants and transients, and the generally lower life expectancies in inner areas (Townsend and Davidson, 1982).

There has also been spatial concentration of secondary health care facilities, and the 1962 Hospital Plan was influential in this (see Chapter 1.4.3). Mohan (1984a) has shown how reorganization has affected different urban areas within the Northeast. Investment in the region has been concentrated in Teesside because this had been identified as a future industrial growth point, and government policy stressed spatially uneven allocation of public sector investment as a precondition for modernization. These and similar reorganization plans elsewhere in the UK have usually not been fully implemented because, in the 1970s, protests over local hospital closures coincided with cutbacks in public spending, especially on capital expenditure. Elsewhere in the Northeast, development of the Freeman Road Hospital on the periphery of Newcastle was linked to closures of smaller and specialized hospitals within the city. The general result of such changes in Newcastle and in other UK cities has been to alter accessibility to health care mainly in favour of car-owning households and against the interests of inner-area residents.

3.6   Urban deprivation and policy

3.6.1   *Economic change, poverty and deprivation*

Poverty and deprivation in UK cities are not new, having been chronicled by 19th-century social observers such as Booth and Rowntree. But in the 1960s and 1970s they were linked to the persistent long-term decline of industrial production in the larger cities. Jobs lost through restructuring in manufacturing have not been replaced – either quantitatively or qualitatively – by service sector expansion. There have been net job losses and rapid increases in unemployment: in 1981 the Inner City Partnership Areas (see Chapter 3.6.2) in Tyneside, London, Birmingham, Merseyside and Manchester had unemployment rates of between 15.5 and 26.0 percent while the UK average was only about 12 percent (Hamnett, 1983). There has also been general replacement of skilled manual jobs by unskilled manufacturing and service jobs, and by expansion of well-paid but selective-entry office jobs. As a result, manual workers' average wages have fallen, while unemployment has been socially selective, falling most heavily on the young, the elderly, males and blacks (see Davies, 1981). In some areas, decline in the formal economy has been partly ameliorated by expansion of the informal economy. In the Isle of Sheppey household budgets are supplemented by resorting to do-it-yourself home improvements, cultivation of allotments and reliance on informal social networks either for mutual assistance or to help discover casual employment (Pahl et al., 1983).

Dispersal of population to the suburbs has also been socially selective, even though many working-class families have been decanted to peripheral local authority housing estates. For those unable to buy their homes, the housing market can be a 'trap': on the one hand most private renting is in inner-urban areas and, on the other hand, the residential mobility of local authority tenants seeking transfers within that tenure is limited. Despite the introduction of small-scale national transfer schemes for council tenants, most of this group are 'trapped' in the sense that they can only move to a small number of local council housing estates.

Inner areas can be characterized as suffering from collective deprivation which Davies (1981) sees as:

> ... the gap between the quality and quantity of opportunities provided by the inner-city environment, and the needs of people sharing the environment. It is not a matter of multiple deprivation – of many people having many problems separately. It is rather an accumulated form of deprivation experienced by those living in inner-city areas, psychic as well as material. Collective deprivation starts with inner-city residents' perception of their environment. The image is one of deterioration – of neglect, decay and dereliction, and of narrow choices in many fields: education, shopping, leisure, jobs and housing. In some instances, the deterioration is real, compared with a generation ago. In others, it is a widening gap between residents' aspirations, their awareness of conditions elsewhere, and the conditions they see around them. (p. 4)

'Conditions elsewhere' refers to the inability of inner-area residents to share in the materialistic and individualistic consumption patterns that are so visible in outer areas. However, 'the conditions they see around them' are real enough. Sim (1984) looked at several different indicators of deprivation for parliamentary constituencies (a scale that differentiates inner and outer areas) and found three major features. First, deprivation assumes different forms in different cities. High rankings on separate indices do sometimes overlap, notably in some London constituencies such as Brent, Hackney and

Hammersmith (Figure 3.4). However, most areas tend to suffer particularly acutely from one type of problem, examples being unemployment in Merseyside and overcrowding in many Scottish cities.

Second, some cities are particularly badly affected, especially Glasgow and London and, to a lesser extent, Merseyside and Birmingham; several of their sub-areas feature in these lists. Belfast was not included in the analysis but it is one of the most deprived cities in Europe. Overall, however, with minor exceptions, it is the largest cities which disproportionately contain most of the more deprived areas in Britain. More specifically, and this is the third feature, inner cities appear to be worse affected (see also Table 3.4). However, the rankings also include some outer conurbation areas, usually those dominated by large, local authority estates. These include Knowsley North in Merseyside, with very high unemployment, some of the Glasgow constituencies with high rates of overcrowding, as well as some outer GLC zones such as Norwood and Ealing. This underlines an important point: there is nothing unique or timeless about the problems of the inner areas. Concentrations of deprivation are the outcome of broader social and economic changes and there is evidence now that a similar combination of economic and social conditions is leading to new spatial concentrations of the unemployed, the poor and the badly housed in peripheral metropolitan areas such as Speke on Merseyside or Killingworth on Tyneside. Such spatial shifts do not occur 'naturally': they are the outcome of investment and managerial decisions within both the private and public sectors.

3.6.2 Policies for deprived inner areas

Poverty, unemployment and deprivation have been features of Britain's inner-urban areas throughout the postwar period, but only came to national attention in the 1960s as the slowdown of national economic growth accentuated the problems of inner cities' economies. Racial tensions had been growing since the late 1950s, following riots in Notting Hill and Nottingham, and had been made a major political issue in the 1964 Smethwick by-election. In the late 1960s, there were again outbreaks of racial violence in the major cities and extreme right-wing groups such as the National Front tried to build up a popular base in these areas. Individual MPs in Westminster also gave prominence to racial issues, particularly Enoch Powell in his notorious speech on 20 April 1968 in which he predicted that, unless action was taken on immigration, then 'Like the Romans, I seem to see the River Tiber foaming with much blood'. The Wilson government reacted by further restricting immigration but it also launched the 1968 Urban Aid Programme, the first major step in developing inner-area policies.

The Urban Aid Programme had two important provisions: first, central government subsidies were made available to allow local authorities to expand

Number of times listed in top 20
ranked areas for seven separate
indicators of urban deprivation

1	·
2	•
3	●
4	◆

Figure 3.4 Parliamentary constituencies figuring in one or more lists of highly ranked deprived areas, 1981 (adapted from Sim, 1984).

services such as housing advice centres and nursery schools in deprived areas; and second, the Community Development Projects (CDPs) were established. These were to combine research on the causes of deprivation with an action programme to encourage self-help among the residents of these areas. They were established on the premise that the problems of deprived areas stemmed from the inherent characteristics of their residents but the CDPs actually demonstrated that the problems of deprived areas stemmed from the process of national and international economic restructuring and the effects of State policies in the fields of housing, education and welfare (see Community Development Project, 1977a, b).

The same message was reinforced, if in apparently less political terms, in the reports of the three *Inner Area Studies* commissioned by the Department of the Environment. These demonstrated how economic change, selective population decentralization and unequal access to housing had combined to produce concentrations of unemployment in the inner areas of London, Liverpool and Birmingham. The response by central government was swift and, symbolically, the speech by Peter Shore, Secretary of State for the Environment, in September 1976, marked a change of direction in government policy. He stated in poetical vein that 'Cities serve and sustain the whole region around them in cultural, social and economic terms. If cities fail, so to a large extent does our society. That is the urgency of tackling the problem, and why it has to be of concern to everyone in this land'. In more prosaic terms, he indicated that decentralization policies would be slowed down while resources would be shifted to inner cities.

This was given concrete form in a June 1977 White Paper, 'Policy for the Inner Cities', which formed the basis for the Inner Urban Areas Act in July 1978. Four specific objectives were identified for inner-city policy: strengthening the economies of inner areas, improving their physical fabric, alleviating social problems and securing a new balance between inner areas and the remainder of the metropolitan areas. The Act established seven Partnership Areas which were to receive between £10 and £25 million per annum from central government, 23 Programme Authorities receiving between £3 and £6 million, and 15 other Designated Districts receiving about £1 million each per annum (Figure 3.5). The Act made available additional funds and development powers for councils in Programme Authorities and Designated Districts but the main emphasis was on the Partnerships. In each of the seven areas selected, representing inner-city zones in the five major conurbations, a Partnership committee was formed between central and local government (Leach, 1985). These were to provide an innovative and integrated approach to policy formulation and implementation. In practice, each Partnership has developed its own distinctive approach and investment programme: in 1981–1982, 43 percent of expenditure in Hackney/Islington was on economic development, 69 percent in Lambeth was on social

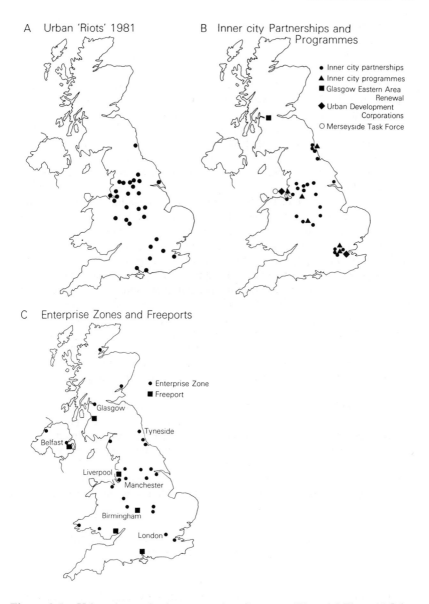

Figure 3.5 Urban riots and urban economic policy areas (*Financial Times*, 13 July 1981).

development and 37 percent in Liverpool was on environmental improvements.

Glasgow was not included among the Partnership Areas as it already had its own special agency for inner-area redevelopment, the Glasgow Eastern Area Renewal (GEAR) Project established in 1976. GEAR was made up of representatives of Glasgow City Council, the Scottish Development Agency, the Housing Corporation, the Greater Glasgow Health Board and the Manpower Services Commission. It covered an area which, in 1951, had a population of 145,000 but that had since plumeted to only 45,000. Almost two-thirds of its expenditure up to 1984 was on housing – a persistent local problem – and only 13 percent was on industrial development (Leclerc and Draffan, 1984).

The potential scope of inner-area policy was always likely to be limited, if only because of the general weakness of area-based approaches when faced with the effects of national and international economic restructuring. However, there have also been specific weaknesses in the policies adopted (Hambleton, 1981). Policies were formulated in narrow terms: pressurized by central government to act and spend quickly, the Partnerships concentrated on series of short-term expenditure programmes, and there has been little serious political discussion of policies. As Parkinson and Wilks (1983) state: '... national policy making for the inner city has been less an interactive process, as has sometimes been claimed by those involved, than it has been government by spasm. The inner city has been elevated or relegated in status on the political agenda and allocated resources according to a variety of criteria, frequently perceived political advantage, but rarely individual or institutional need' (p. 36).

Given political marginalization and the emphasis on short-term programmes, bureaucratic inertia has taken over the initiative. Local authorities' programmes have been mainly prepared on departmental lines, while the Department of the Environment has become the major central government partner. As a result, traditional centre-local relationships have been dominant and there is no real partnership. Partnerships have simply become ways of spending urban policy funds but – as these can amount to more than 10 percent of total revenue in a city such as Liverpool – the amounts involved are not trivial. Since 1979 the Conservative governments have given more emphasis to reversing economic decline and environmental decay in inner cities, so the original broad aims of an integrated approach to economic, social and environmental problems have been almost completely lost.

Frustrated by the slowness of local government (which, of course, has to be electorally responsible for policies), central government in 1979 foisted special Urban Development Corporations (UDCs) on London's and Merseyside's docklands areas. The UDCs were answerable directly to central government and had economic and housing powers akin to those of the New Town corporations. In the case of London a long history of conflict between central and local government lay behind this decision. In the 1960s it was evident that large areas of derelict docks would soon become available for redevelopment. A report commissioned by the Heath government in 1971 had proposed a strategy for commercializing the East End with office developments and medium- to high-income housing in the disused docklands. The plan was bitterly opposed by the Labour-controlled borough councils and, after 1973, by the newly elected, Labour-controlled GLC. They preferred an approach that would secure better housing and suitable jobs for the local communities. The result was prolonged stalemate but, since 1979, the designation of the Docklands Development Corporation, and of an Enterprise Zone for the Isle of Dogs, has firmly shifted the initiative to central government and the private sector.

In 1981 there were further central government initiatives for the inner cities, following several nights of sustained violence and rioting in many cities (see Figure 3.5). Enterprise Zones have already been discussed (see Chapter 3.2.3) and the other initiative was the Merseyside Task Force, established in response to that area's especially acute economic problems and, more immediately, as a reaction to rioting in Toxteth during the early summer. This was an attempt to reformulate the 'partnership' approach so as to give more power to central government. Michael Heseltine, Secretary of State for the Environment, became head of the Task Force. Given the unusual local political conditions that followed the riots, and given also the political weight of Heseltine, the Task Force recorded some important achievements – although at a cost to local democracy. The Task Force has put together interdepartmental funding for a number of projects involving training, housing, land development, and the much publicized, though essentially cosmetic, International Garden Festival. However, Heseltine moved to the Ministry of Defence in 1983 and subsequently the Task Force has been bureaucratized so it is now little more than a regional office of the Department of the Environment (Lindley, 1985).

How effective have area-based policies been as remedies for the economic, social and environmental problems of UK cities? Area-based policies are founded on certain assumptions, including the idea that policies confined to specific areas will encapsulate most deprived individuals. This is not verified by the facts, and Holtermann (1975) showed that, for example, the worst ranked 5 percent of enumeration districts in urban areas contained only 23 percent of houses lacking hot water. Similarly, Educational Priority Areas include only a small proportion of the educationally deprived, while unemployment in large cities is hardly confined to their inner areas.

Another assumption is that the appearance of deprivation in specific areas implies existence of spatial causes. Local conditions may be important but the root causes of inner-city economic difficulties lie in the process of national restructuring, given the UK's changing position in the international division of labour. At best, area policies seem to offer mild painkillers for a patient suffering from a progressive and infectious disease! Hardly surprising, then, that governments faced with persistent deprivation and sporadic outbreaks of urban rioting have had to seek a succession of new painkillers for the patient. Parkinson and Wilks (1985) vividly sum up the experience of inner-area policies in Liverpool:

> Since the late 1960s the city has been the recipient, or victim, of every experiment invented, including Jim Callaghan's traditional Urban Programme, Tony Crosland's Educational Priority Areas, Roy Jenkins' Community Development Projects, the Home Office's Brunswick Neighbourhood Project, Peter Walker's Inner Area Studies, Peter Shore's Inner City Partnership, Geoffrey Howe's Enterprise Zones, and Michael Heseltine's Urban Development Corporations and Task Force. A decade's experience of these programmes had not substantially lessened the city's problems but it had produced acute local scepticism of what it was possible to achieve for Liverpool through 'special initiative'. (p.66)

Similar verdicts probably also apply to the experience of other major cities. Inner-area policies increasingly look less like effective urban policies and more like an exercise in State legitimation. This is all the more apparent when one considers the volume of State expenditure committed to 'urban policies', pathetically small in relation to the needs of people in these areas, and the failure to specify how desired policy objectives are to be attained.

3.7   Urban politics: centre–local relationships

For much of the 20th century local government has operated within a 19th-century framework. In 1945 urban government was already fragmented and divided between county boroughs and urban districts, which also had to function alongside county structures. Two major developments further undermined the system. First, with the expansion of the Welfare State, education services and planning responsibilities, local authorities were called on to undertake a range of complex tasks, but many proved too small or lacking in resources to meet this challenge. Second, economic reorganization, increased personal mobility and spatial decentralization of population made existing, narrowly drawn boundaries hopelessly inadequate for the task of implementing local economic, social and environmental policies.

In periods of expanding local authority programmes, relationships between central and local government were relatively harmonious, although there were occasional conflicts. Examples are the Clay Cross Labour councillors' decision to oppose the Heath government's Fair Rents Act (see p. 34) and, at the end of the 1970s, the opposition of some Conservative-controlled authorities to the Labour government's plans for comprehensive education. However, since 1979 there has been an unprecedented level of centre–local government conflict. To understand this it is necessary to trace the evolution of the local government system in the postwar period.

The need to reorganize local government boundaries first became evident in London. In the 1950s, planning in London was still divided between more than 30 county and metropolitan borough councils and Middlesex County Council. Yet there was a need to implement far-reaching policies to help maintain London's role as an international economic centre, reorganize its transport system and undertake major redevelopment projects. The 1959 Herbert Report underlined deficiencies in London's government and the 1963 London Government Act introduced a new local government system for the capital. The Greater London Council had overall responsibility for coordinating the activities of individual boroughs as well as having its own responsibilities in the fields of housing, planning, transport and emergency services.

A decade later, local government in the remainder of Britain was reformed. In England and Wales, local government structures were investigated by the Redcliffe–Maud Commission, which sought to balance the needs of local democracy, corporate management and a sensible geographical basis for local authorities' boundaries. Much of the debate within and outside the Commission centred on the relative advantages of a two-tier system of subregional units against those of a unitary city-region system (McKay and Cox, 1979). However, the new system proposed in the Heath government's 1972 Local Government Act was largely a political compromise to avoid upsetting traditional (Conservative) rural counties. There were only minor boundary changes in England, although Wales experienced a much more radical spatial reorganization. Scotland, in a separate reform, also obtained a two-tier system, but the upper-tier authorities were regional in scale.

One feature of these reforms would later have a significant bearing on central–local relationships, namely the more radical reform in the metropolitan areas. New two-tier metropolitan counties were established in Tyneside, West Yorkshire, South Yorkshire, Tameside, Merseyside and the West Midlands. Within the metropolitan counties, more power over education and social services was devolved to the districts than in the non-metropolitan counties. In political terms, the reform created six large authorities (to add to the GLC), which potentially would be high spending and would not be Conservative controlled.

There have also been changes in local authorities' traditional right to determine their own expenditure levels, setting their own local rates which were supplemented by central government grants. Until the 1960s, these grants were payable under a series of separate headings, but the rate support grant (RSG) introduced a 'block' payment to cover most local government services, with the exception of housing. The RSG was calculated so as to equalize the costs of providing services in different authorities, but local councils were largely allowed to determine their own expenditure patterns. Therefore, central government crucially had limited control over local authority expenditure.

Given the expanding range of services they provided, local authorities came to account for a large proportion of total public expenditure, equivalent to about 34 percent by 1972–1973. Local authority employment also increased sharply, by some 1.2 million jobs between 1961 and 1978. However, in consequence of the economic decline in many metropolitan areas, their potential rateable bases stagnated and some had to resort to substantial external borrowing. It was against this background that conflict with central government intensified. By the late 1970s, faced with a sterling crisis, the Labour government embarked on major public expenditure cuts and local authority spending was a prime target.

After 1979 public expenditure cuts were an essential element of Thatcher macro-economic policy (see p. 25–6), so further restrictions on local authority spending followed. By 1982–1983 local authority expenditure had been reduced to about 24 percent of total public expenditure, and the relative levels of central government subsidies had also been cutback. The Conservative government was also intent on a policy of privatization to reinforce emerging, more individualized patterns of consumption. As consumption cleavages – especially in terms of ownership of homes and cars and the use of private health and educational services – cut across the traditional class bases of voting patterns (Duke and Edgell, 1984), this was likely to weaken the Labour Party's electoral base. However, implementing these policies brought the government into greater conflict with local authorities, especially Labour-controlled councils.

Since 1979 there have been several major areas of central–local conflict, especially housing (see p. 35–6). The Secretary of State for the Environment has also encroached on local authorities' planning powers, using draft circulars to set out his views on such matters as permitting more development of green belts. However, the key attack on local autonomy has been financial. The first stage was the Local Government, Planning and Land Act 1980, which allowed central government to limit local authorities' spending on particular activities, as well as their total expenditure. Later the government's economic strategy required further restrictions and the Local Government Finance Act 1982 barred the levying of supplementary grants and introduced 'rate capping'. The latter involves penalizing overspending (over centrally determined maximums) by reducing central grant support in the following year. At the same time central government has sought to outflank local authorities by providing direct funding of many local policies, especially the inner-city initiatives. These undermine traditional local democracy because the new bodies have considerable powers – for example in compulsory purchase or in waiving planning laws – without being responsible to local electorates.

These controversial measures have been resisted by some Labour-controlled authorities, leading central government to use the legal system to enforce its policies: for example, the GLC's cheap-fares policy was outlawed by the House of Lords, Norwich City Council was forced to comply with the 'right-to-buy' provisions of the 1980 Housing Act, and Lothian Regional Council was forced to implement expenditure cuts by the threat of appointment of commissioners to run the authority. Local government has become a major area of political conflict and, in 1985, several councils refused to set legal rates (within the maximum demanded by central government). Public galleries have been crowded for stormy council meetings, and there have been well-organized local campaigns to resist the cuts. Boddy (1983) writes: 'These local campaigns, and clashes between central and local government, together with the emergence of the GLC's Ken Livingstone or Lambeth's Ted Knight as media "bogeymen" of the Left, have catapulted local government into the public eye in a way which even T. Dan Smith, Poulson or the Clay Cross Councillors failed to do... there has even been a soap opera (admittedly screened on BBC2) entitled "County Hall" ' (pp. 119–120).

The campaigns are not simply about resisting public expenditure cuts. They are also part of the argument against further shifts from collective to private consumption, and about the need to use public policy to rectify some of the social and spatial inequalities that are so evident at a time of economic restructuring and unemployment growth. Central government's ultimate reply to this challenge would be abolition of local government and substitution of administration through nominated agencies. With the consultative document *Streamlining the Cities* in 1983, this was proposed for the (largely Labour-controlled) metropolitan counties and the GLC and, after a stormy political passage, became law in 1985.

FOUR

The Rural Dimension

4.1 Introduction

After the experiences of the agricultural depression in the 1930s and of supplying the strategic food needs of wartime Britain, both major political parties fought the 1945 General Election committed to increasing agricultural output. This was to be the major influence shaping the countryside for the next two decades. There were initial differences between the parties – Labour seemed more committed to helping agricultural workers and to land nationalization – but these quickly faded and bipartisan politics held until the 1960s. Thereafter, different attitudes to the European Community's Common Agricultural Policy (CAP) led to some divergence in policies for financing agriculture.

However, the context within which agricultural policies were formulated has also changed in the past 20 years. Policies to reduce output – for example the introduction of milk quotas by the EC in 1983 – have begun to replace those to expand output at virtually any cost. The rural conservationist lobby has also gained strength and sought to modify some of the changes brought about by intensification of agriculture, such as drainage and ploughing of marginal areas. Elsewhere, in isolated incidents, holiday and second homes have been burned by extreme nationalist groups in Wales, and fierce local political battles are being fought over the retention of rural buses, health facilities and schools. Finally, almost unthinkable 20 years earlier – the 1980s saw several instances of rural Conservatives in revolt against a Tory government's plans for privatizing housing and transport.

These shifts should be seen in the context of changes in the nature of production in the countryside. Agriculture – as a source of local jobs and income – was in a long slow retreat throughout the postwar period while, by the 1970s, some rural areas had become the focus of relatively rapid employment creation in manufacturing. Elsewhere, the decline of production was matched by a greater role for some rural areas in consumption: they became locations for daily commuters to urban areas, for seasonal or weekend visitors to holiday homes and for retirement homes. The requirements of production and consumption rarely coincide and there have been a number of conflicts over environmental issues: notable examples include applications for quarrying and mining in National Parks, for these can provide local employment although disfiguring the landscape.

The conflicts are sharpened because they occur within a framework of largely negative local authority planning. The 1947 Town and Country Planning Act set up a system of planning limited mainly to land-use matters and to the prevention of 'undesirable' development. This stemmed from the assumption of the 1945 Labour government that most postwar development would be undertaken in the public sector so that the State itself, as principal developer, would provide the positive and social inputs to planning. However, the strategy was annulled by Conservative victory in the 1951 Election. The postwar planning system was also governed by the overriding objective of preserving rural land so that, alongside normal development control procedures, there appeared a set of specially protected areas, including green belts, National Parks (National Heritage Areas in Scotland), Areas of Outstanding Natural Beauty (AONB), Forest Parks and Heritage Coasts (Figure 4.1). Northern Ireland has received different treatment. The recommendations of the Planning Advisory Board in 1947 that five National Parks be designated was never implemented. Now there are a mixture of AONBs and Areas of Special Control. Therefore, local authorities in the UK were limited to a preventative, negative role and the initiative for development passed to the private sector. This had two major implications for housing: first, the general restriction on new housing construction in rural areas, coupled with demand from middle-class newcomers, forced up housing prices; second, planners were able to exercise physical but not social planning. In particular, they could control the types of houses built but not who occupied them. This general planning framework was accorded bipartisan political support after 1950 and was only really challenged by post-1979 Conservative governments intent on further shifting development initiatives to the private sector.

These economic and social processes brought about two fundamental changes in rural areas. First, traditional class, gender and age structures in rural areas were remodelled and social groups with very different needs in terms of their reliance on local schools, local services and local buses, came to reside in the same villages and rural catchment areas. Whereas the rural working class sought improvements to public services and employment provision, the new middle class sought to preserve (or even create) an idyllic rural Britain as the setting for lifestyles based on individual and privatized consumption. Second, the remaking of local social structures was not a uniform process: instead it was dependent on local features such as existing social structures, accessibility levels and potential for recreation. Rural areas – never homogeneous – became differentiated along new lines and it is essential to recognize that there are different types of rural areas characterized by different combinations of, and forms of, production and consumption.

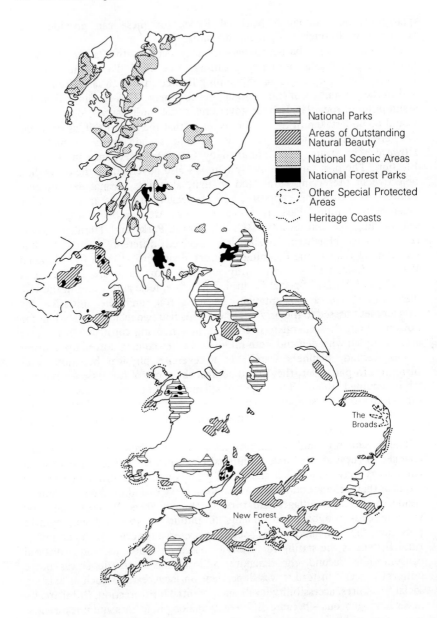

Figure 4.1   Rural areas in the UK with designated special protection status.

4.2 Agriculture: the price of postwar prosperity

4.2.1 Land and land ownership

The ownership of land is notoriously difficult to determine with any precision, but recent estimates indicate a high degree of polarization. While 1 percent of the population own 52 percent of the land in Britain,* 80 percent own only 8 percent of the land (Norton-Taylor, 1982). Landowners can be classified into three types: traditional landed estates, industrial landowners and financial institutions (Massey, 1977). Traditional landed estates own about 40 percent of the land surface of Britain but only about 9 percent of the agricultural area. By far the largest group in this category is the Crown and aristocracy. Crown Estates own some 350,000 acres, while 26 aristocrats have combined holdings of over one million acres: the largest of these in Scotland is owned by the Duke of Buccleuch (277,000 acres), and in England by the Duke of Northumberland (90,786 acres). Capital transfer taxes have led to a break-up of some estates but increasingly they are able to survive intact through adopting various forms of trustee ownership. In addition to the aristocracy, there are also large holdings by the Church of England (170,000 acres), the Oxbridge universities (160,000 acres), the Ministry of Defence (700,000 acres), and the National Trust (over 400,000 acres).

A second group of landowners consists of financial institutions, such as insurance companies and pension funds, for whom investment in farm land is only one element in their portfolios. These institutions were particularly active in the land market in the 1970s and, for example, in 1972 alone they increased their holdings of agricultural land by some 40 percent. Despite some spectacular investments, such as the £20 million spent by the Prudential Assurance Company to acquire the Herefordshire estate of the late Sir Charles Clore in 1979, they own only about 1 percent of all the farmland in Britain. However, this is regionally uneven, and their holdings are concentrated in large estates of prime quality land in eastern England.

The third group comprises industrial landowners – individual farmers who account for about 90 percent of all farm land (but a smaller proportion of all land). Despite owning most agricultural land, this group is in the weakest financial position. Given technological developments in agriculture many family farms are just too small to function effectively (Massey, 1977). However, the total supply of land is fixed and only a very small amount comes onto the market in any one year. The traditional estates hold land for status as much as for economic reasons and they sell reluctantly, if at all, while farmers themselves rarely wish to dispose of their major asset. Furthermore, when land does come onto the market, farmers in some regions have to compete

* The term 'Britain' rather than 'United Kingdom' is used when specific data or examples do not include Northern Ireland.

with the financial institutions. Although the total holdings of the latter are small, in some years they have purchased up to one-half of all farm land on the open market (Norton-Taylor, 1982). Consequently, agricultural land prices have soared; the average sale price has risen from about £200 a hectare in the 1950s to £3717 in England and £2350 in Scotland in 1983. As farmers find it increasingly difficult to acquire more land to make their farms viable, this has encouraged part-time farming.

4.2.2   The State and agriculture

Agriculture accounts for only 2 percent of employment in the UK but it is the most extensive of land uses, provides the basis for a series of agro-processing industries, and has been the single largest source of rural job losses since 1945. State policies are critical in this sector – no other activity has been so consistently and comprehensively protected and subsidized: the subsidy on net production in agriculture is about 40 percent compared to 33 percent for railways and 10 percent for coal mining (*The Sunday Times*, 18 August 1985).

Protection has not always prevailed; indeed, in the late 19th century the State adopted free-trade policies to secure cheap food imports, thereby reducing living costs and, indirectly, urban wages. Only in the 20th century were *laissez-faire* policies reversed; the First World War increased the need for greater agricultural self-sufficiency, and the 1930s agricultural depression also led to demands for interventionist policies. Marketing boards were introduced for milk and for pig meat in 1933, and price subsidies were strengthened, especially for cattle and cereals (Bowler, 1979). During the Second World War agriculture was run, essentially, on command lines and this set the scene for postwar agricultural policy.

The most remarkable feature of postwar rural policies was that, effectively, these became synonymous with agricultural policy. Prior to the 1945 Election, Labour's policies had included a major rural housing programme, land nationalization and programmes to relieve rural poverty (Self and Storing, 1962). However, in office the major bastion of their rural policy was agricultural support, linked to the dubious contemporary assumption that a prosperous agriculture would equate with rural prosperity and conservation of rural landscapes. The Scott Committee accepted the latter view and it became a foundation of postwar land-use planning. The cornerstone of agricultural policy was the 1947 Agricultural Act, which guaranteed prices and markets for producers. Prices were to be determined by market forces but annual price reviews set minimum guaranteed prices for producers. When market prices fell below these, State subsidies made up the difference to the farmers. The guarantee prices were to be set at levels that assured both moderate prices for consumers and 'proper' levels of remuneration for farmers, hence encouraging expansion of output. These were clearly contradictory aims and it was usually expansion of output – and hence relatively high prices – which was prominent. That a Labour government introduced such a favourable package for farmers was not so surprising. Following the depression years, farmers, many of whom operated on a small scale and small margins, really did have '... some claim on the egalitarian impulses of the 1945 Labour government' (Bowers and Cheshire, 1983). Increased production and reduced imports could help ease the UK's chronic foreign currency shortage and balance of payments deficit (see Chapter 1.2). More cynically, Labour also had an opportunity to consolidate the new rural support it had found in the 1945 Election.

Once established, and given the failure to join the EEC in the 1950s, the aim of expansion and the system of guarantee prices both received bipartisan support; they were effective and by 1953 food production was already 53 percent higher than prewar levels. World market conditions, however, changed in the mid-1950s: commodity prices fell and, consequently, the real costs of agricultural support rose dramatically. The Conservative government's response to this was threefold: more emphasis on selective expansion with reduced subsidies for some products, such as pig meat; stronger controls on imports; and more emphasis on stabilizing rather than on just raising prices. However, the costs of agricultural support continued to rise, reaching £340 million in 1961. The Conservative (and, later, the Labour) government's response to this was further import controls. The UK was already shifting to greater protectionism even before it entered the EEC.

Guarantee prices were only one, if arguably the most important, element of agricultural policy. After 1951, in response to initially disappointing increases in output, a series of grants was introduced to subsidize investments in, for example, fertilizers, machinery and bringing marginal land into production. This contributed to an increased ratio of capital to labour and encouraged specialization. However, by the 1970s such policies brought the Ministry of Agriculture into conflict with conservationists when, for example, grants for hill land ploughing were seen to encourage a reduction in rough grazing in areas like Exmoor.

The bipartisan approach to agricultural policy ended after the UK's accession to the EEC in 1973. The system of European Agricultural Guidance and Guarantee Fund (EAGGF) prices led to higher prices for agricultural products (if only because these took more account of the costs of marginal producers) and there were also changes in the means of financing agricultural subsidies. The European Community annually sets target prices for farm products. If market prices decline below these, the Commission intervenes to purchase and stockpile surplus output, covering the costs by levies on imports (to bring these up to EC price levels) and on member states. Within this framework, there is supposed to be 'free trade' in agricultural produce. In practice, however, the UK – in common with other member states – has used the 'green' currency (an official EC 'exchange rate', which differs from the real and fluctuating sterling exchange rate) to influence the cost of food to the consumer and the prices paid to farmers within the UK. The UK government has also occasionally undertaken specific actions to protect UK producers, such as in 1984 when it sought to impair imports of UHT milk, supposedly on the grounds of hygiene.

Over time the costs of the Common Agricultural Policy have risen sharply. By 1979, it was estimated that on average each farm in the Community was receiving about £10,000 per annum in financial support, either directly through production grants and through intervention buying and stockpiling of 'lakes' and 'mountains' of agricultural produce, or through the higher costs imposed on the consumer by import levies. By 1983–1984, over £1700 million per annum was being spent on agriculture in the UK, some £1374 million on market regulation alone. Although £1200 million was covered by EAGGF receipts, a large share of the cost was ultimately borne by the UK Exchequer. In most years since accession to the EC, the CAP has resulted in higher prices for domestic consumers than would probably have prevailed under pre-1973 policies. Therefore, part of the cost of agricultural support has been shifted from the taxpayer (as in the traditional UK system of deficiency payments) to the consumer. This is socially regressive and has contributed to a break-up of the bipartisan approach to agricultural policy. The Conservatives wish to maintain but reform the CAP, while Labour's official policy is a return to deficiency payments.

Despite this recent divergence, agriculture has largely been shaped by bipartisan State policies in the postwar period. Bowers and Cheshire (1983), writing about the role of the Ministry of Agriculture, Food and Fisheries (MAFF), state that:

> Agriculture in the UK has been, and is, a hothouse industry. Without the protection offered it, it would have declined both in output and labour force and land could well, at the margin of cultivation, have gone out of production. MAFF determined its rate of expansion, chose the direction it should take and through a system of subsidies and farm management advice brought it about. (p. 115)

In its own terms the policy has been remarkably successful. Guaranteed, stable prices helped to create an environment of confidence which facilitated long-term investment planning and contributed to a steady rise in output and greater self-reliance in food supplies. Between 1971 and 1983 the UK's self-sufficiency rose from 50 to 62 percent for all foods and from 62 to 78 percent for indigenous foods (*Annual Review of Agriculture*, 1985). However, the social consequences of those policies have been mixed. Payments are proportional to output, so large-scale, efficient farms in the most productive areas have gained most. Agro-industries have also benefited, given the drive to more capital-intensive production. Furthermore, as subsidies increase the return to agriculture, they have contributed to increases in land prices hence benefiting landowners. Those who have benefited least are consumers (especially under the CAP), and farm workers whose interests have been poorly represented in the bipartisan approach. For example, Labour, despite a longstanding manifesto commitment to abolishing tied cottages, only undertook any significant reform of this tenure in 1976.

How have farmers been able to secure such advantageous policies, not only in terms of guaranteed prices but also with respect to rates (which they do not pay) and capital transfer taxes (from which they are partially exempt)? Initially, they benefited from the immediate postwar desire to secure increased food production and self-sufficiency and there was also genuine poverty in many rural areas. Later, they argued that increased agricultural output helped to reduce the UK's recurring balance of payments deficits. However, their continued favoured position can only be explained by reference to agricultural corporatism, the close mutually dependent relationship between farmers' organizations and central government (Grant, 1983). The National Farmers' Union (NFU) is extremely well organized and has forged close and special ties with the Ministry of Agriculture to the exclusion of almost all other interest groups. For example, while the NFU deals directly with the upper tiers of the civil service in the Ministry, agricultural workers' wages are determined by a government quango. Meanwhile, conservation groups have to channel most of their pressures through two Department of the Environment quangos – the Nature Conservancy Council and the Countryside Commission. These are politically marginal, possessing little scope for policy-making; arguably, they deflect the conservationist lobby from the real centres of power (Cox and Lowe, 1984). While the corporatist relationship is at the heart of NFU influence, farmers also draw strength from other sources, especially strong traditional links with the Conservative Party in both Houses of Parliament (Roth, 1973), and excellent public relations.

4.2.3 The organization of agriculture

State policies, changing market demand and the relationship between farming and agro-industries (which have removed much of the processing of inputs and outputs from the farmyard) have brought about significant developments in production. Increases in the size of farms and in capital and labour ratios have resulted in considerable gains in productivity, output and profits, especially for larger farms. This has encouraged further farm enlargement and additional changes in production methods. As a result there have been major developments in farm practices, land ownership and the nature of farm employment (Marsden, 1984).

Given a relatively fixed supply of land (excepting some marginal upland areas), improvements in food self-sufficiency depended on securing greater land productivity. Cox and Lowe (1984), for example, state that in 1946 it took 3.33 square metres of land to produce a standard loaf of bread but by the 1980s this had fallen to only 1.33 square metres. These changes – and a reduction in unit production costs – have been brought about by substitution of capital for labour so that the share of labour in total farm expenses fell from 42 percent in 1948–1949 to 20 percent in 1965–1966 (Massey, 1977). There has also been a 70 percent decrease in the agricultural labour force since 1945.

More capital-intensive farm practices have led to more energy-intensive production, with machinery replacing labour and chemical fertilizers replacing natural ones, although the recent growth of 'organic farming' represents a limited reaction to this. Another response has been increased specialization: the characteristic 'mixed' farm of the immediate postwar years is now rare. By the early 1970s, some 90 percent of full-time farms were classified as being specialized (in up to three products), although part-time farms are more likely to be mixed (Britton, 1974). Specialization is partly a consequence of the shift to more capital-intensive agriculture. While labour is relatively flexible and can be used to plough, hedge or milk, machinery is more task specific: combine harvesters or milking sheds cannot easily be switched between tasks. Given the costs of such machinery and scale economies in their use, there are constant pressures on farmers to increase the acreage devoted to particular products. This can be achieved in two ways – increased specialization or increased farm size – and in practice farmers may adopt both strategies.

There have been significant increases in the size of farms, and a corresponding reduction in their number by about 50 percent, or approximately some 250,000 units, between 1908 and 1980 (Norton-Taylor, 1982). These trends have intensified in the postwar period. Between 1965 and 1975 some 22,000 small holdings disappeared while, in contrast, the percentage of agricultural land occupied by farms larger than 297 acres (120 hectares) increased from 33 to 43 percent (Marsden, 1984). Consequently, 10 percent of farms now account for 50 percent of the food produced in the UK.

There are, however, important regional variations (Figure 4.2) and these can be generalized as the difference between wetter, upland western areas and dryer, lowland eastern areas. Larger-scale farms specializing in cereals tend to be found in the east, smaller farms specializing in livestock in the west. Product differences and scale variations are related: in 1980 the average dairy farm was 111 acres (45 hectares), the average cereal farm 306 acres (124 hectares). Highly mechanized cereal production also offers greater economies of scale than livestock production: Britton and Hill (1975) consider that economies of scale level off for dairy farms at about 100–150 acres, and for cropping farms at about 200–250 acres. Cereal production also requires much

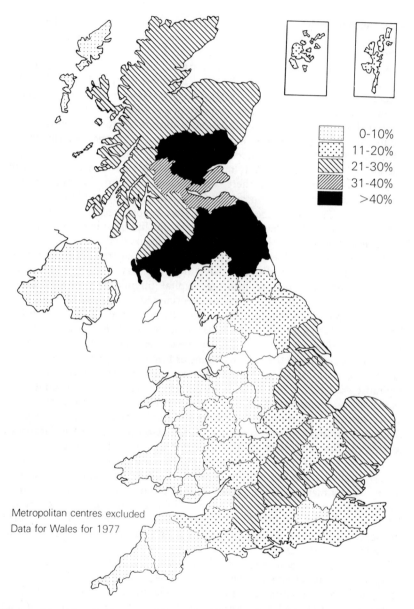

Metropolitan centres excluded
Data for Wales for 1977

Figure 4.2 Farm size in the UK, 1983: percentage of farm holdings larger than 247 acres (100 hectares) (*Agricultural Statistics*, 1984).

larger fields for efficient operation of farm machinery, and much of the recent controversy concerning the removal of hedgerows has focused on eastern England. However, differences between the East and West of the UK go beyond product specialization: the largest concentrations of grade 1 agricultural land are in eastern England and have attracted investment by financial institutions (Munton, 1977). Western areas are characterized more by owner-occupied family farms, which have proven more resistant to the insistent logic of capitalist accumulation leading to greater concentration in production. We return to this later but, first, consider changes in farm tenure.

Whereas in 1919 only 11 percent of farms were owner-occupied, this had reached 66 percent by 1981 (Norton-Taylor, 1982). Much of the growth occurred in the 1920s when there was remarkable fluidity in land markets, and the percentage of owner-occupied farms more than trebled in this decade. Subsequently, the structure of taxation has encouraged further shifts to owner-occupancy. The main counterforce to this has been investment by the financial institutions, for these usually rely on managers.

The 20th century has seen an apparent contradiction in agriculture, however. The dominant trends have been increased specialization and mechanization, leading to growing capital inputs and concentration. Nevertheless, family farms – often owner-occupied – have not only survived, but have grown in relative strength. In 1981 there were 163,000 farms in England and Wales of less than 124 acres (50 hectares); 96,200 of these were smaller than 50 acres (20 hectares); and most were reliant on family labour, rarely employing more than one part-time or full-time employee in addition to casual labour. This is not to say that agriculture has not become more capitalist – it has, but in a form different from the relentless concentration of ownership and increased scale of production evident in manufacturing (see p. 23–4). Instead, large-scale capital has encapsulated agriculture so as to remove the more profitable processing of inputs and outputs from the farmyard, leaving the farm only with direct production on the land (Friedmann, 1980). Fertilizers, equipment and animal feeds are now likely to be produced in factories rather than on the farm itself, while food processing has also been taken over by manufacturing plants. These agro-industries are dominated by some of the UK's largest companies. Unilever, for example, owns the following subsidiaries: BOCM Silcock (the largest animal feed manufacturer in the UK), Bachelor Foods, Bird's Eye, Walls, East Sussex Farmers Ltd, Dale Turkeys, Matteson's Hams and Flora.

There are sound reasons for survival of the family farm as an essential part of agricultural production, however. Private ownership of land is an obstacle to capitalist accumulation in agriculture, unlike in manufacturing. The long seasonal nature of production means that much investment is tied up in land before the returns – in terms of crops or livestock sold – can be realized (Mann and Dickinson, 1978). This has discouraged external sources of capital from investing in agriculture. Factory farming methods, improved crops and livestock breeds are slowly breaking this barrier but, to date, it has remained effective.

Family farms, nevertheless, continue to operate under these same conditions. Many farmers inherit land and, being free of mortgage or tenancy payments, do not pay a true 'rent' on it. They ignore the real costs of capital tied up in land and, even if they did not, would still prefer to remain in farming as 'keeping the family name on the land' can be as important a motivation as profit and loss accounts (Williams, 1973). Costs are also subsidized in other ways: many family farms are part-time, and one or more family members may obtain additional income from a second (non-farming) job. In addition, family farms rely on unpaid family labour, especially by the women on the farm (Bouquet, 1982). The precise contribution of this unpaid labour is variable but Gasson (1980) estimated that in 1970 farm wives contributed at least 5 percent of direct labour in production in England, as well as unpaid labour in running the household and unpaid office work. In tourist areas, they may also act as unpaid chambermaids and cooks for bed and breakfast guests, or may run farm shops and camp sites. Symes and Marsden (1983) confirm this broad picture: wives, on average, provide nine hours of labour per week, divided approximately equally between office duties, outdoor work and other supportive activities. The personal costs for them may include frustrated career aspirations as well as casualization of their contribution to the farm.

4.2.4 Agricultural employment and incomes

There has been a massive reduction in agricultural employment through redundancies, retirement and the attraction of alternative, better-paid jobs in other industries in the 1950s and 1960s. The percentage of the labour force employed in agriculture has fallen steadily from 10 percent in 1891 to about 2 percent at present. More recently, the numbers in agriculture fell from 695,000 in 1973–1975 to 624,000 in 1983 and, within this total, the number of employees fell from 404,000 to 334,000. However, there continue to be significant regional variations (see Chapter 2.2) in the distribution of agricultural employment, which is most important in some counties in Wales, Scotland, the far West and eastern England (Figure 4.3).

There have also been changes in the social composition of those working in agriculture (Table 4.1), mirroring the organizational changes discussed earlier. With the survival of the family farm, the number of farms has remained relatively stable; numbers of farmers, partners and directors were approximately equal in 1973–1975 and in 1983, although there was a shift to part-time activity. A small part of this is accounted for by 'hobby farmers', whose main source of income lies elsewhere and who view the farm more as

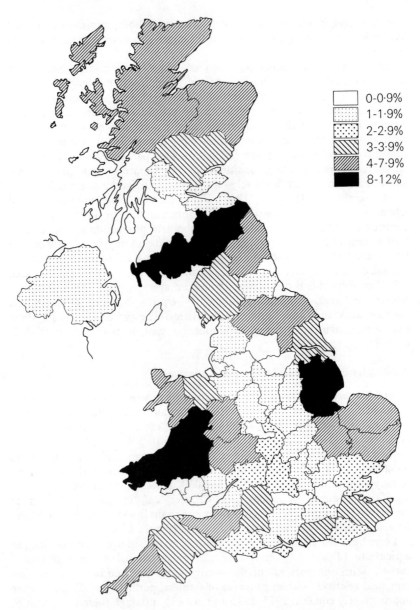

Figure 4.3   Proportion of labour force employed in agriculture, 1981 (1981 Population Census).

Table 4.1   Employment in agriculture, 1973–1975 and 1983

	1973–1975 average (000s)	1983 (000s)	1973–75 to 1983 annual percentage change
Full-time regular			
Hired male	159	122	−23
Hired female	15	11	−26
Family male	45	30	−33
Family female	14	5	−64
Part-time regular			
Hired male	24	19	−21
Hired female	26	23	−11
Family male	16	12	−25
Family female	18	7	−61
Seasonal			
Male	42	57	+36
Female	36	41	+14
Salaried managers	–	8	–
Total no. employed	404*	334*	−17
Farmers, partners, directors			
Full-time	216	203	−6
Part-time	74	87	+17
Total	290	290	0
Total	695*	624*	−10

Source: *Annual Review of Agriculture* (1985).

* Totals are subject to rounding effects in the source document.

recreation than as an economic undertaking (Gasson, 1966). However, more important has been the tendency for 'genuine' farmers to seek an additional source of income outside farming, relegating agricultural activities to weekends and evenings. This practice has implications for the growth of manufacturing industry outside metropolitan areas (see Chapter 4.3).

In contrast, there has been a major reduction in the numbers of farm employees. This is the outcome of increased mechanization, which has permitted significant cost reductions even though agricultural wages have consistently remained well below average wage levels. By 1983 there were only 334,000 employees in agriculture – 280,000 hired workers and 54,000 family members. Almost all categories of farm labour declined during the 1970s, but the largest percentage reductions were in family employees, especially females. Average family size has fallen but many farms simply can no longer offer full-time work for the head of the household, let alone his or her children.

The substitution of capital for labour has not been complete, however. There are still some seasonal activities, such as fruit harvesting, which defy mechanization. Whereas previously such labour came from full-time or part-time employees, it is now provided by seasonal labourers, who increased in number by 14% (females) and 36% (males) between 1973–1975 and 1983. This is a heterogeneous group including gangs of both mobile, highly skilled specialists (for example, sheep shearers) and local, relatively unskilled harvesters (especially for fruit and vegetable crops). Seasonal labour is attractive to farmers as it is flexible, non-unionized and usually paid on a piece rate rather than an hourly rate basis. Even so, 'pick your own' retailing methods are undermining the need for seasonal labour for harvesting some crops.

However, the reduction of wage costs is not usually as important in agriculture as in manufacturing, for labour costs have fallen as a percentage of total production costs but it also reflects a striking paradox of postwar agriculture. At a time of unrivalled prosperity in farming, farm workers have made no significant gains in their wages *vis-à-vis* other groups of employees. Between 1938 and 1973–1977, the incomes of farmers moved from below average to more than twice the average for male manual workers. In contrast, agricultural workers, despite making small gains, still earned less than three-quarters of the average wage, even in the mid-1970s (Bradley, 1984). Farm workers have always been poorly unionized, and their employment in small units in geographically dispersed workplaces continues to make collective action difficult to organize. This has been further reinforced by the importance of family farms: most farms employ one or, at most, a handful of employees who work alongside the farmer in a paternalistic relationship (Newby, 1977). The tied-cottage system also strengthens farm workers' dependency on their employers.

The initial postwar premise that a prosperous agriculture would lead to a prosperous countryside has proved ill founded. Agriculture has been fundamentally reorganized and output has soared, but the farmers have monopolized the benefits. When developments in land prices are also taken into account, then it is evident that agriculture has become increasingly socially polarized.

4.3 Manufacturing and services in rural areas

4.3.1 Rural manufacturing: decentralization and growth

The changing spatial division of labour in the United Kingdom had employment implications for many rural areas (see Chapter 2.2). Keeble (1984) shows that between 1971 and 1978 only rural counties exhibited any evidence of manufacturing growth, with 6.7 percent gains. This was in marked contrast to heavy losses in the conurbations and more urbanized areas (Table 4.2). Fothergill and Gudgin (1982), using more spatially and temporally disaggregated data, provide further insights. The turning point in employment decentralization was the 1960s: in the early years of the decade all areas except London gained employment but, by the late 1960s, growth was evident only in county towns and rural areas. By the early 1970s, county towns were barely holding their own whereas rural areas – despite the impact of the first oil crisis – exhibited relatively strong growth. Essentially, firms have adopted new restructuring strategies in the face of rising costs and international competition. One response – substituting machines for people – and the resulting rise in unemployment have already been discussed (see Chapter 1.3). Another strategy involved exploiting reserves of relatively cheap and flexible labour, often found in rural areas. Small-town locations also offer large firms the possibility of spatial monopoly in local labour markets.

Of course, in detail, the process of decentralization has been more complex than this. The emergence of new divisions of labour has permitted larger manufacturing firms to decentralize parts of their production processes to rural areas, including the assembly stages requiring cheap, unskilled (often, but not necessarily, female) labour. Additionally, some rural areas offer an environment that is favourable for individual consumption and this has

Table 4.2 Employment decentralization in Great Britain, 1959–1975

Area	% change in manufacturing			% change in services
	1959–1966	1966–1971	1971–1975	1959–1975
London	−0.7	−3.6	−5.1	+1.9
Conurbations	+0.2	−1.7	−2.2	+5.9
Free-standing cities	+1.7	−0.1	−1.3	+16.0
Industrial towns	+2.8	−0.2	−0.5	+21.1
County towns	+3.0	+1.1	+0.1	+15.2
Rural areas	+6.0	+1.9	+3.5	+11.4
Great Britain	+1.1	−1.1	−1.8	+10.8

Source: Fothergill and Gudgin (1982).

encouraged complete transfers of smaller firms from urban areas by some entrepreneurs concerned with lifestyles. However, most new firms in rural areas are indigenous new starts rather than transfers (Fothergill and Gudgin, 1982), although the latter may be larger firms offering more jobs. Nevertheless, a large share of the relative decentralization of jobs to rural areas can be accounted for by new local firms. These tend to fall into two categories: either small, highly specialized, high-technology companies locating in areas where the necessary professional and technical personnel already live or to which they can be attracted on environmental grounds; or small, consumer goods firms producing for particular local markets (including tourism) or subcontracting to larger companies.

There are parallels between the decentralization of industry in rural areas and the process of diffuse industrialization observed elsewhere in Europe, especially northeastern Italy (Fua, 1983). Industries in rural areas can draw on a labour force that engages in double-job holding (hence the importance of part-time and seasonal work in agriculture in the UK) and which has relatively little previous industrial work experience. It is therefore likely to be non-militant and flexible in acceptance of work practices, and fairly easily laid off at times of cyclical fluctuations in demand or secular recession.

These developments in rural industrialization are likely to vary both between different types of rural areas and between sectors, as is exemplified by the clothing and advanced electronics industries. The clothing industry is a classic example of relatively labour-intensive production, having been remarkably resistant to the introduction of new technology, although automated design, cutting and sewing machines are now emerging. While a few simple operations can be automated, most processes continue to be based on hand-operated sewing machines. Clothing manufacturing is not necessarily unskilled labour, but traditional reliance on women workers has permitted tasks to be downgraded and it is relatively poorly paid. The industry has been subjected to intense competition both from other advanced economies and from newly industrialized countries throughout the postwar period, but this became particularly intense in the 1970s (Steed, 1981). The survival strategies open to firms were necessarily limited: as there were few opportunities to reduce production costs through increasing mechanization, they had to reduce labour costs directly. These had anyway been under pressure, for expansion of office and other service jobs had increased competition for, and the costs of, the traditional pool of female labour in UK cities. The new female labour reserves were found in the smaller towns, rural areas and some Development Areas. Clothing manufacturing shifted to these zones and away from traditional centres of production in London, West Yorkshire and Lancashire (Massey, 1984). In the face of international competition, the UK clothing industry has also increasingly specialized in small-batch production of short-life, high-fashion products, and rural areas have proven to be especially attractive for this scale of production.

Massey (1983b) has outlined the impact of this type of industrial restructuring in Cornwall, emphasizing how the process differs in some respect from that observed in traditional industrial peripheral areas, such as the Northeast and South Wales, which also had female labour reserves. In Cornwall, traditionally low female participation in manufacturing employment reflects lack of opportunities (especially where quarrying, mining or fishing predominate), availability of seasonal jobs in tourism and agriculture, and difficulties of access to workplaces for women (especially with children) living in dispersed settlements. In the 1960s the number of women officially recorded as working in agriculture fell by 12 percent and this increased the potential female labour reserve. The availability of this pool of labour – with little experience of capitalist wage relations and used to low wages (or even no wages for work on family farms) – contributed to the growth of manufacturing firms in the county in the 1970s.

The advanced electronics industry presents a different picture, especially in East Anglia, which had the fastest employment growth of any region in the 1970s (Gould and Keeble, 1984; see Chapter 2.2). There were marked intraregional variations, firm formation rates in the more rural areas being greater than those in either the small or large towns – 6.3 percent compared to 2.2 percent and 3.4 percent. This can be accounted for by the industrial composition and occupational structure of these areas. Industrial composition is characterized by relatively large numbers of small firms in electronics, mechanical engineering and printing. These industries are not specifically tied to market or raw material locations and, instead, entrepreneurs seem to be attracted by the quality of life offered by rural East Anglia. Such areas also tend to be the existing residences of highly skilled professionals and technicians and this in itself has encouraged local firm formation, especially in the electronics industry. Some three-quarters of the region's high-technology enterprises are located within 30 miles of the city of Cambridge and its university. These firms offer very different types of employment to those in clothing manufacturing, being predominantly white collar.

These two examples are illustrative of the different types of processes involved in rural industrialization. Not all rural areas have offered equally favourable conditions for production, however. Indeed, there is a postwar history of attempts by the State to foster industrial growth in some rural regions; we return to this theme in Chapter 4.3.3.

4.3.2 Service employment: centralization and concentration

The almost continuous postwar growth in service employment has had very different impacts on urban and rural areas. Although there were major gains in service employment in rural areas, these were actually less than those in free-standing cities, industrial towns and county towns (see Table 4.2). The reasons for this become evident if some of the different types of service occupations are considered. Nationally, there has been rapid growth in employment in public administration and little or no growth in the distributive trades (see Chapter 1.3). Rural areas, with higher overall growth rates (see Chapter 4.4), might have been expected to perform better than the more urban areas in terms of the growth and redistribution of jobs in these sectors. Although no comprehensive evidence is available to explain why they have not done so, the reasons seem clear: both public and private sectors have been subject to centralization and concentration.

In the private sector, there is increased concentration of shops and personal services in the towns, while village shops and services (such as hairdressers) have all but disappeared. This has partly been encouraged by local authority planning policies, especially the idea of concentration in key settlements (Cloke, 1979), even where this ran counter to existing settlement patterns as in Northern Ireland (Caldwell and Greer, 1984). More fundamentally, concentration has been the outcome of increased economies of scale requiring fewer but larger distribution units. The process has been facilitated by centralization in companies such as Sainsbury and Tesco, which have the resources for the massive investments required to bring about the new patterns of retailing. These may take the form of city-centre redevelopments or out-of-town hypermarkets but, in either case, the result is the same: a long, slow decline of genuinely rural provision of consumer services.

There are also economies of scale in the provision of public sector services, whether in education, health or social services, leading to concentration of public sector service jobs. Given the sparse population outside the towns, the urban orientation of road networks and declining public transport provision, this has inevitably meant spatial concentration. Thus the majority of employment by local authorities and by public bodies such as the NHS is located in the county and district 'headquarter' towns. Reform of local government in 1974 reinforced this; the effective centralization of power replaced many smaller, more rural councils with a smaller number of larger district councils.

Although most rural areas have tended to act mainly as centres for consumption, some of the more attractive localities have attracted producer services. Office decentralization from London and the Southeast has already been discussed (Chapter 3.2.2) and here it is sufficient to note that some minor gains have been made by small towns, especially in East Anglia, the outer Southeast and the Southwest. Outstanding examples include the transfer of the headquarters of the London and Manchester Insurance Company to Exeter and of John Wiley (the publisher) to Chichester. Given the importance of contacts in the work of these offices, it is not surprising that they are mainly to be found in the larger settlements within rural areas. Finally, tourism can be a source of local employment. Rapid postwar expansion has been based on growth in real incomes, especially in the 1950s and 1960s, increased leisure time as a result of reductions in working hours and retirement ages, and increased personal mobility (Patmore, 1983). While much tourism – both domestic and foreign – is urban based (especially London), rural areas have also shared in the boom. Remoter rural areas in Scotland, Wales and the North and West of England, in particular, have been the focus of such countryside-based tourism and recreation. This has brought some employment to these areas, and indeed, many small towns and villages in the Lake District and North Wales are dominated by the tourist industry. However, such employment has limitations, tending to be seasonal and low waged, although the structure of the industry offers scope for small-scale capital accumulation and firm formation by local entrepreneurs. Tourism also brings wider social conflicts: the growth of holiday and second homes causes difficulties for low-waged locals seeking to buy houses (see Chapter 4.5.1), while the requirements of tourism may not coincide with those of agriculture or rural manufacturing. Tourists may seek access to the countryside while farmers may wish to deny this, and tourists may seek preservation of the landscape while industrialists seek to exploit it (see Chapter 4.7).

4.3.3 State policies for non-agricultural rural development

State policies have been ambivalent with respect to rural industrialization. Concern over rural land losses in the 1930s, followed by the Scott Committee Report in 1942 (recommending that agriculture be given priority in all land-use conflicts in the countryside), led to an essentially negative approach to rural industrialization. This was enshrined in the 1947 Town and Country Planning Act (see p. 117). Industrial development generally received little encouragement and, at best, was directed towards the upper levels of the settlement hierarchy. Industrial estates were developed on the edges of towns, but planning permission was rarely granted for industrial projects in villages or the open countryside (Shaw and Williams, 1981). This approach was consistent with the requirements of middle-class newcomers that rural areas serve mainly as a focus for consumption. It was also favoured by farmers who, at least in the immediate postwar years of tight labour markets, did not wish to see higher factory wages undermining their own secure local supplies of cheap labour (Newby, 1979). Interestingly, in Cornwall at least, local industrial capital also seems to have been antagonistic to further large-scale industrial growth in the county, fearing the effects on local wages of external branch plants (Massey, 1983b). There are parallels here with the attitudes of the NCB in opposing industrial development on the coalfields up to 1958.

Not all rural areas were the focus of middle-class consumption. Many remoter regions remained residual to both production and consumption requirements (except tourism). By the late 1940s there were signs of rising and persistent unemployment in some rural areas, notably in Scotland and Wales. In the early 1950s Scotland acquired Assisted Area status, which was a significant break with the early emphasis of regional policy on the coalfields. Regional policy has been discussed earlier (see Table 2.3), and here it is sufficient to note that, by 1979, Assisted Area status had been granted to rural areas in Scotland and Wales, and to most rural areas in the North and the far Southwest of England (see Figure 2.2). In Northern Ireland the Local Enterprise Development Unit was supposed to give priority to rural areas such as Strabane, which had over 30 percent unemployment by 1983 (Bull, 1984). At the same time there were signs that rural local authorities in the UK were changing their attitudes to rural industrialization in the face of growing unemployment. Local authorities undertook a range of local economic initiatives, either independently or in cooperation with agencies such as the Development Commission, to encourage industrial growth in rural areas. Finally, in response to the emergence of a rural dimension to the UK's postwar economic crises, a number of specifically rural agencies have been established by the State to promote local development.

The three agencies primarily involved with rural development are the Highlands and Islands Development Board, Mid-Wales Development and the Development Commission (with its linked body – the Council for Small Industries in Rural Areas (CoSIRA)). The zones in which these agencies operate are shown in Figure 4.4

The Development Commission is the oldest of these agencies, having been established in 1909 to improve the economic and social structure of rural areas. In the postwar period its activities have evolved so as to reflect changes both in social realities and in the ideology of development. Initially it sought to promote the revival of rural crafts through the Rural Industries Bureau, which reinforced the romanticized view of rural areas as unsuitable for modern industrial production. By the mid-1960s this strategy had been abandoned and CoSIRA was set up in 1968 to help small firms (employing less than 20) in small towns (see Tricker and Martin, 1984). Its role is primarily to provide business advice and information, but it is also a 'lender of the last resort'. By 1984 it had some £19 million on loan (Williams, 1984b), small beer in comparison to expenditure on regional and urban programmes. In addition, the Development Commission uses about 40 percent of its own expenditure for constructing advance factories in England (its activities in Wales and Scotland having been taken over by the Welsh and Scottish Development Agencies; see p. 102–3). Most of its premises are located in small towns, thereby exhibiting the same preference as the other rural agencies for spatially concentrated investment. However, in partnership with local

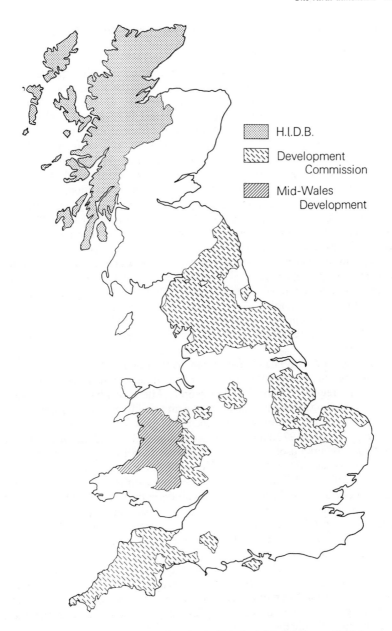

Figure 4.4   Rural development agencies in Britain (after Williams, 1984a).

authorities, it has built small workshops in remoter areas and, since 1982, grants have been made available for converting existing buildings in the countryside to economic uses. Some 930 workshops and factories were completed between 1974 and 1983–1984, providing 2 million square feet of floorspace (Williams, 1984b). Nevertheless, given the limited budget at its disposal (about £19 million in 1984), it has been forced to concentrate investment in the areas with the highest incidence of unemployment. At first these priority areas were designated Special Investment Areas but since 1984 they have been replaced by the less extensive Rural Development Areas. Finally, in keeping with the Thatcherite emphasis on voluntarism, more attention has been given recently to the potential role of rural community councils in encouraging self-help in rural employment creation.

The newest of the three agencies is Mid-Wales Development, established in 1977, although it replaced the earlier Development Board for Rural Wales. It has usually spent about 46–60 percent of its budget on manufacturing and service industries (Williams, 1984a), and has been committed to the development of Newtown as a major growth centre. In common with the other agencies, its apparent neglect of remoter areas has been criticized, although given a limited budget (£10 million in 1984) and faced with cuts in public expenditure, it is possible to sympathize with its desire to achieve economies of scale in investment. As with the other agencies, Mid-Wales Development is dependent on central government funding so its scope for action is ultimately circumscribed.

The Highlands and Islands Development Board (HIDB) was established in 1965 to promote an overall strategy of regional development in the North of Scotland, a region of some 340,000 people. The Board has a wide range of powers including the right to acquire land and buildings so as to promote new economic ventures, and provision of loans and grants; it also offers advice and training. Between 1973 and 1982 it spent some £159 million on grants and loans for economic projects and the largest share of this – £44 million – was spent on tourism, followed by fisheries with £37 million and manufacturing with £14 million (Williams, 1984a). The Board initially favoured a growth area strategy based on Fort William, Inverness and Caithness. These received a large part of the Board's investments in housing and factories, while an additional 27 rural development points were considered suitable for economic growth. Some large-scale, capital-intensive projects were also promoted as propulsive local industries. More recently, in line with government emphasis on voluntarism, the HIDB has also been more active in encouraging community employment initiatives. For example, by 1983 it had provided initial funding for 14 community cooperatives creating jobs for 40 full-time and 150 part-time employees in horticulture, fisheries, manufacturing and other projects (Williams, 1984b).

According to its own estimates, the HIDB created 16,362 jobs between 1973 and 1982, with 5698 of these surviving into 1982 (Williams, 1984b). Population losses have been stemmed and incomes have started to catch up with the national mean, although this is partly due to North Sea oil developments. However, the growth centre strategy has been criticized for neglecting more rural areas; the critique was given additional force by the recent closure of two prestige projects, the Fort William pulp mill and the Invergordon aluminium smelter. Now more attention is being directed to remoter rural areas in order to encourage indigenous industrial potential. Nevertheless, the Board's powers and financial resources are too limited, given the scale of the problems faced, for it is trying to stem rural depopulation and ameliorate rural poverty in an area with exceptional difficulties. It has sought to tackle these problems by creating employment in tourism, fisheries and manufacturing projects. However, it has not been able to tackle a fundamental requirement – the need for agricultural reform, especially in the crofting areas. Many large estates in the Highlands are economically underutilized as they are primarily seen as a focus for individual consumption by their owners. Economic development requires that these should be broken up and brought into production, but the strength of the landowners is such that they have successfully resisted all attempts by the HIDB to gain 'last resort' powers of compulsory purchase.

This review of rural economic initiatives is hardly comprehensive and to it must be added both EC and local authority ventures. The EC provides some additional support to agriculture and other economic initiatives in what it terms areas with 'less-favoured' status. On the grounds of soil infertility, low economic potential and low or dwindling population, some 18.7 million acres, or 42 percent of the agricultural land in the UK, is thus classified, mainly in Wales, Scotland, Northern England and Northern Ireland. In addition, since 1982 the EC has provided 40 percent of the finance for a special £20 million five-year Integrated Development Programme for the Western Isles. Rural councils have also developed a range of local policy initiatives, including financial assistance to new firms, provision of sites and premises, subsidies for building conversions and infrastructure provision and, especially important in Scotland, fostering community businesses (Tricker and Bozeat, 1983).

Northern Ireland has received separate treatment. The Industrial Development Organization has had primary responsibility for promoting industrial growth points. As a reaction to growing unemployment in rural areas, the Local Enterprise Development Unit was established in 1971, empowered to aid small manufacturing businesses in rural areas in the province. By 1983 some 1500 projects had received assistance (Bull, 1984) but investment has mainly been channelled to larger settlements (Busteed, 1976) and, since the late 1970s recession, to Belfast.

All these measures try, in some small way, to modify the social consequences, and influence the pattern, of restructuring in the UK. Their efforts may make some significant local contributions to job creation but their budgets are small and they are likely to remain marginal in comparison to the need for employment creation. More important may be their largely unintentional effects on class composition and social relationships in rural areas.

4.4   Population and social polarization in rural areas

Rural areas serve the individual consumption needs of three distinctive groups: those who work in the cities but live in the countryside, those who worked in the cities but have retired to the countryside, and those who use the countryside occasionally for recreational or tourist purposes. Changes in the nature of, and the balance between, production and consumption have brought about modifications in rural social structure and in aggregate population changes.

The population of the countryside had been in long slow decline after 1861 and there were concerns about the social consequences of rural population losses in the interwar years. However, in the postwar period these trends were reversed and, from 1951, the population of rural areas, in aggregate, increased (Lawton, 1973). A number of more accessible rural areas had experienced population gains since the 1920s with the extension of commuting, but 1951 marked the end of nearly a century of aggregate decline. The geographical pattern of change, however, continued to be diverse and many rural areas, especially in remoter regions, still lost population throughout the 1950s and 1960s. In the 1970s rural population gains were further accentuated and became more geographically widespread, incorporating most counties.

The overall position is summarized in Table 4.3, which shows the clear emergence of the remoter, largely rural districts as the most rapidly growing areas in the UK, outstripping even the more accessible rural areas in the Southeast. This is confirmed by Champion's (1981) cluster analysis of population changes at the district level (Figure 4.5). Whereas in the 1960s there were massive population gains in the rural growth areas of the Southeast and eastern England, by the 1970s there were large gains of 7–13 percent throughout rural Britain, including most of Scotland and Wales. Two remoter Scottish districts – Badenoch and Strathspey, and Ross and Cromarty – actually featured among the ten fastest growing areas in the UK in the 1970s.

Population changes and migration have been accompanied by major social changes in the countryside. In many areas, the net migration flows can be broken down into the movements of two very different social groups. Out-migration continues as a result of agricultural decline while the limited

Table 4.3 Population change in England and Wales, 1961–1981

	Percentage change	
	1961–1971	1971–1981
England and Wales (all districts)	5.7	0.5
Resorts and seaside districts	12.2	4.9
Mixed urban-rural and more accessible rural areas:		
Outside the Southeast	21.9	8.8
Inside the Southeast	22.1	6.7
Remoter, largely rural districts	9.7	10.3

Source: Office of Population Censuses and Surveys.

number and restricted range of jobs available in manufacturing and services meant that school-leavers and young adults have found it difficult to fulfil employment aspirations locally. For example, a study in Norfolk showed that only 18 percent considered that the type of job they preferred could be found within reasonable travelling distance of home (Drudy and Wallace, 1971). In addition, increased dominance of individual over collective consumption (see Chapter 4.5) has meant that rural areas lack many of the services, shops and recreational facilities (such as cinemas and clubs) that young people require; lacking private transport, they also have poor access to these in nearby towns and cities (Phillips and Williams, 1984b).

The counterflow of in-migrants involves very different social groups; in crude terms, the old are replacing the young and the middle class are replacing the working class, so that rural gentrification and senescence are occurring. The largest group of incomers are probably the commuters and, although commuting is by no means a postwar phenomenon, it has been considerably extended in recent years, facilitated by improvements in private transport. Spence et al. (1982) estimated that only 4 percent of the British population in 1971 lived in local authorities so remote that these did not send at least some commuters to the major urban areas. Some newcomers may be reluctant commuters, constrained by the lack of suitably priced housing in urban areas; this applies particularly to manual workers in the Southeast (Pahl, 1975). For others, notably the middle class, the urban to rural move is tied to lifestyle developments whereby house and garden and surrounding physical environment gain paramount importance.

Rural areas have also attracted retirement migrants. There is a growing proportion of the elderly in the UK (16 percent over pensionable age in 1981) and a significant number of these – especially among the middle class and skilled working class – are house owners and may have favourable pension arrangements. These provide the conditions for post-retirement migration or,

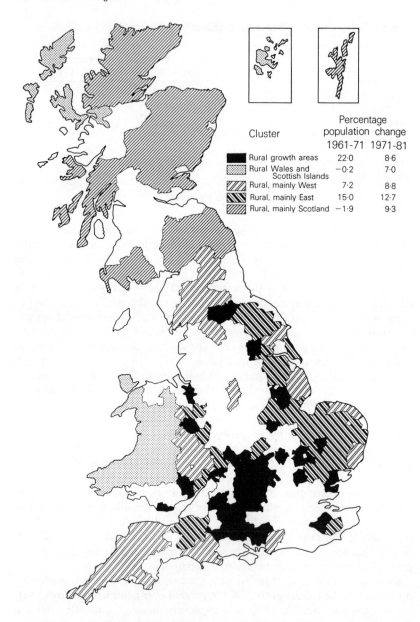

Cluster	Percentage population change	
	1961-71	1971-81
■ Rural growth areas	22·0	8·6
▨ Rural Wales and Scottish Islands	−0·2	7·0
▨ Rural, mainly West	7·2	8·8
▨ Rural, mainly East	15·0	12·7
▨ Rural, mainly Scotland	−1·9	9·3

Figure 4.5   Rural population changes, 1961–1981 (after Champion, 1981).

in response to redundancies, early-retirement migration. The two main retirement migration flows are to coastal areas and to small inland towns, especially in the South and West (Law and Warnes, 1976). Again, this is a group opting for a lifestyle that maximizes individual consumption, especially with respect to the quality of housing and physical environment available in some rural areas. These moves are undertaken despite the absence of adequate collective consumption facilities in recipient areas, evident, for example, in chronic shortages of health care facilities in many coastal retirement areas or in poor public transport facilities in many country towns. There are also financial advantages for migrants leaving the Southeast, given lower house prices in other regions. In this way owner-occupiers can secure substantial capital gains, which is one means of supplementing pensions.

Migration does bring about a change in rural social structures but, arguably, it intensifies rather than fundamentally alters social class cleavages in many regions. Newby (1980) argues that this occurs in East Anglia where there is a tradition of paternalistic, employee–employer relationships. The cleavage between the new middle class and the local rural working class supplements, but does not replace, this traditional relationship. The farm worker had a subordinate position in the traditional occupational community but was also highly integrated into the local social structure, with status based on skill at work rather than on income or pattern of consumption. In contrast, members of the new middle class are far more likely to make judgements on the basis of conspicuous consumption. On occasion, this actually brings the farmer and the farm worker closer together for both prefer the old scales of social status but, usually, especially in the struggle for local political power, farmers are more likely to be aligned with middle-class newcomers against the local working class.

The basic class structure may not have been fundamentally changed, but the presence of the new middle class does have important implications for the rural working class. There is sharp income polarization (Table 4.4) operating on two dimensions – a divergence between manual and non-manual workers and between men and women. However, all manual groups in rural areas have incomes below the equivalent UK average while the reverse is true for non-manual groups. This suggests that the better-off middle class may choose to live in rural areas while the worse-off working class are constrained to live there. With above-average (urban) wages, the middle class are in a strong position to outbid the rural working class in local housing markets and they are also likely to influence the balance between individual and collective consumption. Hence, Newby (1980) describes the position of the rural working class as '... a residual population ... left stranded in the countryside' (p. 268).

Table 4.4   Income polarization in rural areas

| | £ average gross weekly earnings | |
	Rural areas	UK
Full-time male		
Non-manual	215.2	163.1
Manual	117.2	121.9
Full-time female		
Non-manual	104.1	96.7
Manual	66.3	74.5
Part-time female		
Non-manual	48.7	43.5
Manual	21.7	33.0

Source: Bradley (1984).

4.5   Housing, transport and consumption in rural areas

The forms of individual and collective consumption in rural areas have been affected by a number of factors. Prime among these are changes in social structure and income polarization, which have influenced levels of both individual and aggregate local needs and resources. This is particularly important in rural areas because, unlike cities – where social polarization also exists (see Chapter 3.4.2) – the middle class and the working class, the rich and the poor, live almost side by side. They live in the same villages, or at least the same parishes, and therefore potentially share the same shops, personal services, welfare services and transport facilities. Potential conflicts are probably most acute over public transport and housing, for here the interests of the two groups impinge directly on each other. The conflicts are partly acted out in economic terms with the middle class outbidding locals for housing and failing to support bus services, but they also have a political dimension. Debates over subsidizing public bus services or financing new local authority estates are recurrent items on the agendas of most rural councils (Newby, 1980). Furthermore, the conflicts are more acute because they occur against a background of largely negative local authority planning that permits little new development.

4.5.1   Rural housing

National housing policies have been drafted mostly to meet the needs of urban areas. For example, there has been a consistent failure to make adequate allowance in the price yardsticks devised by central government for council house building for the higher construction costs of rural areas (Dunn et al.,

1981). The Thatcher government failed to appreciate the rural consequences of the 1980 Housing Act provisions on council house sales (Phillips and Williams, 1984a). Since the mid-1960s there has also been an emphasis on area-based approaches to housing policy but General Improvement Areas and Housing Action Areas were developed as responses to specifically urban problems (see Chapter 3.3). Blanket approaches to areas of housing with similar physical deficiencies had some logic in inner-city locations but were clearly inappropriate to rural areas.

Rural areas do have a high incidence of poor-quality housing, however; the 1981 English Housing Condition Survey showed that, compared to the national mean, rural areas had 10 percent more unfit dwellings and their repair costs were 49 percent higher. The poor-quality housing in rural areas tends to be dispersed and there are also variations within individual areas; while standards are quite good in more accessible, commuter zones, there tends to be a stock of older and potentially deficient dwellings in remoter districts. These problems have been exacerbated by recent cutbacks in housing expenditure (see Chapter 1.4.1); for example, a survey of 63 predominantly rural districts in England and Wales showed that completions fell from about 27,000 in the mid-1970s to just over 16,000 in 1981 (Rural Voice, 1982).

The key to interpreting housing issues lies in the relationships within and between tenures. Given the role of many rural areas as locales for individual consumption, there has been a massive increase in owner-occupation in the postwar years. This is partly accounted for by national expansion of this tenure but owner-occupation levels in rural areas are well above those in urban areas. (Dunn et al., 1981). This is consistent with a shift to home-based recreation and leisure and the desire, therefore, to maximize a household's private space (Kemeny, 1980). In addition, home ownership confers financial advantages but many white-collar and better-paid manual workers wishing to buy their own homes have been constrained to move to more rural areas to find suitably priced dwellings. Rural dwellings are also used for tourism or recreation, in other words as second or holiday homes. There are now about 150,000 second homes in Britain (Sarre, 1981). Although equivalent to only 1 percent of the total dwelling stock of the UK, holiday homes are unevenly distributed; in the Lake District the proportion reaches 11 percent (Clark, 1982), while it exceeded 70 percent in some Cornish villages in 1981.

The outcome of these changes is that in many areas – both commuter and tourist zones – there is intense demand in the housing market; this is particularly acute in tourist areas, where planning restrictions often severely limit new additions to the housing stock. The middle class are usually able to outbid the rural working class who, anyway, find it difficult to obtain mortgage finance (see Chapter 3.3 for similar problems faced by the urban working class). It is therefore increasingly difficult for young, manual, working-class families to secure a foothold in the rural owner-occupied housing market and many are forced to move from their villages to acquire a suitable home. The pressures are especially acute in tourist areas, and second homes have been a particular cause for concern. In Wales, this has been linked by the Welsh Nationalist Party to the issue of preserving cultural identity and, in extreme cases, there have been arson attacks on holiday homes. Second homes have also been a major issue in the Lake District; the Lake District National Park Authority as well as Cumbria County Council have sought to use Section 52 of the 1971 Town and Country Planning Act to ensure that planning permission is given for new houses only where these will be occupied by people with local jobs or those who will reside locally. Gwynedd County Council has also sought to restrict second homes by withdrawing rates relief on these. However, central government in the 1980s has strenuously opposed all such ventures in social planning, and has tried to restrict local authorities to narrower, land-use development control responsibilities. The Secretary of State for the Environment, Michael Heseltine, explicitly stated in 1981 that 'Planning is concerned with the manner of the use of land, not the identity or merits of the occupiers' (quoted in Gilg, 1982, p. 37). The initiative for development is being securely anchored in the private sector, concerned above all with profit rather than housing need.

With their partial exclusion from owner-occupation, the rural working class are necessarily reliant on rented dwellings. Private rentals have been in decline nationally (see Chapter 1.4) and the supply in rural areas is, at best, limited. A number of other features also undermine the suitability of private renting as a long-term housing solution for rural families. These include a high proportion of winter lets (as higher rents can be obtained from tourists in the summer), and large numbers of caravans and mobile homes, often in poor condition. There are also an estimated 100,000 agricultural tied cottages and these, too, tend to be of relatively poor quality. Furthermore, until the Rent (Agriculture) Act 1976 there was little security of tenure for occupants and job dismissals usually meant eviction. Of course, some farmers do need to have workers 'on site', especially given the unsociable hours that are required on livestock farms, but tied cottages also constitute an effective means of social control. In summary, then, the private rented sector has only a limited and diminishing role in meeting rural housing need.

Local authority dwellings have a critical role in housing provision for the lower paid, but the proportion of council houses is lower in rural than in urban areas, accounting for only about one-fifth of the stock. The reasons for this can be found in the particular nature of production and consumption in rural areas, as well as local politics. While rural areas served mainly as a focus for agricultural production, local councils were often reluctant to build council houses as this would weaken control over the agricultural labour force

(Newby, 1979). There was also a less visible crisis in the reproduction of labour power in rural than in urban areas, and it was in the latter that the initial pressure for local authority housing occurred, both from working-class movements and from industrial capital. Later, when the requirements of individual consumption became paramount, the new middle class (who frequently had replaced farmers as local councillors) opposed council house building in the smaller villages on conservation grounds. Economies of scale in construction, local government reform and centralization of decision-making in 1974, and cutbacks in government housing expenditure have also encouraged rural councils to concentrate new housing in fewer but larger estates, usually in the main towns (Phillips and Williams, 1982).

Local authority housing provision has therefore been relatively limited in rural areas, particularly at the lower levels of the settlement hierarchy. Therefore, many families have found it difficult to obtain suitable council houses in their home villages and there has been evidence of frustrated demand, and of reluctant centralization of successful applicants in a few towns, as is illustrated by data on housing stock, letting and preferences from a case study of South Hams, Devon (Table 4.5). This has serious implications for the ability of the rural working class to secure a place in rural housing markets and to improve their accessibility to friends, relatives, shops, services and jobs. The position has been exacerbated by public expenditure cuts since the mid-1970s (see Table 1.4) and, in the 1981 survey of rural districts referred to earlier, only 18 percent of housing completions were in the public sector (Rural Voice, 1982).

Decollectivization of housing has been reinforced by the Thatcher government's attempt to recommodify housing by encouraging council house sales under the 1980 Housing Act (see p. 35). This has particularly serious implications for rural authorities, for prior to 1980 the rate of council house sales was already greater in rural than in urban areas, being 4.6 per 1000 in districts with populations over 150,000 compared to 9.4 per 1000 in districts with less than 50,000 (Phillips and Williams, 1984a). Sales have also been greater in the smaller rural settlements, for the eventual resale value of individual council houses in attractive villages is usually higher than for properties in large estates. In passing the 1980 Housing Act, the Thatcher government pushed the normally compliant Conservative rural councils too far too quickly, especially those in attractive tourist regions where there was potential for resale as second homes. Their concerted opposition eventually forced a small concession from the government, in recognition of special social problems in these regions. District councils were allowed to impose restrictive clauses on the resale of houses located in National Parks, Areas of Outstanding Natural Beauty and Designated Rural Areas. In practice public expenditure cutbacks and limitations on the use of capital receipts from sales have restricted the possibilities of repurchasing. Nevertheless, this was the

Table 4.5   Local authority housing in South Hams, Devon, 1979–1981

Settlement classification under the 1981 Settlement Plan	Total local authority housing stock (%)	Completions 1976–1979 (%)	Availability of voids for letting (%)	Area preferences of applicants (%)
Area centres	51.3	80.2	64.8	63.0
Selected local centres	11.0	1.8	9.4	8.7
Non-classified areas	37.7	18.0	25.8	28.3
Total	100.0	100.0	100.0	100.0

Source: Phillips and Williams (1983).

first major sign that the government's privatization plans would, at times, bring them into conflict even with rural Conservative councils.

As part of the government's strategy for greater reliance on voluntarism, resources have been shifted from the public sector to the voluntary housing movement. Initially, the implications of this were felt less in rural than in urban areas, where most housing association activity had been located anyway (see Chapter 3.3). The Housing Corporation has recently encouraged more rural initiatives but there is no evidence that the scope of these can adequately substitute for general cuts in housing expenditure. Two features of voluntary housing provision in rural areas are noteworthy (Richmond, 1985). First, being based on local initiative, development is haphazard and bears little relationship to the spatial incidence of need. Second, there has been increased centralization of control over the voluntary sector, especially since the Housing Corporation became its primary source of external funding after 1964. Under the Thatcher government this has led to what Richmond terms 'residualization of housing association activity'. They are being shifted from their initial dual purpose of providing for general and special needs (including low-cost renting for those on low incomes). Instead, finance increasingly is being channelled either to special 'residual' needs projects (as for the elderly) or to building for sale. This move to recommodify housing provision has been reinforced by the Housing and Building Control Bill 1984, which extends the right to buy to many housing association tenants. Once again these measures were opposed by Tory representatives in the Houses of Commons and House of Lords, and the right to buy was eventually refused to tenants of charitable associations.

4.5.2 Rural transport

Two major features of postwar transport policy have been encouragement of private transport and, within public transport, concentration on principal road and railway routes with, inevitably, an intercity focus. Rural areas have rarely figured in transport debates in terms of their production needs and, instead, the emphasis has been on some subsidization of rural routes on welfare grounds. Rural areas have been especially vulnerable to the consequences of government decision-making as was illustrated by the Beeching programme of railway closures. Private transport in rural areas is also subject to such external decision-making. Distances are greater and petrol costs are often higher, so the overall costs of private motoring can be considerably greater in rural than in urban areas. Changes in vehicle or petrol taxation rates can be particularly sensitive. David Penhaligon, MP for Truro, reacting to the 20p per gallon increase in the March 1981 Budget, said that '... if you really want to harm the economy of rural areas, there is nothing more effective than putting up the price of petrol' (quoted in Gilg, 1982, p. 23).

Such macro-economic changes have a differential impact on social groups living side-by-side in the countryside. Public transport has always been less comprehensive in rural than in urban areas and this partly accounts for higher rural rates of car ownership: the General Household Survey of 1980 showed that 70 percent of households in rural areas compared to 58 percent in Britain as a whole owned at least one car. However, the high level of car ownership has a feedback effect on public transport for they are locked together in a vicious circle. Increased car ownership leads to less use of public transport so that revenue falls, resulting in rising prices and reduced services, which causes further shifts from public to private transport. There were clear differences in changing costs between 1961 and 1980; railway fares increased by a ratio of 7.25, bus fares by 7.9 and costs of running a motor vehicle by only 5.5.

The postwar history of public transport has been one of long, slow decline in services and the disappearance of routes. Change has been most dramatic for railways, and the 1962 Beeching Report proposed closure of 2000 stations and 5000 route miles of track. When the Labour government halted the programme in 1967, most of the cuts had already been implemented (Phillips and Williams, 1984b, pp. 142–145). However, the difference between Labour and Conservative policies is more a matter of rhetoric than of reality and neither has really challenged the supremacy of private transport. Nevertheless, public expenditure cuts and privatization proposals in the 1980s may lead to further cuts in rural services and this has already been proposed in the 1982 Serpell Report. Reductions in bus services have been less dramatic but just as real; for example, between 1965 and 1975 the number of country buses remained constant but the number of passenger journeys fell by about 30 percent, thereby encouraging bus companies to reduce services further. As a result, many villages have no bus service or, at best, one or two buses each day. In rural Wales, for example, most parishes do not have suitable daily services for taking residents to and from work (Nutley, 1980). Government response in the 1980s has been twofold: experimentation in privatizing bus services and voluntarism; for example, the Transport Act 1980 eased taxation rules on car-sharing schemes for journeys to work.

With the decline in bus and rail services, the onus in securing adequate transport has shifted to the individual. Car ownership, however, is dependent on income and occupation (Figure 4.6): in 1983 only 7 percent of self-employed household heads had no car compared to 58 percent of unemployed household heads. Given the polarization of incomes in rural areas, the disparity may be even more acute, especially when ownership of two or more vehicles is considered. The 'transport poor' (Wibberly, 1978) are not just defined by incomes, however. Most households own only one car and, therefore, to the list of transport poor should be added most women, children and the elderly. For a variety of social and physical reasons, they do not normally have access to a car and must rely on often inadequate, public transport.

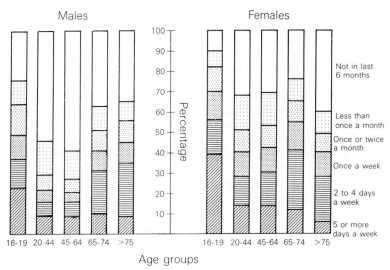

Figure 4.6 Social aspects of car-ownership levels and public transport usage (Central Statistical Office, 1985).

4.6   Social class, accessibility and rural welfare

Service provision, in terms of both shops and private services and essential collective services such as health and education, is an important constraint on the quality of life. Again it is important to stress that the social structure of different types of rural areas influences access to services, not least because social classes living in close physical proximity have different and competing need in terms of individual and collective consumption.

The organization of the Welfare State in particular areas is largely determined by national policies (see Chapter 1.4) but there are some distinguishing features in rural areas. The middle-class voters and councillors, who often dominate rural councils, tend to be more reluctant than their urban counterparts to supplement central Exchequer expenditure on public services with local rates; for example, in England in 1984–1985 local rate-borne expenditure was about 10 percent higher in metropolitan than in non-metropolitan areas. Furthermore, in the recent conflicts between local and central government over public expenditure, rate capping (under the Rates Act 1984) has involved authorities in 'urban' rather than rural areas (Jones and Stewart, 1983). With continued centralization of financial control these differences may be lessened, but the historic differences in accumulated investments in school, community and cultural facilities will only slowly be eroded.

Another important element of rural service provision is centralization. Dispersed rural populations necessarily require an element of selectivity in service provision. In practice, this has meant centralization, a tendency reinforced by the population decline in many rural areas before the 1970s. Recently there have been signs that rural authorities are resisting further cuts in public services. Pressure was put on the Post Office to withdraw threatened massive closures of sub-post offices and on British Telecom to consult with local councils before withdrawing public telephone boxes. But the overall rundown of public services continues. The process has been accentuated in some rural areas by a tendency for middle-class newcomers to use private health and education services, which reduces effective demand (if not need) for local State provision. Pressures to reduce costs also led to greater concentration for there are thought to be substantial economies of scale in providing many services. Increased private personal mobility for the majority of households has been a prerequisite for these locational shifts but, by the same token, increased burdens have fallen on those reliant on public transport. Newby (1980) poignantly summarizes the plight of the disadvantaged:

> The poor and the elderly have not 'chosen' to live in their villages in any meaningful sense; they have been stranded there by three decades of rural social change and by growing public indifference to their plight. They lack the resources

to convert their needs into demands, yet it is to demand rather than need that most rural public services respond. (p. 276)

Two such public services – health and education – are considered in more detail. Education is one of the most sensitive services, not least because a primary school is often considered an essential ingredient of a thriving community. Village schools have been under pressure from two sources. First, there are economies of scale in provision. For primary schools, costs per capita fall very sharply with increased size until about 50 to 60 pupils are reached, but thereafter level off. Second, the potential number of enrolments for village schools has fallen even in some villages where overall population levels may have increased, because of changes in local social structure. Retirement migrants have no children of school age and middle-class commuters may prefer to send their children to private schools. As a result, school rolls in many villages have fallen, or have continued to remain, below critical cost thresholds for economic viability. Education usually accounts for about 60–70 percent of most counties' expenditure, so it is schools that have often borne the brunt of public expenditure cuts. A series of case studies document school closures in rural areas in the postwar period; for example, Moseley (1979) found that some 80 primary schools had been closed between 1951 and 1971 in Norfolk. More recently, with further rounds of public expenditure cuts, Rural Voice (1982) reports that whereas, nationally, there had been 25 school closures in 1979, this number had risen to 79 by 1981. Provision of non-statutory pre-school facilities has been even poorer in rural areas.

Centralization has also characterized the health service. The NHS hospital policy has involved formalization of a hierarchy of provision, linked with closure of the bottom – and the main rural – tier of cottage hospitals (see p. 47). Public opposition halted the programme in the 1970s and community hospitals are now favoured, albeit with a limited range of (increasingly expensive) capital equipment (Phillips, 1981). While economies of scale and increased reliance on private transport have contributed to concentration, privatization of medical care has added to inequality of provision. Access to private medicine is obviously socially inequitable but there are also spatial inequalities in the distribution of facilities – hardly surprising as new private hospitals cost about £100,000 per bed to build. While all four of the Thames Health Areas had more than 20 private hospital beds per 100,000 of population in the early 1980s, the levels in the more rural Southwest and East Anglia regions were 12.2 and 10.9 respectively (Mohan, 1984b).

It is not just hospitals that have been subject to centralization. Primary health care provision has been characterized by the concentration of doctors into group practices and health centres (see pp. 46–8). Such arrangements may be effective in urban areas but in rural areas they imply that more villages will become devoid of even the simplest health provision. A study of over 200 small settlements (populations less than 500) in the mid-1970s showed that 87 percent had no doctor's surgery and none had a dentist or optician (Leschinsky, 1977). In both health and education services, the benefits and costs of reorganization fall unevenly on social classes, gender and age groups.

To some extent similar centralization tendencies occur in commercial services, again facilitated by increased personal mobility. Bulk purchasing and low labour costs have allowed supermarkets and hypermarkets to undercut considerably the prices in village shops. The ability of most households to benefit from more centralized retailing depends on a number of conditions: car ownership provides access, deep freezes permit occasional bulk purchasing trips, and changes in work practices (with few employees having to work at weekends) permit family shopping outings on Saturdays to nearby towns. However, working-class access to such centralized services is far inferior to that enjoyed by the more mobile middle class.

As a result, village services have been caught in the familiar vicious circle of reduced demand, higher costs, rising relative prices and further falls in demand. Many rural areas have lost their shops, Post Offices and other services; for example, a 1979 survey in England and Wales showed that 800,000 people lived in parishes without a sub-post office, 700,000 had no food shop and 250,000 had no basic services whatsoever. In remoter areas in Scotland the numbers of parishes with shops and Post Offices fell by 50 percent between 1960 and 1980 (MacKay and Laing, 1982). Where some provision survives, it is likely to be a general store concentrating on basic foodstuffs; the range of goods available is usually limited while prices are often higher than in nearby towns. Even mobile services – for long the standby of many villages – have been in decline. In Somerset the proportion of parishes with more than six tradespeople making regular deliveries fell from 93 to 30 percent between 1950 and 1980 (Moseley and Packman, 1984). Some mobile services, such as laundry deliveries and visiting cinemas, have virtually disappeared.

There has been no serious attempt in the UK to subsidize services provision despite the fact that this constitutes an important component of the quality of rural life. Instead, self-help is often stressed by central government as an alternative strategy. There are notable examples, such as parish councils running pubs and community volunteers staffing village shops, buses and even schools. These can be of immense value to individual households. However, there is a limit to voluntarism and it is unlikely to replace systematically the range of services provided by either the public or the private sector. Similarly, the 'self-service economy' (Gershuny and Miles, 1983) in which manufactured household goods replace service outlets offers only limited relief to rural residents. Access to such manufactured goods is conditioned by income anyway (see Chapter 1.4) but, moreover, there is no evidence that they can replace food shops and Post Offices, let alone education, health or social services.

By and large it is the same social groups and the same types of areas that suffer from poor access to jobs and to different services. Together they amount to a vicious circle of multiple deprivation, and herein lies one of the great paradoxes of rural areas. It is remoter areas that usually show up worst in most analyses of multiple deprivation (see Knox and Cottam, 1981, on Scotland and Hoare, 1982, on Northern Ireland), but severely deprived households also exist in the most accessible areas, even those characterized essentially as loci of middle-class individual consumption. They are deprived because of their place in the economic and social order; living in the accessible countryside does not necessarily ameliorate this. Indeed the very presence of the new middle class with their individualistic consumption patterns and privatized lifestyles may be one contributory factor in the withdrawal of collective services that adds to working-class deprivation.

4.7 Whose countryside?: rural politics

Two major features of rural politics in the postwar period are largely unerring support for the Conservative Party and the importance of single-issue politics, especially in relation to the environment. This is in marked contrast to the more overtly class-based local politics of urban areas.

In most postwar elections the rural counties have voted solidly against Labour and for the Conservatives (or Unionists) so that the phrase 'shire MPs' has become a synonym for Tory representatives in the House of Commons. Conservatives have also polled well in most rural local authority elections, and in their 1977 landslide victory in the county council elections in England and Wales, for example, they secured overall control in 36 of the 47 non-metropolitan counties, with Labour retaining absolute majorities only in Durham, Mid Glamorgan and West Glamorgan which, anyway, had significant industrial bases.

The two major exceptions to Tory dominance are the first and last major elections to be held in the period covered by this book. The 1945 General Election result saw a startling nationwide electoral shift to Labour, which even carried along rural constituencies in an emotional response to the interwar industrial and agricultural depressions. This was short-lived and was followed by over 30 years of relatively constant rural support for Conservatism, broken only by 'residual' rural Liberal support in such regions as the Southwest and Mid Wales. Only since the Thatcher governments took power has this solid voting block started to weaken, particularly with the rise of the Liberal–SDP Alliance, a special threat to Conservatives in rural areas.

This reached a new high point in the May 1985 county council elections which, arguably, saw a redrawing of the rural electoral map. After these elections in the non-metropolitan counties in England and Wales, the Conservatives held an absolute majority in only nine areas, the same number as Labour; the Alliance had a clear majority in one county while, as a result of their overall net gains totalling over 120 seats, some 26 other counties were politically 'hung' (Figure 4.7). In part, the government was reaping a return on national issues but there was also a distinctive rural backlash, and Alliance gains were greater in the rural South than the rural North. This backlash must be seen in the context of public expenditure plans having led to proposals for such unpopular measures as charging for school buses.

Non-party politics have also been prominent in rural areas. This had always been evident at the local level and, for example, in district councils with populations below 50,000 (predominantly very rural), only 27 percent of councillors in England and Wales belonged to the Labour and Conservative Parties in 1982. The remainder were Liberals, SDP, ratepayers and independents, although there is an assumption that the latter two categories are often 'conservative' if not, 'Conservative' in inclination. Perhaps more important has been the prominence of single-issue politics and the dramatic rise in the number of pressure groups organized around these, either on a permanent basis – for example the Ramblers' Association – or on an *ad hoc* basis in reaction to local developments. Examples of the latter type include groups opposed to proposed sites for London's third airport, or the unholy alliance of rural conservative environmental groups and those in 'urban' deep-mining areas against proposed open-cast coal-mining schemes.

In a sense, the growth of pressure groups has been a function of the expansion of State interference in the countryside (Leat, 1981). Whereas 100 years ago individuals could dispose of land as they wished, unchallenged by public opinion, in the 20th century individual property rights have been undermined by the State, especially through the planning system. This, in turn, has been a focus for amenity and conservation group pressure. Planners have been relatively receptive to pressure groups if only because the final detailed forms of developments are open to negotiation, without fundamentally challenging the authority of the planners as ultimate decision-makers. The growth of environmental groups is impressive. Prior to 1965 no more than 12 such nationally based groups had been formed in any decade but 23 were established between 1966 and 1975 (Lowe and Goyder, 1983). On a broader basis, the Civic Trust Register reveals the existence of some 1135 local and national amenity and civic societies in the late 1970s (Leat, 1981). Their role in local politics has increased throughout the postwar period, but this was formalized and encouraged in particular by the 1969 Skeffington Report on public participation.

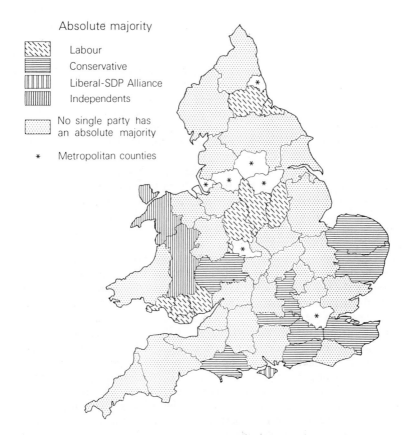

Figure 4.7   County council election results in England and Wales, May 1985.

Who do the pressure groups really represent? Amenity groups have a very large membership, estimated at some two million (although a half of these are in one organization, the National Trust) but Lowe and Goyder (1983) have shown that there is a distinctive class bias in both membership and leadership. While managerial and professional groups constitute 14 percent of the total population of England and Wales, they represent 25 percent of the membership of the Royal Society for the Protection of Birds and 72 percent of the National Trust's members. The leadership of such groups is overwhelmingly drawn from the middle class, especially the upper-middle class. At local level it is often the new middle class who provide the leadership of these groups. Indeed, conservation issues can be seen as central to the preservation of lifestyles based on individual consumption – that is, protecting the immediate environs of the home and the surrounding countryside.

The question of leadership leads to consideration of which class interests are represented by pressure groups – especially given the close proximity in which the middle and working classes live in rural areas. Available evidence is inconclusive but suggestive: studies in Norfolk (Newby, 1979), Suffolk (Buller and Lowe, 1982) and Surrey (Connell, 1978) have all shown that amenity groups' activities have favoured the needs of the new middle class while acting against those of the working class for cheaper housing and more jobs. In the Scottish Highlands a rather different situation exists for here the powers of landowners have been less effectively challenged by middle-class amenity groups. It is significant that, early in the postwar period, the five National Parks proposed for Scotland by the Ramsay Committee were never implemented, unlike their English and Welsh equivalents. This was due to strong resistance by the landowners, worried by the spectre of land nationalization, and to the relative weakness of local amenity groups. There was evidence also of some concern about the need to permit economic development in the Highlands in order to provide jobs so as to stem depopulation (Shucksmith and Lloyd, 1983). However, despite the absence of National Parks designations and vociferous middle-class groups, development in many parts of the Highlands has been frozen by the owners of large estates themselves (see p. 175) in order to preserve their private recreational interests.

Not all local issue politics have been resolved to the detriment of the rural working class. Many rural working-class people support the aims of the conservation lobby (Lowe and Goyder, 1983), while many pressure groups have fought for the retention of vital services such as village schools or Post Offices. But it is difficult not to believe that, by and large, it is the interests of the new middle class that have been better served by these movements.

FIVE

Conclusions:
Retrospect and Prospect

In the postwar era the UK has lost an empire and experienced continuous relative decline in its role in the international political and economic order. Manufacturing has lost its competitiveness in the face of pressures from developed countries, such as Japan and West Germany, and from newly industrialized countries such as Taiwan and Korea: by 1983 there was even a net deficit on trade in manufactured goods. The new role of the UK economy is less easily analysed. While the UK remains an important centre for international finance and banking, more indicative of its new status in the international division of labour is the growth of short-term labour emigration (especially to the Middle East and West Germany) and the fact that tourism is now the largest growth industry. These changes have implications for the economy in aggregate and for specific localities within the UK. They are important not just in terms of shifting patterns of employment but also in terms of the changes in class composition which have been an integral part of economic change; these have had differential impacts on regions and individual localities within them. The recurrent economic difficulties lie at the root of a series of modernization policies, especially in the 1960s and, in recognition of the failure of these, massive public expenditure cuts from the mid-1970s. The differential spatial effects of these changes are illustrated by the way in which economic restructuring in the 1950s and 1960s brought about some regional convergence in manufacturing, to be followed in the 1970s by new spatial inequalities as industry collapsed in the conurbations.

It is within this context that the links between production and consumption have been viewed. Postwar economic changes have led to some income convergence in the UK, although wealth differentials remain considerable. However, with the steady growth of unemployment over the past two decades, a more profound division has reasserted itself – between those in paid employment and the unemployed. It is those with no income, or a very low income, who have least access to private transport (and therefore reduced personal mobility), to owner-occupied housing (and the capital gains this can offer) and to a range of consumer durables such as videos and dishwashers (not to mention second homes or yachts). Many of these seem to be essential ingredients in the evolution of more privatized, home-based patterns of consumption and lifestyles. There is evidence that even the Welfare State, which was designed to help construct a more egalitarian and caring society, has failed to ameliorate these inequalities. Despite apparent adherence to principles of universal and equal access to education and health care facilities, there have been considerable social and spatial inequalities in their provision. Cuts in public expenditure since the 1970s have exaggerated these differences, for emphasis is being shifted to private sector provision (based on the ability to pay) and to fragmented provision through voluntarism.

The UK in the 1980s is a divided society and this division can be observed on a variety of dimensions. First and foremost, it is socially divided between the 'haves' and 'have-nots' and this is a fundamental reflection of class position and of the type of job held, if any. Perhaps the single most depressing feature of the postwar UK has been the seemingly inexorable rise of unemployment, which has been socially selective by race, gender, age and social class. Those who have suffered most have been blacks, males, school-leavers and the over-50s, and semi- and unskilled workers. These are also the groups who have suffered most from long-term unemployment which has been so tragic for individuals and so divisive for society. The UK is now a long way from the more egalitarian society that a war-weary populace had voted for in the form of the 1945 Labour government. Owner-occupation, foreign holidays, cars, television sets and membership of health and leisure clubs may have become accessible to most members of the middle class and some of the working class, but they remain painfully elusive for many: single-parent families, black and white unemployed youngsters, redundant manual workers and low-paid service employees, to name only the most obvious.

The picture is not entirely gloomy. Access to education and health services has improved dramatically; local authority housing is more widely available than in 1945 (although now in decline); some aspects of sexual and racial discrimination have been made illegal; and use of the environment is more carefully regulated (if at a social cost). Most social groups have benefited from these and other changes in the Welfare State since 1945. There have also been specific gains for women. Greater participation in waged labour offers more independence while the proliferation of consumer durables (such as automatic washing machines and dishwashers) has taken the sheer drudgery out of many domestic tasks. However, this is not to say that women have achieved economic and social equality. Their jobs are often undergraded and underpaid in comparison to those of men; there is more sharing but hardly an equal division of domestic labour; and it is women who usually suffer from mobility deprivation in single-car households. Their circumstances are changing, as is popularly symbolized by the Greenham Common women's opposition to cruise missiles, but barriers to equality of opportunity are still considerable in workplaces, the home and the community. Equally, it is important to remember that while increased participation in waged work has provided a degree of emancipation for many women, the specific ways in which most women, especially married women, were incorporated into waged labour had important broader effects – for example, in providing a labour reserve that was vital in industrial and class restructuring, in reproducing UK society as an unequal – though rather differently unequal – society.

Many of these divisions in UK society have distinctive spatial dimensions. At the regional level, there has been a narrowing of lifestyle differences between the North and the South, and some convergence of economic structures. But standards of living are, on most indicators, consistently higher in the Southeast than in the rest of the country, and unemployment patterns in the 1980s bear an all-too-familiar resemblance to those of the 1930s, in both absolute levels and regional distribution. There are also differences at the urban level, with cities such as Belfast, Glasgow and Liverpool being considered among the most deprived areas in Western Europe. Within cities, the great gulf is between inner and outer areas, sharply distinguished by their job prospects and consumption patterns. It is the suburbs and commuter villages, above all, which symbolize the shift to more privatized, home-based lifestyles. At the same time, the increasing incidence of deprivation and unemployment in some outer areas (especially large, peripheral, local authority estates) reminds us that the distribution of these is neither static nor spatially immutable. Rural areas also exhibit deep social cleavages both between farm workers and farmers (especially owner-occupiers who have benefited from escalating land values) and between middle-class newcomers and the local working class population.

The immediate prospects for any substantial reduction in these divisions are not encouraging for a number of reasons. First, the economic outlook suggests that unemployment is likely to increase, thus adding to the numbers of 'have-nots'. Second, in an era of economic austerity, there is little realistic prospect that more redistributive State policies will be adopted. Instead it is likely that the middle class will continue better to utilize declining health and education services, while being able to supplement these and other basic services with private sector provision. They will also probably continue to monopolize many of the 'externalities' redistributed by the planning system, such as preservation of selected urban and rural areas. Finally, the growing importance of inherited wealth – especially housing – for middle-class and some working-class families will tend to sustain existing social polarization and reinforce hereditary elements of the class structure. As a result, many of the tensions in UK society – displayed so vividly in the urban riots of 1981 and 1985 – may become even more embittered.

Was all this necessary? Was the economic decline of the UK irreversible and could the internal divisiveness have been avoided or, at least, ameliorated? The answer is equivocal: given the loss of the Empire and the surrender of economic hegemony to the USA, a change in the UK's economic role was inevitable. This would have been reinforced by the rise of the newly industrialized countries as well as by the expansion of industrial capacity in continental Europe. However, the decline need not have been so precipitate if, for example, sustained and coherent investment strategies had been undertaken in either the public or private sectors. However, this would have required hard choices to be made: would the State pursue short-term or long-term employment goals, and would expenditure be directed to technical education or agricultural subsidies, for example? This was probably beyond the reach of the postwar social democratic consensus, which sought the impossible: greater egalitarianism without upsetting the established social order, and greater State control of the economy without unduly restricting private capital. Instead, the consensus produced a whole series of compromises such as stop-go economic policies, coexistence of private and public health and education facilities, and regional and urban economic policies that lacked any real powers.

The consensus only really started to break up in the 1970s when the failure to produce economic growth was badly exposed in the economic crisis of the mid-1970s and this resulted in enforced public expenditure cuts. This made many of the hard choices, previously avoided by the social democratic consensus, more difficult to evade. As Drucker and Parry (1985) state: 'That is why politicians of both Left and Right are exploring increasingly radical solutions and inviting a cautious electorate to join them in high-risk strategies which were inconceivable in the recent past' (p. 49). The most prominent of these strategies has been Thatcherism – 'electoral ideology actually put into practice'. But this has failed to produce the desired economic results, even in its own terms. There has been deregulation, decentralization and an assault on trade union power, but the end-product has been massive and prolonged unemployment rather than the anticipated surge of private entrepreneurship and economic growth. The hard choices facing the government have become even harder. Reduced revenue from taxation has been matched by an enormous leap in unemployment and social security payments. Drastic choices have had to be made and the Thatcher government has not been afraid to take at least some of these: law and order has been favoured over education, nuclear weapons over the health service. Yet, the long-run relative economic decline of the UK has continued in the 1980s, and the cost has been a more divided society with an enlarged embittered minority.

What does the future offer? The Labour Party seems caught in a trap. The more radical socialist alternatives prepared by the Left do not seem able to gain sufficient electoral support to be feasible in the near future. Instead, Labour under Neil Kinnock is '... picking up some of the Tory themes of modernisation and competitiveness and seeking to make them its own, though in more human form' (Rutherford, 1985). Put more bluntly, Labour is trying to capture the middle ground of politics in electoral terms – a middle ground moved to the right by the impact of Thatcherism itself – through adopting Thatcherism with a human face. Whether this will be electorally successful is made more difficult to predict by the effects of the rise of the SDP–Liberal Alliance, itself a throwback to Butskellism and the social democratic consensus.

Consideration of the Alliance brings us back to the links between spatial scales; national and regional electoral performances are intimately linked with each other, and with the economic and social outlook for particular regions. Were the Alliance in the next General Election to increase its share of the vote in constituencies predominantly but not exclusively to the south of the Severn–Wash line, to the point where it won many of those seats where it came second in the 1983 General Election, then it could hold the balance of power in a hung Parliament. It is even possible that it could form the largest party were it to win seats in the South while Labour also gained seats elsewhere from the Conservatives. On the other hand, were the Conservative Party successfully to defend its massive majority in the South while Labour held onto its strongholds in the industrialized (or deindustrialized) North, with the non-Conservative vote split as in 1983, then Margaret Thatcher could be returned for a third term with a massive Parliamentary majority. It is a measure of the mountain that the Labour Party had to climb after 1983 that to win an absolute majority in the next election, it needed to take 117 seats from the Conservatives, including the Prime Minister's in Finchley (Harris, 1984, p. 282).

The implications of this are immense. For Labour to capture enough seats to form a government, it now has to win from both the Alliance and Conservatives in the South. To do so would – at a minimum – require formulating policies that fail to prioritize the interests of its traditional constituencies in the North and West. For the Conservatives to retain power, the principal priority is to hold onto the South, formulating national economic and industrial policies that favour the interests of its supporters there, while being able to cut regional and welfare policies that are of greatest significance to those living north or west of the Severn–Wash line. For the Alliance to win enough seats to hold the balance of power or, possibly, even form a government, it would have to formulate a similar package of policies, aimed at similar interests. Given any of these three scenarios, the prospect for those living in regions with above-average unemployment levels and below-average incomes and living conditions or in depressed inner-city localities within the affluent South is more of the same – or worse. The division between the two halves of the UK is likely to be reproduced and, indeed, widened, and this remains our conclusion, regardless of whether the spatial focus is directed to inter-regional difference or is shifted to the contrast between urban and rural areas.

BIBLIOGRAPHY

Abel-Smith, B. and Titmuss, R. (1956) *The Cost of the National Health Service*. Cambridge: Cambridge University Press.

Allen, D.E. (1976) 'Regional Variations in Food Habits'. In Oddy, D.J. and Miller, D.S. (eds) *The Making of the Modern British Diet*. London: Croom Helm.

Ambrose, P. (1977) 'Access and Spatial Inequality'. *Fundamentals of Human Geography Unit 24*. Milton Keynes: Open University.

Ambrose, P. and Colenutt, B. (1975) *The Property Machine*. Harmondsworth: Penguin.

Anderson, J. (1983) 'Geography as Ideology and the Politics of Crisis: the Enterprise Zone Experiment'. In Anderson, J., Duncan, S. and Hudson, R. (eds) *Redundant Spaces in Cities and Regions?* London: Academic Press.

Annual Review of Agriculture (1985) London: HMSO.

Atkinson, A. (1983) 'UK Trade in Manufactured Goods'. *Barclays Review*, LVIII, 4, 'Centre Spread'.

Austrin, T. and Beynon, H. (1980) *'Global Outpost: the Working Class Experience of Big Business in the North East of England 1964–79*. Durham: University of Durham, Department of Sociology.

Ball, M. (1983) *Housing Policy and Economic Power*. London: Methuen.

Barclays Review (1981) 'Productivity – International Comparisons'. *Barclays Review*, LVI, 3, 'Centre Spread'.

Barclays Review (1982) 'The Changing Structure of the UK Balance-of-Payments 1970–81'. *Barclays Review*, LVII, 3, 'Centre Spread'.

Barclays Review (1983) 'UK Trade in Manufactured Goods'. *Barclays Review*, LVIII, 4, 'Centre Spread'.

Barnett, A. (1982) 'Iron Britannia: War over the Falklands'. *New Left Review*, 134, 1–96.

Beresford, P. and Pearson, K. (1985) 'Dollar Sales Leave all Logic Behind'. *The Sunday Times*, 10 March 1985.

Bevan, A. (1952) *In Place of Fear*. London: Heinemann.

Beveridge, W. (1942) *Report on the Provision of Social Insurance, Medical and Allied Services*. Cmnd 6404. London: HMSO.

Beynon, H. (1985) 'Introduction'. In Beynon, H. (ed.) *Digging Deeper*. London, Verso.

Blackstone, T. (1980) 'Education'. In Bosanquet, N. and Townsend, P. (eds) *Labour and Equality*. London: Heinemann.

Bloomfield, G.T. (1981) 'The Changing Spatial Organization of Multinational Corporations in the World Automotive Industry'. In Hamilton, F.E.I. and Linge, G. (eds) *Spatial Analysis, Industry and the Industrial Environment, Vol. II*. Chichester: Wiley.

Boal, F.W. (1982) 'Segregating and Mixing: Space and Residence in Belfast'. In Boal, F.W. and Douglas, J.N.H. (eds) *Integration and Division*. London: Academic Press.

Boddy, M. (1976) 'The Structure of Mortgage Finance: Building Societies and the British Social Formation'. *Transactions of the Institute of British Geographers*, New Series 1, 58–71.

Boddy, M. (1980) *The Building Societies*. London: Macmillan.

Boddy, M. (1983) 'Centre-Local Government Relations: Theory and Practice'. *Political Geography Quarterly*, 2, 119–138.

Bosanquet, N. (1980) 'Labour and Public Expenditure: an Overall View'. In Bosanquet, N. and Townsend, P. (eds) *Labour and Equality*. London: Heinemann.

Bouquet, M. (1982) 'Production and Reproduction of Family Farms in South-West England'. *Sociologia Ruralis*, 22, 227–249.

Bowers, D. (1982) 'Aspects of the Housing Market'. *Barclays Review*, LVII, 3, 'Centre Spread'.

Bowers, J.K. and Cheshire, P. (1983) *Agriculture, the Countryside and Land Use: an Economic Critique*. London: Methuen.

Bowler, I. (1979) *Government and Agriculture: a Spatial Perspective*. London: Longman.

Bradley, T. (1984) 'Segmentation in Local Labour Markets'. In Bradley, T. and Lowe, P. (eds) *Locality and Rurality*. Norwich: Geo Books.

Britton, D.K. (1974) 'The Structure of Agriculture'. In Edwards, A. and Rogers, A. (eds) *Agricultural Resources: an Introduction to the Farming Industry of the United Kingdom*. London: Faber and Faber.

Britton, D.K. and Hill, N. (1975) *Size and Efficiency in Farming*. Farnborough: Saxon House.

Brown, A. (1962) *The Tory Years*. London: Lawrence and Wishart.

Brown, C. (1984) 'Patterns of Employment Among Black and White People in Britain'. *Employment Gazette*, 92, 304–307.

Brown, C.J.F. and Sheriff, J.D. (1979) 'De-industrialization: a Background Paper'. In Blackaby, F. (ed.) *De-industrialization*. London: Heinemann.

Brown, R. (1984) 'Work'. In Abrams, P. and Brown, R. (eds) *UK Society*. London: Weidenfeld and Nicolson.

Bryer, R.A., Brignall, T.J. and Maunders, A.T. (1982) *Accounting for British Steel*. Aldershot: Gower.

Bull, P. (1984) 'Economic Planning for Rural Areas in Northern Ireland'. In Jess, P.M., Greer, J.V., Buchanan, R.H. and Armstrong, W.J. (eds) *Planning and Development in Rural Areas*. Belfast: Queens University.

Buller, H. and Lowe, P.D. (1982) 'Politics and Class in Rural Preservation'. In Moseley, M.J. (ed.) *Power, Planning and People in Rural East Anglia*. Norwich: Centre for East Anglia Studies.

Burgess, R.G. (1984) 'Patterns and Processes of Education in the United Kingdom'. In Abrams, P. and Brown, R. (eds) *UK Society*. London: Weidenfeld and Nicolson.

Busteed, M.A. (1976) 'Small-Scale Economic Development in Northern Ireland'. *Scottish Geographical Magazine*, 92, pp. 172–181.

Byrne, D. and Parson, D. (1983) 'The State and the Reserve Army: the Management of Class Relations in Space'. In Anderson, J., Duncan, S. and Hudson, R. (eds) *Redundant Spaces in Cities and Regions?* London: Academic Press.

Caldwell, J.H. and Greer, J.V. (1984) *Physical Planning in Rural Areas of Northern Ireland*. Belfast: Queen's University Belfast, Occasional Paper no. 5.

Cameron, G.C.C. (1980) 'The Economies of the Conurbations'. In Cameron, G.C. (ed.) *The Future of the British Conurbations*. London: Longman.

Carney, J., Hudson, R. and Lewis, J. (1977) 'Coal Combines and Inter-Regional Uneven Development in the UK'. In Massey, D. and Batey, P. (eds) *Alternative Frameworks for Analysis*. London: Pion.

Castles, S., Booth, H. and Wallace, T. (1984) *Here for Good: West Europe's New Ethnic Minorities*. London: Pluto.

Central Health Services Council (1969) *The Functions of the District General Hospital*. London: HMSO, Department of Health and Social Security.

Central Statistical Office (1978) *Social Trends 9*. London: HMSO.

Central Statistical Office (1981) *Regional Trends 12*. London: HMSO.

Central Statistical Office (1982) *Social Trends 13*. London: HMSO.

Central Statistical Office (1985) *Annual Abstract of Statistics*. London: HMSO.

Centre for Agricultural Strategy (1980) *The Efficiency of British Agriculture.* Reading: University of Reading, CAS, Report no. 7.

Centre for Urban and Regional Development Studies (1984a) *The Changing Location of Employment 1971–81.* Newcastle: University of Newcastle, Centre for Urban and Regional Development Studies, Functional Regions Factsheet 18.

Centre for Urban and Regional Development Studies (1984b) *Population Change 1971–1981.* Newcastle: University of Newcastle, Centre for Urban and Regional Development Studies, Functional Regions Factsheet 2.

Champion, A.G. (1981) 'Population Trends in Rural Britain'. *Population Trends,* 26, 20–23.

Channon, D. (1973) *The Strategy and Structure of British Enterprise.* London: Macmillan.

Churchill, D. (1985) 'Big Rise in Corporate Mergers'. *Financial Times,* 3 May 1985.

Clark, G. (1982) *Housing and Planning in the Countryside.* Chichester: Wiley.

Clarke, J. (1984) 'There's No Place Like... Cultures of Difference'. In Massey, D. and Allen, J. (eds) *Geography Matters!* Cambridge: Cambridge University Press.

Cloke, P.J. (1979) *Key Settlements in Rural Areas.* London: Methuen.

Coates, D. (1980) *Labour in Power?: a Study of the Labour Government 1974–1979.* London: Longman.

Cochrane, A. (1983) 'Local Economic Policies: Trying to Drain the Ocean with a Teaspoon'. In Anderson, J., Duncan, S. and Hudson, R. (eds) *Redundant Spaces in Cities and Regions?* London: Academic Press.

Community Development Project (1977a) *The Costs of Industrial Change.* London: CDP Inter-Project Editorial Team.

Community Development Project (1977b) *Gilding the Ghetto.* London: CDP Inter-Project Editorial Team.

Connell, J. (1978) *The End of Tradition.* London: Routledge and Kegan Paul.

Cox, G. and Lowe, P. (1984) 'Agricultural Corporatism and Conservation Politics'. In Bradley, T. and Lowe, P. (eds) *Locality and Rurality.* Norwich: Geo Books.

Crossman, R. (1976) *The Diaries of a Cabinet Minister, Vol. 2.* London: Hamish Hamilton.

Currie, D. (1983) 'World Capitalism in Crisis'. In Hall, S. and Jacques, M. (eds) *The Politics of Thatcherism.* London: Lawrence and Wishart.

Danson, M.W., Lever, W.F. and Malcolm, J.F. (1980) 'The Inner City Employment Problem in Great Britain, 1952–76: a Shift-Share Approach'. *Urban Studies,* 17, 193–210.

Davies, H.W.E. (1981) 'The Inner City in Britain'. In Schwartz, G.G. (ed.) *Advanced Industrialisation and the Inner Cities.* Lexington, Mass.: Lexington Books.

Dawson, J.A. (1982) 'The Growth of Service Industries'. In Johnston, R.J. and Doornkamp, J.C. (eds) *The Changing Geography of the United Kingdom.* London: Methuen.

Denham, C. (1984) 'Urban Britain'. *Population Trends,* 36, 10–18.

Dennis, N. (1970) *People and Planning.* London: Faber.

Department of Economic Affairs (1965) *The National Plan.* London: HMSO.

Department of Education and Science (1980) *Statistics of Teachers in Service in England and Wales.* London: HMSO.

Department of the Environment (1972) *Studies of Rural Transport in Devon and West Suffolk: Report by the Steering Groups.* London: DoE.

Department of Employment (1981) *Census of Employment.* London: HMSO.

Department of Health and Social Security (1979) *Review of Health Capital: a Discussion Document on the Role of Capital in the Provision of Health Services.* London: DHSS.

Department of Transport (1976) *National Travel Survey, 1975/6.* London: Department of Transport.

Dicken, P. (1982) 'The Industrial Structure and the Geography of Manufacturing'. In Johnston, R.J. and Doornkamp, J.C. (eds) *The Changing Geography of the United Kingdom.* London: Methuen.

Doherty, J. (1983) 'Racial Conflict, Industrial Change and Social Control in Post-War Britain'. In Anderson, J., Duncan, S. and Hudson, R. (eds) *Redundant Spaces in Cities and Regions?* London: Academic Press.

Drake-Brockman, P. St.-L. (1984) *Recent Manufacturing Employment Decline in London: a Study of Four Boroughs.* Durham: Unpublished BA dissertation, Department of Geography, University of Durham.

Drucker, H.M. and Parry, R. (1985) 'Britain'. In Ridley, F.F. (ed.) *Policies and Politics in Western Europe.* London: Croom Helm.

Drudy, P.J. and Wallace, D.B. (1971) 'Towards a Development Programme for Remote Rural Areas: a Case Study in North Norfolk'. *Regional Studies,* 5, 281–288.

Duke, V. and Edgell, S. (1984) 'Public Expenditure Cuts in Britain and Consumption Sectoral Cleavages'. *International Journal of Urban and Regional Research,* 8, 177–201.

Dunn, M.C., Rawson, M. and Rogers, A. (1981) *Rural Housing: Competition and Choice.* London: Allen and Unwin.

Edwards, A. (1979) *The Newly Industrializing Countries and their Impact on Western Manufacturing Vols. 1 and 2.* London: Economist Intelligence Unit.

Edwards, E.G. and Roberts, I.J. (1980) 'British Higher Education: Long Term Trends in Student Enrolment'. *Higher Education Review*, 12, 7–43.

Electronics Location File (1985) *Outlook for the British Electronics Industry in 1984*. Richmond, Surrey: Urban Publishing Company.

Elias, P. and Keogh, G. (1982) 'Industrial Decline and Unemployment in the Inner City Areas of Great Britain: a Review of the Evidence'. *Urban Studies*, 19, 1–15.

Eyles, J. and Woods, K.J. (1983) *The Social Geography of Medicine and Health*. London: Croom Helm..

Farrell, M. (1980) *Northern Ireland: the Orange State*. London: Pluto.

Firn, J. (1975) 'External Control and Regional Development: the Case of Scotland'. *Environment and Planning A*, VII, 393–414.

Fleming, M. and Nellis, J. (1982) 'A New Housing Crisis?' *Lloyds Bank Review*, 144, 38–53.

Forrest, R. and Williams, P. (1984) 'Commodification and Housing: Emerging Issues and Contradictions'. *Environment and Planning A*, 16, 1163–1180.

Fothergill, S. and Gudgin, G. (1978) *Regional Employment Statistics on a Comparable Basis 1952–75*. London: Centre for Environmental Studies, Occasional Paper no. 5.

Fothergill, S. and Gudgin, G. (1982) *Unequal Growth: Urban and Regional Employment Change in the U.K.* London: Heinemann.

Fothergill, S. and Gudgin, G. (1983) 'Trends in Regional Manufacturing Employment: the Main Influences'. In Goddard, J.B. and Champion, A.G. (eds) *The Urban and Regional Transformation of Britain*. London: Methuen.

Frank, A.G. (1980) *Crisis in the World Economy*. London: Heinemann.

Friedmann, H. (1980) 'Household Production and the National Economy: Concepts for the Analysis of Agrarian Formations'. *Journal of Peasant Studies*, 7, 158–184.

Fröbel, F., Heinrichs, J. and Kreye, O. (1980) *The New International Division of Labour*. Cambridge: Cambridge University Press.

Froud, R. (1985) 'Public Spending and Borrowing'. *Barclays Review*, May, 33–36.

Fua, G. (1983) 'Rural Industrialisation in Later Developed Countries: the Case of Northeast and Central Italy'. *Banco Nazionale del Laveoro*, 147, 351–377.

Gamble, A. (1983) 'Thatcherism and Conservative Politics'. In Hall, S. and Jacques, M. (eds) *The Politics of Thatcherism*. London: Lawrence and Wishart.

Gasson, R. (1966) *The Influence of Urbanization on Farm Ownership and Practice: Some Aspects of the Effects of London on Farms and Farm People in Kent and Sussex.* Kent: Wye College, Studies in Rural Land Use, Report no. 7.

Gasson, R. (1980) 'Roles of Farm Women in England'. *Sociologia Ruralis,* 20, 165–180.

Gershuny, J.I. and Miles, I.D. (1983) *The New Self-Service Economy.* London: Frances Pinter.

Giggs, J.A. (1979) 'Human Health Problems in Urban Areas'. In Herbert, D.T. and Smith, D.M. (eds) *Social Problems and the City: Geographical Perspectives.* Oxford: Oxford University Press.

Gilg, A.W. (1982) 'Annual Review'. In Gilg, A.W. (ed.) *Countryside Planning Yearbook 1982.* Norwich: Geo Books.

Glennester, H. (1972) 'Education and Inequality'. In Townsend, P. and Bosanquet, N. (eds) *Labour and Inequality.* London: Fabian Society.

Goddard, J.B. (1979) 'Office Development and Urban and Regional Development in Britain'. In Daniels, P. (ed.) *Spatial Patterns of Office Growth and Location.* Chichester: Wiley.

Gould, A. and Keeble, D. (1984) 'New Firms and Rural Industrialization in East Anglia'. *Regional Studies,* 18, 189–202.

Grant, W. (1983) 'The National Farmers' Union: the Classic Case of Incorporation'. In Marsh, D. (ed.) *Pressure Politics: Interest Groups in Britain.* London: Junction Books.

Gray, F. (1976) 'Selection and Allocation in Council Housing'. *Transactions of the Institute of British Geographers,* New Series 1, 34–46.

Gray, J. (1985) 'U.K. House Prices – the Big North-South Divide'. *Financial Times,* 3 August 1985.

Hall, P. (1975) *Urban and Regional Planning.* Harmondsworth: Penguin.

Hall, P. (1980) Transport in the Conurbations'. In Cameron, G.C. (ed.) *The Future of the British Conurbations.* London: Longman.

Hall, P. (1984) 'Enterprises of Great Pith and Movement'. *Town and Country Planning,* 53, 296–297.

Hall, P., Thomas, R., Gracey, H. and Drewett, R. (1973) *The Containment of Urban England.* London: Allen and Unwin.

Hall, T. (1980) *King Coal.* Harmondsworth: Penguin.

Hambleton, R. (1981) 'Implementing Inner City Policy: Reflections from Experience'. *Policy and Politics,* 9, 51–71.

Hamnett, C. (1983) 'The Conditions in England's Inner Cities on the Eve of the 1981 Riots'. *Area,* 15, 7–13.

Hamnett, C. (1984) 'Housing the Two Nations: Socio-tenurial Polarization in England and Wales, 1961–81'. *Urban Studies*, 43, 389–405.

Hamnett, C. (1985) 'Inner City Decline'. *Unit 18 D205 Human Geography Course*. Milton Keynes: Open University Press.

Hamnett, C. and Randolph, W. (1984) 'The Role of Landlord Disinvestment in Housing Market Transformation: an Analysis of the Flat Break-up Market in Central London'. *Transactions of the Institute of British Geographers*, 9, 259–279.

Hannah, L. (1976) *The Rise of the Corporate Economy*. London: Methuen.

Harris, R. (1984) *The Making of Neil Kinnock*. London: Faber and Faber.

Henry, M. (1984) 'Company Finances and Investment in the United Kingdom'. *Barclays Review*, LIX, 3, 90–93.

Herbert, D.T. (1976) 'Urban Education: Problems and Policies'. In Herbert, D.T. and Johnston, R.J. (eds) *Spatial Perspectives on Problems and Policies*. London: Wiley.

Hillman, M. with Henderson, I. and Whalley, A. (1973) *Personal Mobility and Transport Policy*. London: Political and Economic Planning Broadsheet 542.

Hoare, A.G. (1982) 'Problem Region and Regional Problem'. In Boal, F.W. and Douglas, J.N.H. (eds) *Integration and Division*. London: Academic Press.

Hogg, J. (1985) 'Consumer Spending in the United Kingdom – a Shifting Pattern'. *Barclays Review*, LX, 2, 37–42.

Holland, S. (1975) *The Socialist Challenge*. London: Quartet.

Holtermann, S. (1975) 'Areas of Urban Deprivation in Great Britain: an Analysis of 1971 Census Data'. *Social Trends*, 33–47.

Hood, N. and Young, S. (1979) *The Economics of Multinational Enterprise*. Harlow: Longman.

Hudson, R. (1984) 'Capital Accumulation and Regional Problems: a Study of North East England'. In Hamilton, F.E.I. and Linge, G. (eds) *Spatial Analysis, Industry and the Industrial Environment, Vol. III*. Chichester: Wiley.

Hudson, R. (1985) 'Nationalized Industry Policies and Regional Policies: the Role of the State in Capitalist Societies in the Deindustrialization and Reindustrialization of Regions'. *Society and Space* (in press).

Hudson, R. and Lewis, J. (1982) *Regional Planning in Europe*. London: Pion.

Hudson, R. and Sadler, D. (1983) 'Region, Class and the Politics of Steel Closures in the European Community'. *Society and Space*, 1, 405–428.

Hudson, R. and Sadler, D. (1985) 'Coal and Dole: Employment Policies in the Coalfields'. In Beynon, H. (ed.) *Digging Deeper*. London: Verso.

Hudson, R., Rhind, D. and Mounsey, H. (1984) *An Atlas of EEC Affairs.* London: Methuen.

Jacques, M. (1983) 'Thatcherism – Breaking out of the Impasse.' In Hall, S. and Jacques, M. (eds) *The Politics of Thatcherism.* London: Lawrence and Wishart.

Jessel, S. (1978) 'What Did Halsey Propose?' In Field, F. (ed.) *Education and the Urban Crisis.* London: Routledge and Kegan Paul.

Jones, G. and Stewart, J.D. (1983) *The Case for Local Government.* Hemel Hempstead: Allen and Unwin.

Keeble, D. (1984) 'The Urban-Rural Manufacturing Shift'. *Geography*, 69, 163–166.

Keegan, W. (1984) *Mrs Thatcher's Economic Experiment.* Harmondsworth: Penguin.

Kemeny, J. (1980) 'Home Ownership and Privatization'. *International Journal of Urban and Regional Research*, 4, 372–388.

King, R. (1984) 'Population Mobility: Emigration, Return Migration and Internal Migration'. In Williams, A. (ed.) *Southern Europe Transformed.* London: Harper and Row.

Knox, P.L. and Cottam, M.B. (1981) 'Rural Deprivation in Scotland: a Preliminary Assessment'. *Tijdschrift voor Economische en Sociale Geografie,* 72, 162–175.

Law, C.M. (1980) *British Regional Development since World War I.* Newton Abbot: David and Charles.

Law, C. and Warnes, A.M. (1976) 'The Changing Geography of the Elderly in England and Wales'. *Transactions of the Institute of British Geographers,* New Series 1, 453–471.

Lawton, R. (1973) 'Rural Depopulation in Nineteenth Century England'. In Mills, D.R. (ed.) *English Rural Communities.* London: Macmillan.

Lawton, R. (1982) 'People and Work'. In House, J.W. (ed.) *The UK Space.* London: Weidenfeld and Nicolson.

Leach, S. (1985) 'The Monitoring and Evaluation of Inner City Policy'. *Regional Studies*, 19, 59–63.

Leat, D. (1981) 'The Role of Pressure Groups in Rural Planning'. In Gilg, A.W. (ed.) *Countryside Planning Yearbook 1981.* Norwich: Geo Books.

Leclerc, R. and Draffan, D. (1984) 'The Glasgow Eastern Area Renewal Project'. *Town Planning Review*, 55, 335–351.

Lee, T.R. (1977) *Race and Residence: The Concentration and Dispersal of Immigrants in London.* Oxford: Clarendon Press.

Leschinsky, D. (1977) *Health Services in Rural Areas.* London: National Federation of Women's Institutes.

Lindley, P.D. (1985) 'The Merseyside Task Force'. *Regional Studies*, 19, 69–73.

Lipietz, A. (1977) *Le Capital et Son Espace*. Paris: Maspero.

Lipietz, A. (1980) 'The Structuration of Space, the Problem of Land and Spatial Policies'. In Carney, J., Hudson, R. and Lewis, J. (eds) *Regions in Crisis*. London: Croom Helm.

Lipietz, A. (1984) 'Imperialism or the Beast of the Apocalypse'. *Capital and Class*, 22, 81–116.

Lloyd, P.E. and Mason, C.M. (1978) 'Manufacturing Industry in the Inner City: a Case Study of Greater Manchester'. *Transactions of the Institute of British Geographers*, 3, 66–90.

Lonsdale, S. (1985) *Work and Inequality*. London: Longman.

Lowe, P. and Goyder, J. (1983) *Environmental Groups in Politics*. London: Allen and Unwin.

McCallum, J.D. (1979) 'The Development of British Regional Policy'. In Maclennan, D. and Parr, J. (eds) *Regional Policy: Past Experience and New Directions*. Oxford: Martin Robertson.

McCrone, G. (1969) *Regional Policy in Britain*. London: Allen and Unwin.

McKay, D.H. and Cox, A.W. (1979) *The Politics of Urban Change*. London: Croom Helm.

MacKay, G.A. (1979) 'Regional Development and North Sea Oil and Gas'. In Maclennan, D. and Parr, J.B. (eds) *Regional Policy: Past Experience and New Directions*. Oxford: Martin Robertson.

MacKay, G.A. and Laing, G. (1982) *Consumer Problems in Rural Areas*. Glasgow: Scottish Consumer Council.

MacKenzie, S. and Rose, D. (1983) 'Industrial Change, the Domestic Economy and Home Life'. In Anderson, J., Duncan, S. and Hudson, R. (eds) *Redundant Spaces in Cities and Regions?* London: Academic Press.

Madge, J. and Brown, C. (1981) *First Homes: a Survey of the Housing Circumstances of Young Married Couples*. London: Policy Studies Institute, no. 600.

Mandel, E. (1978) *The Second Slump*. London: New Left Books.

Mann, S.A. and Dickinson, J.A. (1978) 'Obstacles to the Development of a Capitalist Agriculture'. *Journal of Peasant Studies*, 5, 466–481.

Manpower Services Commission (1985) *Labour Market Quarterly Report* (March). Sheffield: Moorfoot MSC.

Marquand, J. (1979) *The Service Sector and Regional Policy in the United Kingdom*. London: Centre for Environment Studies Research Series no. 29.

Marsden, T. (1984) 'Land Ownership and Farm Organisation in Capitalist Agriculture'. In Bradley, T. and Lowe, P. (eds) *Locality and Rurality*. Norwich: Geo Books.

Massey, D. (1977) 'The Analysis of Capitalist Landownership: an Investigation of the Case of Great Britain'. *International Journal of Urban and Regional Research*, 1, 404–424.

Massey, D. (1978) 'Regionalism: Some Current Issues'. *Capital and Class*, 6, 106–125.

Massey, D. (1983a) 'Contours of Victory, Dimensions of Defeat'. *Marxism Today*, July, 16–19.

Massey, D. (1983b) 'Industrial Restructuring as Class Restructuring: Production Decentralization and Local Uniqueness'. *Regional Studies*, 17, 73–89.

Massey, D.B. (1984) *Spatial Divisions of Labour: Social Structures and the Geography of Production*. London: Macmillan.

Massey, D.B. and Meegan, R.A. (1978) 'Industrial Restructuring Versus the Cities'. *Urban Studies*, 15, 273–288.

Mauser, W.A.P. (1985) *The British Economic Base 1985*. London: Federation of Civil Engineering Contractors.

Meegan, R. (1982) 'Telecommunications Technology and Older Regions'. *CES Paper 7*. London: CES Ltd.

Mellor, J.R. (1977) *Urban Sociology in an Urbanized Society*. London: Routledge and Kegan Paul.

Merseyside Socialist Research Group (1980) *Merseyside in Crisis*. Manchester: Manchester Free Press.

Ministry of Health (1962) *A Hospital Plan for England and Wales*. Cmnd 1604. London: HMSO.

Mohan, J. (1984a) 'State Policies and the Development of the Hospital Services of North East England, 1948–1982'. *Political Geography Quarterly*, 3, 275–295.

Mohan, J. (1984b) 'Geographical Aspects of Private Hospital Developments in Britain'. *Area*, 16, 191–199.

Moore, B. and Rhodes, J. (1973) 'Evaluating the Effects of British Regional Economic Policy'. *Economic Journal*, 83, 87–110.

Moseley, M.J. (1979) *Accessibility: the Rural Challenge*. London: Methuen.

Moseley, M. and Packman, J. (1984) 'Mobile Services and the Rural Accessibility Problem'. In Clark, G., Groenendijk, J. and Thissen, F. (eds) *The Changing Countryside*. Norwich: Geo Books.

Munton, R.J.C. (1977) 'Financial Institutions: Their Ownership of Agricultural Land'. *Area*, 9, 29–37.

Nairn, T. (1976) *The Break-up of Britain*. London: New Left Books.

National Coal Board (1950) *Plan for Coal*. London: NCB.

National Coal Board (1974) *Plan for Coal*. London: NCB.

National Economic Development Council (1963a) *Growth of the United Kingdom Economy to 1966*. London: HMSO.

National Economic Development Council (1963b) *Conditions Favourable to Faster Growth*. London: HMSO.

Newby, H. (1977) *The Deferential Worker*. London: Allen Lane.

Newby, H. (1979) *Green and Pleasant Land?* London: Hutchinson.

Newby, H. (1980) 'Urbanization and the Rural Class Structure: Reflections on a Case Study'. In Buttel, F.H. and Newby, H. (eds) *The Rural Sociology of the Advanced Societies: Critical Perspectives*. London: Croom Helm.

Norcliffe, G.B. and Hoare, A.G. (1982) 'Enterprise Zone Policy for the Inner City: a Review and Preliminary Assessment'. *Area*, 14, 265–274.

Norton-Taylor, R. (1982) *Whose Land is it Anyway?* Wellingborough: Turnstone Press.

Nutley, S.D. (1980) 'Accessibility, Mobility and Transport-Related Welfare: the Case of Rural Wales'. *Geoforum*, 11, 335–352.

Ormerod, P. (1980) 'The Economic Record'. In Bosanquet, N. and Townsend, P. (eds) *Labour and Equality*. London: Heinemann.

Pacione, M. (1979) 'Housing Policies in Glasgow since 1880'. *Geographical Review*, 69, 395–412.

Pahl, R.E. (1975) *Whose City?* London: Longman.

Pahl, R.E. (1984) *Divisions of Labour*. Oxford: Basil Blackwell.

Pahl, R.E., Flynn, R. and Buck, N.H. (1983) *Structures and Processes of Urban Life*. London: Longman.

Parboni, R. (1981) *The Dollar and its Rivals*. London: Verso.

Parkinson, M.H. and Wilks, S.R.M. (1983) 'Managing Urban Decline – the Case of the Inner City Partnerships'. *Local Government Studies*, 9, 23–39.

Parkinson, M.H. and Wilks, S.R.M. (1985) 'Testing Partnership to Destruction in Liverpool'. *Regional Studies*, 19, 65–69.

Patmore, J.A. (1983) *Recreation and Resources: Leisure Patterns and Leisure Places*. Oxford: Basil Blackwell.

Peach, C. and Shah, S. (1980) 'The Contribution of Council House Allocation to West Indian Desegregation in London, 1961–78. *Urban Studies*, 17, 333–341

Phillips, D.R. (1981) *Contemporary Issues in the Geography of Health Care*. Norwich: Geo Books.

Phillips, D.R. and Williams, A.M. (1982) *Rural Housing and the Public Sector*. Aldershot: Gower.

Phillips, D.R. and Williams, A.M. (1983) 'Rural Settlement Policies and Local Authority Housing: Some Observations from a Case-Study of South Hams, Devon'. *Environment and Planning A*, 15, 505–513.

Phillips, D.R. and Williams, A.M. (1984a) 'Public-Sector Housing in Rural Areas in England'. In Clark, G., Groenendijk, J. and Thissen, F. (eds) *The Changing Countryside*. Norwich: Geo Books.

Phillips, D.R. and Williams, A.M. (1984b) *Rural Britain: a Social Geography*. Oxford: Basil Blackwell.

Pickvance, C.G. (1981) 'Policies as Chameleons: an Interpretation of Regional Policy and Office Policy in Britain'. In Dear, M. and Scott, A.J. (eds) *Urbanization and Urban Planning in Capitalist Society*. London: Methuen.

Pinch, S. (1979) 'Territorial Justice in the City: A Case Study of the Social Services for the Elderly in Greater London'. In Herbert, D.T. and Smith, D.M. (eds) *Social Problems and the City: Geographical Perspectives*. Oxford: Oxford University Press.

Pugliese, E. (1985) 'Farm Workers in Italy: Agricultural Working Class, Landless Peasants or Clients of the Welfare State?' In Hudson, R. and Lewis, J. (eds) *Uneven Development in Southern Europe*. London: Methuen.

Radice, H. (1984) 'The National Economy – a Keynesian Myth?' *Capital and Class*, 22, 111–140.

Randolph, W. and Robert, S. (1981) 'Population Redistribution in Great Britain, 1971–81'. *Town and Country Planning*, 50, 227–230.

Ratcliffe, J. (1976) *Land Policy: an Exploration of the Nature of Land in Society*. London: Hutchinson.

Redfern, P. (1982) 'Profile of Our Cities'. *Population Trends*, 30, 21–32.

Regional Studies Association (1983) *An Inquiry into Regional Problems in the United Kingdom*. London: RSA.

Rex, J. (1973) *Race, Colonialism and the City*. London: Routledge and Kegan Paul.

Rhind, D. and Hudson, R. (1980) *Land Use*. London: Methuen.

Richmond, P. (1985) *The State and the Role of the Housing Association Sector in Rural Areas: a Case Study in Devon*. Exeter: University of Exeter, Unpublished PhD Thesis.

Robinson, V. (1980) 'Asians and Council Housing'. *Urban Studies*, 17, 323–331.

Robson, B. (1969) *Urban Analysis: A Study of City Structure*. Cambridge: Cambridge University Press.

Rodger, I. (1984) 'Risks at the Cutting Edge'. *Financial Times,* 4 October 1984.

Rostow, W.W. (1978) *The World Economy: History and Prospect.* London: Macmillan.

Roth, A. (1973) 'The Business Background of MPs'. In Urry, J. and Wakeford, J. (eds) *Power in Britain.* London: Heinemann.

Rowthorne, B. (1983) 'The Past Strikes Back'. In Hall, S. and Jacques, M. (eds) *The Politics of Thatcherism.* London: Lawrence and Wishart.

Rural Voice (1982) *State of the Countryside 1982.* London: Rural Voice.

Rutherford, M. (1985) 'Labour Escapes from its Past'. *Financial Times,* 19 April 1985.

Sadler, D. (1984) 'Works Closure at British Steel and the Nature of the State'. *Political Geography Quarterly,* 3, 297–311.

Sandles, A. (1985) 'Foreign Tourists to Spend 6 bn'. *Financial Times,* 1 May 1985.

Sarre, P. (1981) *Second Homes: a Case Study in Brecknock.* Milton Keynes: Open University, Faculty of Social Science Publications.

Sayer, A. (1984) *Method in Social Science: a Realist Approach.* London: Hutchinson.

Self, P. and Storing, H. (1962) *The State and the Farmer.* London: Allen and Unwin.

Shanks, M. (1977) *Planning and Politics.* London: Allen and Unwin.

Shaw, G. and Williams, A.M. (1981) 'The Regional Structure of Structure Plans'. *Planning Outlook,* 23, 2–7.

Shoard, M. (1980) *The Theft of the Countryside.* London: Temple Smith.

Short, J. (1981) *Public Expenditure and Taxation in UK Regions.* Farnborough: Gower.

Short, J.R. (1982) *Housing in Britain: the Post-War Experience.* London: Methuen.

Short, J.R. and Bassett, K.A. (1981) 'Housing Policy and the Inner City in the 1970s'. *Transactions of the Institute of British Geographers,* 6, 293–312.

Shucksmith, D. and Lloyd, M. (1983) 'Rural Planning in Scotland: a Critique'. In Gilg, A.W. (ed.) *Countryside Planning Yearbook 1983.* Norwich: Geo Books.

Shutt, J. (1984) 'Tory Enterprise Zones and the Labour Movement'. *Capital and Class,* 23, 19–44.

Sim, D. (1984) 'Urban Deprivation: Not Just the Inner City'. *Area,* 16, 299–306.

Smith, D.M. (1979) *Where the Grass is Greener: Living in an Unequal World.* Harmondsworth: Penguin.

Smith, P. and Brown, P. (1983) 'Industrial Change and Scottish Nationalism since 1945'. In Anderson, J., Duncan, S. and Hudson, R. (eds) *Redundant Spaces in Cities and Regions?* London: Academic Press.

Spence, N., Gillespie, A., Goddard, J., Kennett, S., Pinch, S. and Williams, A. (1982) *British Cities: An Analysis of Urban Change*. Oxford: Pergamon Press.

Stafford, A. (1981) 'Learning not to Labour'. *Capital and Class*, 15, 55–78.

Steed, G.P.F. (1981) 'International Location and Comparative Advantage: the Clothing Industries and Developing Countries'. In Hamilton, F.E.I. and Linge, G.J.R. (eds) *International Industrial Systems*. Chichester: Wiley.

Symes, D.G. and Marsden, T.K. (1983) 'Complementary Roles and Asymmetrical Lives: Farmers' Wives in a Large Farm Environment'. *Sociologia Ruralis*, 23, 229–241.

Taylor, P.J. (1979) ' "Difficult-to-Let", "Difficult-to-Live-in", and Sometimes "Difficult-to-Get-Out-of": an Essay on Provision of Council Housing, with Special Reference to Killingworth'. *Environment and Planning A*, 11, 1305–1320.

Thompson, E.P. and Smith, D. (eds) (1980) *Protest and Survive*. Harmondsworth: Penguin.

Townsend, P. (1980) 'Social Planning and the Treasury'. In Bosanquet, N. and Townsend, P. (eds) *Labour and Equality*. London: Heinemann.

Townsend, P. and Davidson, N. (1982) *Inequalities in Health*. Harmondsworth: Penguin.

Tricker, M. and Bozeat, N. (1983) 'Encouraging the Development of Small Businesses in Rural Areas: Recent Local Authority Initiatives in England'. *Regional Studies*, 17, 201–204.

Tricker, M. and Martin, S. (1984) 'The Developing Role of the Commission'. *Regional Studies*, 18, 507–514.

Wainwright, H. (1984) 'Women and the Division of Labour'. In Abrams, P. and Brown, R. (eds) *UK Society*. London: Weidenfeld and Nicolson.

Wibberley, G. (1978) 'Mobility and the Countryside'. In Cresswell, R. (ed.) *Rural Transport and Country Planning*. London: Leonard Hill.

Wilkinson, M. (1985) 'UK Living Standards Trail in World League'. *Financial Times*, 2 January 1985.

Williams, G. (1984a) 'Development Agencies and the Promotion of Rural Community Development'. In Gilg, A.W. (ed.) *Countryside Planning Yearbook*. Norwich: Geo Books.

Williams, G. (1984b) 'Promoting the Rural Economy: the Role of Development Agencies in Remoter Rural Areas'. *Regional Studies*, 18, 73–88.

Williams, P.R. (1976) 'The Role of Institutions in the Inner London Housing Market: the Case of Islington'. *Transactions of the Institute of British Geographers*, New Series 1, 72–82.

Williams, P.R. (1978) 'Building Societies and the Inner City'. *Transactions of the Institute of British Geographers*, 3, 23–35.

Williams, W.M. (1973) 'The Study of Family Farming'. In Mills, D.R. (ed.) *English Rural Communities: the Impact of a Specialised Economy*. London: Macmillan.

Williamson, W. and Byrne, D.S. (1979) 'Educational Disadvantage in an Urban Setting'. In Herbert, D.T. and Smith, D.M. (eds) *Social Problems and the City: Geographical Perspectives*. Oxford: Oxford University Press.

Wilson, H. (1974) *The Labour Government, 1964–70*. Harmondsworth: Penguin.

Wood, C.M., Lee, N., Laker, J.A. and Saunders, P.J.W. (1974) *The Geography of Pollution: a Study of Greater Manchester*. Manchester: Manchester University Press.

Woods, K. (1982) 'Social Deprivation and Resource Allocation in the Thames Regional Health Authority'. London: University of London, QMC, Geography Department, Occasional Paper no. 20.

Yergin, D. (1980) *Shattered Peace: the Origins of the Cold War and the National Security State*. Harmondsworth: Penguin.

PLACE INDEX

SUBJECT INDEX